Nonmodern Practices

Nonmodern Practices

Latour and Literary Studies

Edited by Elisabeth Arnould-Bloomfield and
Claire Chi-ah Lyu

BLOOMSBURY ACADEMIC
NEW YORK • LONDON • OXFORD • NEW DELHI • SYDNEY

BLOOMSBURY ACADEMIC
Bloomsbury Publishing Inc
1385 Broadway, New York, NY 10018, USA
50 Bedford Square, London, WC1B 3DP, UK

BLOOMSBURY, BLOOMSBURY ACADEMIC and the Diana logo are
trademarks of Bloomsbury Publishing Plc

First published in the United States of America 2020
This paperback edition published 2022

Volume Editors' Part of the Work © Elisabeth Arnould-Bloomfield and
Claire Chi-ah Lyu, 2020
Each chapter © of Contributors, 2020

Cover design: Nicholas Motte

All rights reserved. No part of this publication may be reproduced or transmitted in any form or by any means, electronic or mechanical, including photocopying, recording, or any information storage or retrieval system, without prior permission in writing from the publishers.

Bloomsbury Publishing Inc does not have any control over, or responsibility for, any third-party websites referred to or in this book. All internet addresses given in this book were correct at the time of going to press. The author and publisher regret any inconvenience caused if addresses have changed or sites have ceased to exist, but can accept no responsibility for any such changes.

Library of Congress Cataloging-in-Publication Data
Names: Arnould-Bloomfield, Elisabeth, editor. | Lyu, Claire Chi-ah, editor.
Title: Nonmodern practices : Latour and literary studies /
edited by Elisabeth Arnould-Bloomfield and Claire Chi-ah Lyu.
Description: New York : Bloomsbury Academic, 2020. | Includes bibliographical references and index. | Summary: "This interdisciplinary collection explores the many ways in which Bruno Latour's relational philosophy enables us to extend and even transform radically the way we think, read, and write in the field of humanities today"– Provided by publisher.
Identifiers: LCCN 2020013045 | ISBN 9781501354281 (hardback) | ISBN 9781501354304 (pdf) | ISBN 9781501354298 (ebook)
Subjects: LCSH: Criticism.
| Criticism–Methodology. | Latour, Bruno–Philosophy.
Classification: LCC PN81 .N56 2020 | DDC 801/.95–dc23
LC record available at https://lccn.loc.gov/2020013045

ISBN:	HB:	978-1-5013-5428-1
	PB:	978-1-5013-6927-8
	ePDF:	978-1-5013-5430-4
	eBook:	978-1-5013-5429-8

Typeset by Integra Software Services Pvt. Ltd.

To find out more about our authors and books visit www.bloomsbury.com
and sign up for our newsletters.

Contents

Foreword *William Paulson* vii

Introduction: For a "Literary Anthropology" *Elisabeth Arnould-Bloomfield* 1

Part One Early Modern Tradition from a Latourian Relational Perspective

1 "Nonmodern Humanism": A Relational Reading of Latour and Montaigne *Jan Miernowski* 27
2 Practices of Early Modern Orientalism: A Latourian Perspective *Oumelbanine Zhiri* 49

Part Two Reassessing Literary and Political Modernity with Latour

3 Nonmodern Flaubert *William Paulson* 69
4 Latour, Stengers, and Nonmodern Poetry *Claire Chi-ah Lyu* 89
5 Kafka's Whipper and Joyce's Pandybat: Reading Scenes of Discipline with Latour *Gabriel Hankins* 113
6 Michelet's Nonmodernity *Maxime Goergen* 131

Part Three Latour's Contributions to the Field of Contemporary Animal Studies

7 Landing in Animal Territories *Vinciane Despret* 153
8 Composing with the "Animal Side" *Elisabeth Arnould-Bloomfield* 175

Part Four Issues of Practical Concern Related to Latour's Thinking

9 Latour's Interpretation of Donald Trump *Graham Harman* 197
10 Literary Worlds: Indigenous and Western Network Ethnography *Stephen Muecke* 217

Afterword: On the Ambiguities of the Modern *Rita Felski* 231
Notes on Contributors 245
Index 248

Foreword

William Paulson

The instant I read that I saw another universe and I became another man.
Jean-Jacques Rousseau, *Confessions*

Unlike Jean-Jacques learning of the essay contest that would provoke him to write about politics, I did not fall down in an ecstatic trance, my shirt-front bathed in tears of felicity, when I first spotted a copy of *We Have Never Been Modern* on a bookstore shelf. That moment in October 1993 nonetheless marked one of the decisive turns of my intellectual life. Give credit to Bruno Latour, his translator Catherine Porter, and Harvard University Press: the title and the description on the back cover conveyed a crucial core of the book's argument. What if modernity, instead of being superseded by a prefixed and ambiguously antithetical avatar of itself, had never really happened? What if science and the humanities, the "two cultures" that I (in a small way, on the margins of literary theory) had tried to follow Michel Serres and Henri Atlan and Ilya Prigogine in bridging, were not grounded on the opposing bedrocks of nature and society but were instead a set of practices devoted to producing or projecting a dualistic world?

If we take seriously the possibility that we have always been, and are still, nonmodern, our intellectual landscape looks surprisingly different. And so do literature and literary studies, invested as they have been for at least two centuries in being (or at least having been) modern. A year after first reading Latour, I told a conference of nineteenth-century French studies scholars that "we have never been nineteenth-centuryists": we could not really consider "our" century more modern than its predecessors, nor could we in turn claim to be more modern, or more critical, than the figures and texts we studied. (They listened politely but, unsurprisingly, have gone on acting like *dix-neuviémistes*.) But it soon struck me that there was far more at stake in Latour's challenges than periodization or disciplinary boundaries.

The massive intellectual investment in considering literature to have been modern more or less amounted to considering literature to have been Literature. Having once designated whatever was written down, at least the serious or enduring parts of what was written down, literature came to refer primarily to the "imaginative" genres (mainly poetry, fiction, drama). When preceded by words like "English" or "French," it designated a corpus of texts going back to the middle ages, beginning with early writings in an identifiable state of a modern "national" language. Its boldest theorists, from the Jena Romantics to Mallarmé to Paul de Man, saw literature as autonomously powerful, powerful by virtue of autonomy: capable of producing a distinctive kind of knowledge by exploring the powers of literary language.

But if we question, with Latour, the "modernist settlement," we must question as well many of the basic assumptions of literary culture about the specialness of literature, or language, or indeed the symbolic/cultural order in general. The modern sense of the aesthetic as a distinctive field, or of art "for art," implies that a Great Divide is crossed when we pass into art or literature—we have transcended the everyday, messy tasks of organizing and making sense of the world with whatever means are at hand in favor of a higher, more distinguished mode of representation or invention. The figural and the literal, or narrativity and textuality, or simply good old Art and Life—these and a host of similar oppositions appear as the endpoints of modern polarities comparable to that of Nature and Society in *We Have Never Been Modern*. A nonmodern analysis would thus assert that these are not fundamental modes of being out of which actually existing entities are made via some sort of combination or dialectic, but are instead idealizations produced at no small cost via a disciplined process of purification—precisely the work that modern literature's theorists and publicists were engaged in.

Nonmodern literary study will not reject the insights of formalism and semiotics, but will not take them to be the royal road of critique, ideological or otherwise. Words matter, but they matter in a less unique way than was generally thought in modern literary culture. They matter along with other entities that matter. If language were *the* essential site or medium of the construction of reality, then arguments among a structuralist, a deconstructionist, and a "traditional humanist" (whatever that disgraced straw man might once have been) must have been truly fundamental: *existential* in the way that this word has slipped away from its *-ism* and become allied to *threat*. But if reality is made of everything, the entire gamut of actants or actors admitted by Latour, all the future "stuff," for example—galaxies, the Alps, isotopes, neighbors, gossip, pasta—that Italo Calvino once described as packed in "All at One Point" before the Big Bang, then those "French theory" debates amounted to squabbles over crumbs occasionally falling from the table, or (to put it in a vulgarly quantitative way) the last 5 percent of all the forces, forms, and constraints that shape our world. This may perhaps be the most intellectually and discursively sophisticated 5 percent, but sophisticated in the way of a court elite that doesn't realize, in its delusions of refinement and centrality, that outsiders can just as well see it as a tiny province or subculture.

If we now can see things this way—or more specifically, if the process of scholarly review has allowed the above paragraph to be published—that is surely not just because Bruno Latour's work has become known, but because literary studies cannot (and could never) be fully defined by the modernist process of purification. In the first place, many of the writers and theorists who asserted the specialness of literature did so as antimoderns: for them, literature was a privileged site of opposition to scientific, technical, and economic modernity. In addition, the disciplinary construction of literary studies, especially in the national literatures such as English and French, led to a curious coexistence of the modern and the nonmodern. These disciplines defined their canons in terms of a historical narrative running from the Middle Ages to (almost) the present day—a modern construct, to be sure, but one that preserves the premodern: the writings of Shakespeare and Montaigne are never really relegated to an outdated past, as they would be in a truly modern discipline. The study of literature, as organized, thus enacts a kind of nonmodernity by the inclusiveness of its historical scope.

More important, however, is the simple fact that for all of the definitional distinctions and attempts at purification that have characterized literature for a good two centuries now, writers (and scholars) have gone on doing what users of language have always done: putting words together in ways that affect their listeners or readers, that help make sense of parts of the world (or that contest the sense making already carried out by others). Just as for Latour the modern world has produced human/nonhuman hybrids and collectives of spectacular variety and complexity while claiming to separate nature and culture, so the works of modern literature and criticism continually articulate words and world, just as premodern utterances used to do. Moreover, literary scholars have not hesitated, in the decades since the heyday of high theory, to pursue their work of hybridization by running roughshod over the boundaries between the literary and the nonliterary, the elite and the popular, the linguistic and the visual. We may have tried hard to be modern, but for the most part we are not doing so anymore.

Lastly, the import of Bruno Latour's central insights, or at least of the questions he has raised, seems only to grow with each passing year. His thesis that "the social" is not a purely human matter becomes ever more robust as we see the public sphere disrupted (if not ruined) by social media and related innovations. Having let memes and trolls and bots into our polity, we are obviously not the same collective with cheap silicon-based information processing devices that we were without them. And the need to acknowledge and counteract humanly produced climate change reminds us in the starkest possible way that there is no such thing as "humanity" (or "humanities") separated from the material and nonhuman world—no society or culture (or "literature" or "discourse") that is not bound up with the "collective of humans and nonhumans."

Can one evoke such dire circumstances and then commend a collection of academic essays to the reader's good will? Yes—because each field of inquiry needs to make its own kind of contributions, on its own terms. Latour's words matter because they can contribute to restructuring or rearticulating the collective of which they—and humanities scholars, and the Earth's oceans and atmosphere—are constituent parts. As Elisabeth Arnould-Bloomfield points out in her introduction, the essays collected here amount to a heterogeneous set of experiments in modifying intellectual outlooks and practices. Globally, we still have not learned enough from Latour, not figured out how to make his insights truly operative in enough contexts. Transformative as his words may have been for a few individuals, they will only truly matter to the extent that their effects become legion or, in his own term, collective. And to this project, the present volume, no less than comparable undertakings in other locales, is a needed and emblematic contribution.

December 30, 2019

Introduction: For a "Literary Anthropology"

Elisabeth Arnould-Bloomfield

I

This volume engages anew with William Paulson's 2001 question—"what happens to literary and cultural criticism under the assumption of nonmodernity?"[1] A few years ago, Paulson's query brought Bruno Latour's nonmodern philosophy into literature. It suggested that Latour's thought might be relevant to the renewing of our current reading practices and that it could bring new blood into critical habits that might be wearing thin.[2] Almost two decades later, Paulson's inquiry is barely gaining ground. Latour may have, during that time, transformed science studies, the social sciences and philosophy, but his presence in the literary field is still lagging behind. There are only a handful of publications or conferences dedicated to his work, no "Latourian studies" units in departments, and Latour is often viewed with suspicion by cultural critics and scholars of the left. But there are also notable exceptions, and a few voices are currently making a case for the relevance of Latour's thinking in today's literary critical practices. In addition to Paulson, Rita Felski, Graham Harman, and David Alsworth have all advocated for the important role Latour's thought could play in the renewal of our theoretical and critical practices.[3] They have shown how Latour's relational ontology gives renewed "ontological salience to all classes of beings,"[4] and shifts our modern and postmodern understanding of representation and agency. Actor network theory, they argue, has the potential to bring distinctly new solutions to current impasses in the humanities. Its refusal of critique and reductionism as well as attention to the empirical can give new energy and heart to our interpretative and reading practices.

The texts in this collection take up issues raised in these earlier studies and aim to contribute to a general assessment of Latour's relevance to literary criticism. They are, however, largely experimental and are not meant to offer a systematic reflection on Latour's ability—or inability—to address literature's unique "Mode of Existence."[5] They do not offer a sustained portrayal of what a new Latourian critical program might look like, nor do they seek to define and apply a literary actor network theory to our canon. What they do—in a more modest but also practical fashion—is to query and compose with Latour's thought to see what kind of co-creation might emerge. This pragmatism comes with a fair amount of thematic heterogeneity: the following contributions span literary periods, genres, and themes. They also belong to varying subfields, specialties, and approaches—from animal studies and ecological politics to questions of literary history and critical methodology. Yet this diversity, however motley it may seem, is also an aspect of Latour's philosophy and epistemology. For Latour, the critic is not the one who debunks and purifies but the one who assembles and offers participants areas in which to gather. Multiplying points of view and "matters of concern" on a topic is an essential aspect of Latour's nonmodern critical ethos. And this is indispensable not because of a need for mere pluralism but because the very work of the nonmodern is to attach and reassemble. The nonmodern critic, writes Latour, is the one who "deploys instead of unveiling, adds instead of subtracting."[6] Unlike the anti- or postmoderns who criticize the modern Constitution but do not "mov[e] on to the empirical studies of the networks," the nonmodern "takes simultaneously into account the modern Constitution and the population of hybrids that that Constitution rejects and allows to proliferate."[7] Her role then—our role—is to re-entangle all elements modern critique has separated (nature, society, and text) as well as multiply mediations and assemblages to give voice and freedom to different practices.

II

As the title of *We Have Never Been Modern* makes clear, Latour's analysis of modernity differs substantially from the various strands of critique that make up the post-enlightenment Western tradition. Unlike most anti- or postmoderns, Latour does not set out to denounce modern "disenchantment," its scientistic turn, or the commodification of its "culture industry." He is also less concerned with identifying what modernity *is* than figuring out what it *does*, and what kind of "Constitution" legislates its practices. Traditional historians of ideas ascribe the origin of the modern revolution to changes such as the advent of experimental science, humanism, or Kantian metaphysics. But Latour is as mistrustful of interpretations that see modernity as a "radical break" as he is of monocausal explanations that attribute this break to a single source. Instead of looking for modernity's specific moment, cause, and philosophical flavor, he settles instead on what appears to guarantee all other explanations of modernity: the nature–culture dualism.

Modernity, Latour argues, is a division of world and knowledge into two distinct realms: the factual realm of mechanical matter accessible only to science, and the human realm of mutable politics and representations. Although it appears to most moderns as a natural division of labor and an obvious "double ontological distinction,"[8] this partition is much less organic yet more powerful. Its critical power stems from its clear yet reversible dualist framework, which allows moderns to switch at will between claiming the superiority of the cultural side over nature and leveraging nature against humans. The moderns, writes Latour, have found a way to be invincible because they are "able to reverse [their] principles without even the appearance of contradiction."[9] They may profess that nature is purely transcendent, and society constructed, only to reverse course and argue that society's laws are absolute and nature constructed. This reversibility is neither an accident nor a mistake. It is an essential trait of the modern Constitution as Latour sees it emerging in the polemics opposing Boyle's invention of factual science and Hobbes birthing of incontrovertible politics—both occupy two positions at once since Boyle makes "pure science" out of a wholly socially constructed (experimental) cloth and Hobbes wants politics that are so immanent and rational as to be natural.[10] It is also at work in the critical ruptures and revolutions that redefine each stage of modernity as a new and contradictory intellectual era. Latour shows, for example, that the first enlightenment used the newly minted laws of nature in order to bring some scientific clarity to what it perceived as the epistemological muddle of the premoderns. But he also shows that its second, nineteenth-century phase rejected the naturalization of this first period and gave social and political sciences the task to parse out "the biases of ideology" from the truth of human freedom.[11] As for later, twentieth-century modernity, it is not free of these reversals but totalizes or de-realizes their dialectics in the works of anti- and postmoderns. Regardless of period or position, the structure and power of the modern Constitution lie in this double posture that keeps mobilizing nature at the heart of social relationships or the socially constructed aspect of nature, even as it "leave[s] Nature infinitely remote from human beings."[12]

The modern Constitution owes the power of its critique, and the universality of its reach, to an ability to occupy all critical positions at once. It is this aptitude at reversing and multiplying its stances which allows the moderns to cancel out polarities and to work in the middle where "everything happens by way of mediation, translation and networks."[13] This middle, it is true, does not exist, since it is, Latour writes, "unthinkable."[14] Yet it allows moderns to use the powerful resources of natural–cultural hybrid production while claiming to be working from an altogether different critical framework. Latour notes, for example, that the West did not so much overpower other natures-cultures with its rational order as it sold them on the separation of nature and power while overcoming their traditional networks with "large scale [...] productions of hybrids."[15] This uncontrolled production of quasi-objects is the major difference between moderns and premoderns. The latter produce limited hybrids within carefully controlled natural–social networks, while the former produce countless new hybrids by mixing together "much greater masses of humans and nonhumans, without bracketing anything and without ruling out any combinations."[16]

This paradoxical diagnostic of the modern Constitution as a dual and reversible set of practices is what gives Latour's analysis its originality and power. It is also the source of his controversial statement that "we have never been modern." Although this claim has been read by some as a somewhat flippant denial of Enlightenment, it is clearly both less glib and more far-reaching. Latour does not argue with traditional readings of modernity as the revolutionary (Copernican) division between nature and human knowledge. But he argues that these readings are partial and that, relocated within the full, two-tiered, structure of the modern Constitution, they lose their acumen. To modern, antimodern, and postmodern readers located within the first half of the Constitution, the critical revolution is still ongoing through a succession of ever more purified stances—such as the antimodern rehabilitation of nature or the postmodern skeptical recusal of reality. To less "critical" readers—science studies practitioners, "anthropologists of the moderns"[17]—who acknowledge the Constitution's second set of hybrid practices, it has never fully happened. For them, we have indeed never been modern because the purifying split between humans and nonhumans has not—and could never have—fully materialized. No temporal and logical break was ever successful at parsing out new purified subjects and objects from the imbroglios of premodern knowledge because all things are, in the human world, multiple and hybrid. Boyle's air pump and the mixed objects of experimental science are not substantially different from Amerindian natural–cultural webs. Only two things distinguish these classes of hybrids, according to Latour. (1) They are different in scale, not kind. Modern networks are not controlled and saturated like those of the premodern or traditional nature-cultures. They involve looser and bigger webs of actors; yet, this increase allows "scarcely anything more than small extensions of practices, slight accelerations in the circulation of knowledge"[18] and a paradoxical expansion in the "socialization of nonhumans."[19] (2) The second, more crucial, difference between these hybrids is one of precedence: moderns start with purified representations of hybrid mediations and acknowledge them only insofar as they can be told apart: pre- and nonmoderns reverse the process and begin with mixed objects and mediations to work out how they construct representations, showing both the promises and limits of the societies that create them.

If Latour calls moderns and their Constitution "nonmodern," then, it is hardly for the sake of paradox. It is because the modernity we usually identify with a revolution in science and politics is itself a politically powerful invention of the Constitution's upper level, and because modernity in a larger—less purified—sense is itself an admixture of conceptual discriminations feeding a lower layer of translations. The exact nature of this relationship between the first and second levels of the Constitution is not entirely clarified in the book—Latour only suggests that the two levels are mutually constitutive and that the repression of hybrids makes their intermixing more frequent. What is clear, however, is that all purifications can be shown to contain a blend of human and nonhuman elements and that there is, for Latour, no exception to the rule of universal translation. All objects are co-constituted by matter and mind. Everything, including those things we see as real and primary—rocks, stars, whales, microbes—is made of the entanglement of various material and conceptual agents. Such entanglement has nothing to do with the still dualist belief in some sort of representation of matter by mind. Nor should it be seen as the synthesis or combination of two discrete objects. It is true that Latour's vocabulary can be ambiguous. The word "hybrid," for example, appears to name the admixture of two discrete things. But Latour is a true "relationist": like Deleuze, Barad, or Haraway, he gives priority to the relation over its terms and sees it as a process wherein two entangled agencies co-elaborate each other. For him, relations create entities rather than the other way around. And his hybrids are not the heterogeneous collusion of two separate actors, but the condition and process of their emergence—Barad calls this process "intra- (rather than inter-) action."[20]

This relational principle is at the core of Latour's ontology and epistemology. It structures a world very different from the more dualistic cosmos of the moderns: a world in which all "actors" are hybrid and caught in a dynamic process of relations between various "collectives" or "networks." This world is not made of various entities with more or less substantial properties—natural and artificial, subjective and objective. It is made of concrete actors defined as the distribution of a force rather than the position of a substance. These actors encounter "a motley armada of forces, humans among them."[21] They engage with all in the trials that define and constitute them; and all are equally reshaped (translated) by these relational flows, which compose the world. Everything, for Latour, is in composition with everything else. Nothing exists by itself. Even nature and culture are actors among others in various networks.

Latour's relational ontology—more commonly known as "Actor Network Theory"—has profound implications for knowledge. One of the most crucial and transformative aspects of this theory is the immanent character of all objects and networks. In Latour's nonmodern cosmos, children, raindrops, archbishops, rocks, philosophers, concepts—or any other haphazard actors Latour likes to include in his inventories—all have "the exact same ontological footing."[22] They are all participants in a "democracy" of human and nonhuman actors and are defined by the mediations and alliances they form within their networks. The epistemological ramifications of this "flat ontology"[23] are as wide-ranging as they are significant and begin with a radical representational shift. Latour has repeatedly described, in his studies of modern science and philosophy, the problematic power of the optical metaphor and its representational apparatus. Such optical schemes are based on a dualist model with a fixed geometry. The observer is away from the object of her gaze and her view is both contingent upon and hindered by this transcendent position. Her perspective on phenomena may be clouded by her own bias or distorted by her knowledge, but it is always threatened by the mediations involved.[24] Such representational setup, with its dream of transparency and saltatory scheme,[25] makes the very work of knowledge invisible. By contrast, in Latour's immanent networks, observers are *inside* their web of relations as well as *immanent* and *mobile*. So are objects and ideas. And because knowledge is no longer defined by the mirroring of an object by a subject, it no longer sees its mediations as obstacles but as connectors. Knowing now happens in the middle: in the relations and alliances that recompose objects in their webs. It is no longer invested in the subject and object poles, but in the visible processes of translations. This resettlement entails, of course, a profound shift in the workings of truth. Truth is now contingent upon translation and fabrication, not purification. It depends on multiplying, not paring down connections. And since it no longer deals with "things in themselves" but with "the way these things are tied with our collectives and subjects,"[26] it is itself disseminated throughout networks. For Latour, truth or "reference" circulates along material-semiotic chains and is therefore as mobile as it is constructed. It is "nothing, *but* a chain of translations without resemblance from one actor to the next."[27]

Latour gives an excellent, if playful, example of this "circulating reference" when he opposes what he calls the "gas metaphor" to the "gaze" or optical metaphor of traditional representationalism.[28] The gas we put in our tanks, he argues, hardly refers to the "'real oil' out there."[29] It can only be understood in a network that connects it "to the oil field of Saudi Arabia" and "a series of cracking, transformations, transportations, refineries etc." that can hardly be conceived as "impedimenta" masking "the reality of the final product."[30] "The reality of oil in Saudi Arabia is proven by the number of transformations it undergoes before ending up as gas in your tank."[31] And this process, which "outlines the circulation and fluidity of the reference and [...] the impossibility of interrupting the flow,"[32] also shows that the "truth" of gas—like most truths—cannot be understood with a dualist model but within the mediations and circulation of a network.

Now the "gas metaphor" is hardly more sophisticated than the gaze one. Latour is quick to point out its limits and to show its unsuitability for understanding objects such as animals "who are more than the raw material of our knowledge about them" and participate in it.[33] It is more than likely that the trope is also insufficient to clarify cultural and literary objects, which are also more complex than gas, and respond as well to the questions we ask them. But we need not limit ourselves to this metaphor to investigate the role Latour's truth-in-network can play within literary studies. Latour's transformative approach has much larger implications for understanding literature and criticism. Because it upsets the representationalist, as well as anti-representationalist, ontology and epistemology of modern and postmodern thinking, it deeply affects both our theories of literature and practices of interpretation. And it challenges us to come up with critical approaches capable of accounting for the special brand of material-semiotic practices associated with Latour's networks. In what follows, we reflect upon the impact of Latour's nonmodern approach on literary studies. In addition to questioning how Latour's associative reconfiguration of the world, knowledge, and politics can transform the work of literary hermeneutics, we also wonder what kind of nonmodern "anthropology" can allow us to assess the exact role of literature and its criticism.

III

Literature or its criticism does not appear to be one of Latour's main concerns. He never disparages literary works which he considers to be a rich testing ground for his performative brand of sociology. But he "ignores or explicitly rejects many of the themes that have occupied literary scholars in recent decades: representation, the linguistic turn, textuality, the symbolic, negativity, alterity."[34] What Latour dismisses, in other terms, are those fundamentals that keep us bound to the post-Kantian division of world and thought. He is particularly critical of those theories that have overvalued language and semiotic processes and radicalized modern skeptical tendencies.[35] This criticism is not in itself original. Challenges to modernity are as many as they are diverse. What is more radical is Latour's nonmodern, outsider's perspective and its ability to cut to the quick of our debates. We often hear, today, about the exhaustion of the humanities. Many of our polemics and methods have lost their edge or seem stuck in the centuries-old feedback loop between nature and society, writing and politics. Latour's "de-modernizing" ignores these debates and goes beyond them to the very dualisms that feed them.[36] His approach, which he defines as "anthropological," focuses on natural–cultural hybrids. And because it relies on the study of material-semiotic objects rather than the old representationalist toolbox, it leads to very different questions and readings. This new "anthropology" is not readily defined, however, particularly when it comes to studying literary artifacts. Fitting modern literature and its critical readings into the nonmodern mold is like trying to fit a square peg into a round hole. And approaching "literature" and "critique" in *nonliterary* and *noncritical* ways is likely to prove a challenge.

Latour describes this very challenge in *We Have Never Been Modern* when explaining the difficulties of his new "anthropology."[37] Anthropology is, for the author, the main paradigm for his new network analysis. It is the least dualist of all human sciences and the only knowledge capable of bringing together plant and animals, family ties, ancestors, and the cosmos in a single study of natural–cultural networks. But, as Latour also explains, it is a highly imperfect paradigm which highlights, rather than eliminates, the difficulties of thinking non-dualistically within our modern tradition. Because it is conceived by Westerners to study other societies, it excludes science from its queries and sees premodern collectives as cultural "readings" of our immutable nature. Try as one might, it is impossible to remedy this asymmetry: we can't simply step out of the modern framework and go "beyond nature and culture."[38] And restoring symmetry by turning science and nature into cultural artifacts is not a solution either, as Latour explains. It simply shifts explanatory powers to society and its constructivist stance remains asymmetrical.

A very similar asymmetry destabilizes all efforts to study literature with a nonmodern—or anthropological—perspective. Literature, like science, is borne of the Western divide. It was conceived, early in our history, as the chattier and more speculative twin of the scientific "Book of Nature."[39] And it was fully birthed, a little later, from the empirical "bifurcation" that separated nature into the two distinct domains of matter and perception—what is and what we see. As is well-known, this split between matter and phenomenon became the foundation of Kant's aesthetic with its privileging of subjective experience. And this final Copernican split between an inaccessible nature—known only to science—and the world we perceive—rewritten by us—created the modern literature we know with its inner worlds, slippery words, and solipsistic writing.

This quick sketch is perhaps enough to show how asymmetrical modern literature is and has always been—*at least in theory*. Borne of a differential that turned it away from nature and toward human cultural representations, it has developed the critical personality we know well: both self-conscious and skeptical of its own representational and interpretive powers. The story of modern literature is that of a gaze turned inward: toward its own reflection and auto-*poiesis*.

Not surprisingly, there is also a parallel but opposite version to this story. From the nineteenth century on, the formalist drift away from nature has been complemented by a concurrent pull toward it. But these attempts to restore symmetry have all turned out to be equally polarized. Realists and naturalists have indeed tried to bring natural sciences to bear on the workings of the human world, but these efforts did not reconnect nature and society. Instead, they "naturalized" society by applying to it the laws of natural selection and shifted transcendence onto the natural pole. (One could also show the same movement back and forth across the nature–culture gap in those textualist theories that make language wholly autonomous but end up "materializing" it to keep it ontologically significant.)

I am rehearsing a familiar literary history. Historians and critics have often remarked upon these bipolar tendencies of modern literature. But Latour's anthropological perspective allows for a deeper insight into our "constitutive" inability to restore balance to literature's asymmetry. It helps us see clearly that no amount of pole switching, dialectics, or synthesis could restore symmetry to literary theory within our modern framework. This paralysis of our modern critical theories and practices is especially visible in today's literary studies. Most forms of social and cultural critique borrow their tools from those of "deconstruction, social construction, discourse analysis, postmodernism."[40] They practice a constructivism that relies on "powerful social explanations from the social neverland" (power, gender, class, economic) but remain staunch skeptics and debunkers of all things factual.[41] Latour is well-known for the scorns he heaps on the most extreme cultural critics and their disdain for matters of fact. But Baudrillard, Bourdieu, and other "marshals of simulacra" as he calls them are not the only critics divorced from reality.[42] Even those who, like Foucault or Butler, attempt to link discursive practices to materiality—that of the body, for example—are unable or unwilling to explain precisely how one might account for the simultaneous enactment of biological and historical forces.[43] As for the recent, and welcome, critical turn toward animals and the environment, it is equally plagued by the polarization between constructivists, realists, and postmodern skeptics. Scholars in these fields are still debating whether their nature is real, socially constructed, or radically "other."[44] And if nature or animal studies seem to be finally moving in the right, pragmatic, direction, it is because of the recent contribution of relational thinkers such as Latour, Stengers, or Haraway.[45]

What is the way out? How do we break the modern mold and begin to think literary studies more symmetrically with Latour? As the latter suggests, the only solution is to find a nonmodern position from which to destabilize this dualist apparatus and its operations. We mentioned earlier how Latour describes this position as a "median point" from which all things appear as hybrid or "factish." From this perspective, things-in-themselves are no longer separated from their phenomena. They are all both natural and cultural and can be seen—as Latour's ethnologist might see them—as *quasi-objects*: totem-like artifacts that bind together facts, social ties, the symbolic, and the spiritual. And it is from this hybrid standpoint that Latour redefines the twofold operation of his nonmodern anthropology: (1) to retrace hybrid networks and their work of mediation and (2) to describe the differential that purifies and distributes the terms of the modern settlement.

Latour's median point is an equally fine point of departure for us, modern literary anthropologists. Starting from a hybrid perspective is undoubtedly the only way to avoid the polarizations of our critical methods. And Latour's twin strategy is a comprehensive approach that promises to help us tackle both the covert and overt side of nonmodernity. The first part of his program—network analysis—restores symmetry to our divided critical stance and uncovers the relational webs it dissimulates. The second—Constitutional analysis—stays focused on the modernity of our artifacts and their metaphysical dualisms. As promising as it is, however, this program is also a tough one to follow for literary critics. The expression *literary anthropology*, for example, is seductive. But it is also a contradiction in terms since the symmetrical perspective of Latour's anthropology can never be coterminous with the asymmetrical perspective of modern literature. It also goes without saying that there is no uniquely *literary* or *textual* network analysis since all the actors that make Latour's networks are made, equally, of a mix of matter and signs. This question of literary specificity, or lack thereof, is important and should be at the center of any thinking about Latour and literature.[46] How do we follow Latour's protocols without losing our own way? How are we to read networks and remain literary critics?

To answer these queries, it may be best to begin with an example. Network analysis is always empirical and therefore distinctive, and starting locally will help us make sense of the above conundrum. Ponge's "Oyster" is a good place to start.[47] This particular poem—or any other of the *objeux*[48] (poetic-play/thing) included in *Le parti-pris des choses*—is a good example of hybrid co-elaboration of things and words, and it offers us an equally suitable "median point" from which to base our new perspective. In the Pongian "object/poem," both the thing—with its active resistance to naming (its "parti-pris")—and the text—with its tendency toward autonomy (its linguistic solipsism)—are immanent and entangled. There is no transcendence of word over thing or thing over word as they both elaborate each other in the same process of troping and translating. What is more, this mutual co-elaboration of matter and figure offers a striking nonmodern rewriting of traditional representationalism. Instead of staging the grasping of an object by a subject, the entangled *mise-en-abyme* of poem and thing suggests that Oyster and poem do not *precede their poetic encounter* but are secondary and purified products of the poem's relational performance.[49] This scrambling of the traditional representationalist structure gives priority to mediation over purification and hybridity over entity. As such, it redistributes our habitual understandings of both agency and reference. Poetic agency is now "composite"[50] and no longer reserved to the writer or his text. Conversely, reference "circulates" and no longer hails from the world out there. The product of this hybrid redistribution is precisely what Latour calls a network: a motley crew of actors who translate each other and vie for agency in an ever-moving process of transformations.

Ponge's hybrid poetic offers us a clear standpoint from which to restore critical symmetry and recompose the relational networks divvied up by the moderns. It helps us stay clear of the critical debates that endlessly argue for the priority of things over words or the privilege of words over things. And it invites us to retrace instead, step by step, moment by moment, the series of transformations, transmutations and translations that cross the gap between matter and form and "make it come to matter."[51] This process of composition is the same whether we consider Latour's study of "comparative pedology," Haraway's description of companion species meetings, or the flesh-and-word tropings of Ponge's "Oyster."[52] It involves reconnecting the "figures that help us grapple inside the flesh of world-making entanglements"[53] and being attentive to the "vascularization"[54] that links these entanglements to other networks.[55] This painstaking process is not unlike the close readings we are familiar with. Yet it is different in at least two ways. Network analysis is much more encompassing than any close-reading protocol. It is also, and this is the crucial difference, ultimately "empirical"— in the radical sense that William James and Latour give the term. Traditional readings, whether close or not, remain largely beholden to a hermeneutic that privileges human experience in all its subjective, cultural, or linguistic forms. This is not the case for network analysis where the subjective holds no special status, and meaning belongs to all of the actors in the network, regardless of their nature. This redistribution of roles has obvious consequences for the ways we read. The question of choice between subjective and objective readings, for example, becomes moot, as does the traditional alternative between reading for content or reading for form. More importantly, nonmodern networks—and their anthropology—can no longer be defined as simply "textual." Granted, linguistic mediations may be more frequent and proportionally more prevalent in the "philological" networks we study. But they are not the only ones, nor are they privileged givers of meaning. Ponge's poems do prioritize linguistic mediations, in part because they treat language as both actor and object. But their tropes are not the only mediators nor are they purely linguistic. Metaphors do play a big role in the poems, but so do rocks, cooking advice, ancient cosmology, heraldry, pearls, not to mention a modern writer preoccupied with words. All these quasi-things "trope" each other in a complex macrocosmic and microcosmic exchange of the concrete and the abstract, the ordinary and the metaphysical.

A Latourian reading of Ponge would recompose this mixed assemblage and describe its "contact zones." It would also stay away from any suggestion—common among modern and postmodern critics—that all these actors are figures of speech or otherwise reducible to the phenomenal experience of the writer. For Latour, nothing can be reduced to anything else and troping, like interpreting, "is not a privilege of language or humans but a property of the world itself."[56] All the actors in a poem—whether or not they can speak—have equal hermeneutic weight. They are all vectors and agents of understanding, and this interpretive democracy is both a loss and a boon for literary scholars: a loss, because a criticism that no longer relies on the privilege of text and interpretation loses its autonomy along with its polemical power;[57] a gain, because this democratization of interpretive agency—as well as the redistribution of reference—defines a more collaborative as well as connected way of reading. Felski, who astutely compares this shared hermeneutic with the co-elaboration of a creature's *umwelt*, underscores both the bi-directionality and the embodied nature of the connections between readers and their cultural artifacts. The latter, she argues, "become part of a body-centered web of relations to phenomena that bear meaning for us."[58] In this relational complex, the difference between subject and object becomes moot. Reading, on this new, relational understanding, is an empirical process that emphasizes connections over verification and gives renewed agency to all manners of hybrids. It brings the reader face to face with a "crowd of squabbling, jostling, interconnected actors playing their parts" and places her as well within that performance to compose, translate, and interpret.[59] This methodological sketch is, of course, hardly programmatic. Its generality underscores the difficulty of approaching hybrid networks specifically. Felski, who also takes stock of this difficulty in her two essays on Latour and literary studies, offers an interesting solution to the lack of specificity of network analysis.[60] Instead of trying to solve the impossible question of the nature of literary networks, she focuses her analysis on the modalities of their mediations: what Latour calls their "modes of existence." This solution, which heeds Latour's shift from substance to relation, is indeed rooted in his recent "Inquiry into Modes of Existence"[61] which examines ways of beings, customs, and affects that make up a particular relational practice. Literary modalities are not those of sociology or science studies. Each discipline has singular models of veridiction, ambitions, reading protocols, literature as well as others. And "while we can agree," writes Felski, "that literary texts are connected to countless things that are not literature, [we must also acknowledge that] there cluster around literature certain ways of talking, experiencing, acting, interpreting and evaluating."[62] These ways have to be surveyed, historicized, and also changed according to nonmodern practices. Felski suggest, for example, that we replace and retool old hermeneutic modalities with new ones such as "curating, conveying, composing," or "attachment."[63]

Felski's modal approach is compelling and helps us understand how to read networks more specifically. I would, however, add an important second step to this emerging program. As you may remember, Latour's anthropological approach is always a two-step process: a study of networks followed by a Constitutional analysis. This second moment is a critical one in Latour's analysis. It allows him to take the modern distribution of nature and culture as a theme rather than a tool and to study its metaphysical foundations along with its historical settlements and objects. It is also for us a crucial step in the move from modern to nonmodern literary criticism because networks may undo the divisive work of the Constitution, but they remain in dialog with its structure and artifacts. As Paulson's work shows, reconnecting criticism to wider networks cannot be done without looking first at the history of modern literature, its language and relation with science. What literary critic would, for example, study the poetic networks of a Ponge poem without considering the dualist debates surrounding his poetry and his use of language? These debates need not inform directly a hybrid reading of the "Oyster." But they are certainly essential to understanding the representational pull that shadows these texts and our readings.

Constitutional analysis is an intricate part of any nonmodern approach of literary criticism. It shows us how literature is borne—and perpetually reinvents itself—as polarized within the modern parenthesis. By bringing together specific modern artifacts with nonspecific network analysis, it also helps us stay anchored within our field and alleviates our anxieties about the programmability of nonmodern literary studies. New critical trends do indeed need, as Paulson writes, "research programs to win the rights of citizenship in the academic community."[64] Constitutional analysis can provide at least a partial agenda. It asks us to study 'the many ways in which the notion of modernity and post-modernity have been used in literary, artistic and cultural studies.'[65] Paired with Felski's modalization of network analysis, it advances an already significant and sizeable agenda.

IV

"What does it mean, then, to rethink literary studies under the assumption of nonmodernity?"

We put Paulson's question to the contributors of this volume and left it open. We wanted it to play the role of the twenty-third bowl set out as an experiment by the ethologist Thelma Rowell. For Rowell (and Haraway), setting an extra twenty-third bowl when there are only twenty-two sheep to feed "make(s) it possible for something unexpected to happen." It asks the question:"what *else might be* happening?"[66] rather than "what *is really* going on?" Likewise, we wanted this query to reshuffle critical cards, open the readings to new attachments and unknown worlds. These chapters are the unpredictable and hybrid answers we received.

In his opening chapter, Jan Miernowski makes the surprising claim that Latour's nonmodern practice bears some of the fundamental traits of premodern humanism. He defines such practice with five theses: in politics, the humanist is not locked up in an ivory tower of scholarship, but, on the contrary, is fully engaged in the public debate; in metaphysics, the humanist does not presuppose the superiority of Man, but rather searches for what is human within the marvelous variety of beings; in exegetical work, the humanist is not so much a philosopher as a philologist; in rhetoric, the humanist is not content with mere words, but cultivates eloquence in order to change reality; in theology, the humanist is not indifferent to the matters of faith; on the contrary, belief is the humanist's primary concern. Miernowski proves Latour's "nonmodern humanism" by comparing Latour's study of Pasteur's "war on microbes" with Montaigne's epistemological and discursive skepticism in the *Essays*.

Oumelbanine Zhiri approaches orientalism in terms of mediation rather than purification. She takes issues with the sharp division Edward Said introduces between modern orientalism and its premodern version. According to Said's influential view, Orientalism produced the difference between East and West and justified the latter's domination of the former. Zhiri argues, however, that this view, which helped demystify modern imperialism's cultural production, can be seen as teleological when projected onto earlier periods. To avoid this trap, she proposes a Latourian relational approach to read an episode of encounter between the famed Dutch scholars Thomas Erpenius and Jacobus Golius with the Moroccan Ahmad al-Hajari. She traces the networks of hybrid and scientific exchanges that connect East and West which produced the works of early modern European Orientalists, destabilizing rigid binaries as well as the way in which post-medieval Europe defined itself by way of scientific modernity in opposition to the non-West.

For William Paulson, Bruno Latour's questioning of the "modernist settlement," his undoing of modernity's dualisms, can be extended to fundamental polarities of modern literature, such as experience and discourse, realism and formalism, referentiality and autonomy. Paulson takes up Flaubert, who is a touchstone of literary modernity both as realist and textualist: indeed, Flaubert is understood to epitomize both extremes of a modernist polarity, as if he were simultaneously (or by turns) Zola and Mallarmé. Paulson asks: if Flaubert is nonmodern, can literature have been modern? Concentrating on *Madame Bovary*, Paulson critiques the construction of Flaubert as modern, focusing on the readings of novelist-critics (Zola, Sarraute, and Vargas-Llosa). He also analyzes Flaubert's self-characterization: declaring himself antimodern and modern, the novelist often describes himself as something else, which in some cases we can now call nonmodern. Paulson shows that Flaubert's novels would not be possible if their aesthetic were as one-sided as his interpreters (and often he himself) have claimed.

Claire Chi-ah Lyu's chapter explores what modern poetry and poetic criticism might look like if we have never been modern. It takes issues with the formalist theory of self-referential language that keeps poetry apart from the nonhuman material world and argues that the new interpretive context of climate change—which foregrounds the global and inevitable imbrication of discourse, politics, and nature—challenges us to find an alternative way of defining poetry: not uniquely as the epitome of insular, autonomous discourse but as a hybrid genre that entangles language, thought, body, affect, and the nonhuman material world. By pairing two modern figures, Blanchot and Mallarmé, with two nonmodern thinkers, Stengers and Latour, Lyu proposes to reorient poetry from modern representational purification to nonmodern performative mediation so as to inquire into how poetry can relate us to, rather than separate us from, the nonhuman world.

Gabriel Hankins reads two classic modernist scenes of disciplinary power through the lens of Latourian sociology, in explicit counterpoint to the approaches of Michel Foucault and Pierre Bourdieu. The first example is the episode of the Whipper in Kafka's *The Trial*, which the chapter explores as a case study in the material life of governance. The scene of the pandybat in Joyce's *A Portrait of the Artist as a Young Man* is the second case, along with other scenes of disciplinary and governmental power in this fundamental modernist bildungsroman. In both cases, Hankins reads against the classical and critical sociological accounts of disciplinary power in order to discover new actors and agents at work within these key scenes in the literature of the disciplinary state.

Maxime Goergen starts with an analysis of Latour's concept of nonmodernity against the backdrop of the ideological reshuffle of the late 1980s in France. In particular, he demonstrates that the concept of nonmodernity must be understood in relation to contemporary reassessments of the legacy of the French Revolution and argues that Latour's works allow a critical reappraisal of the nineteenth century, which is presented here as the paradoxical heyday of nonmodernity. Using key "modern" figures like Baudelaire, he illustrates that it is especially in its aesthetic practice that the French nineteenth century must be reassessed as nonmodern. Goergen argues in favor of a literary history of nonmodernity and analyzes the works of one of his potential paragons, the historian Jules Michelet. Close readings of Michelet suggest that the literary text can be defined as the very crucible of nonmodern practices.

Extending Latour and Strum's hypothesis regarding the complex dimension of animal political societies, Vinciane Despret explores the notion of territory as a form of the social that is inscribed in space. By examining what could constitute a territory for a bird, she investigates the ways in which inhabiting a space manufactures sociality as a created bond. For Despret, the creation of territories involves not only geopolitical behaviors but also the capacity to respect forms: each territory is the manifestation of the political invention of a form that composes relations with other forms. In making us aware of other ways of inhabiting and thus of making the world, Despret seeks to enact the lesson Latour has taught her, which is to "learn from other species that there are other ways of existing."

Elisabeth Arnould-Bloomfield reconnects Jean-Christophe Bailly's contemplative vision of the animal world with a more pragmatic and hybrid approach. Taking Bailly's 2007 text, *The Animal Side*, as a test study, she questions its "equal but separate" portrayal of the animal world and suggests using Latour's relational thought to bridge the human and nonhuman sides of the divide. As recent revisions of animal science and epistemology have intimated, it is possible to critique human exceptionality and rethink our proximity to animals without having to turn animals into inaccessible others. Latour's relational epistemology and the pragmatic ethology of Vinciane Despret are charting the course of a "middle knowledge": a knowledge that does not reduce animals to objective aliens or subjective phenomena but operates in the natural–cultural space of interspecies relations. Arnould-Bloomfield's aim is to show that bringing Latour's and Despret's empiricism into contact with Bailly's overly careful epistemological stance allows us to rehabilitate the idea of a transitive yet respectful knowledge of animals.

Graham Harman examines the surprisingly constructive response Latour gives to the tenure of Donald J. Trump as the forty-fifth president of the United States. The chapter begins by reconstructing Latour's shift from an early-career commitment to power politics in the manner of Thomas Hobbes to a model of political consensus around an unknown object, as inspired by John Dewey and Noortje Marres. A brief account is then given of Latour's article "Two Bubbles of Unrealism," published in the immediate aftermath of the 2016 presidential election, which argues that Trump's supporters and opponents have both failed to face up to reality. Harman then turns to Latour's 2018 book, *Down to Earth*, in which Trumpism is treated as a rare political innovation—consisting not in fascism, but in escapism—that needs to be countered with new ideas. In closing, Latour's model of human/world entanglement is contrasted with that of Karen Barad.

In the final chapter, Stephen Muecke presents Paddy Roe (c. 1912–2001), a Nyigina elder in the Indigenous community of Broome, Western Australia. He documents how Roe's storytelling was recomposed as Australian literature, and Roe himself as an author (1983, 1984). The ethnographic description of this process seeks to highlight the differences between traditional oral literary production and the culture of the Australian publishing industry. The analysis, along the lines of Latour's *Inquiry into Modes of Existence*, includes the heterogeneous factors that contribute to the achievement of the work. For example, Roe's "literary world" is inconceivable without the grounding of the "dreaming" (*bugarrigarra*), but "fiction" is not an operative category in his culture. The chapter describes the series of technological, textual, and performative factors involved in the translation of artful oral narratives into artful written literature.

In her afterword, Rita Felski investigates how Latour's claim that "we have never been modern" speaks to humanists. She highlights the ambiguities of the modern: a term that is variously used to describe economic and material conditions, philosophical worldviews, aesthetic sensibilities, everyday cultural experiences, and relationships to time. Modernity is commonly associated with increasing rationalization and standardization, but also with dissidence, uncertainty, and ambiguity. For Felski, Latour's *We Have Never Been Modern*, which focuses on the scientific and philosophical meanings of modernity, does not fully engage this history of conflicting meanings. Her contribution brings Latour into dialog with recent discourses of "multiple modernities," which stress the differing cultures of modernity as shaped by race, gender, and sexuality. She finds, however, that Latour's ideas can be exceptionally useful in clarifying the role of purification and periodization in shaping the development of literature and literary criticism.

Notes

1 William Paulson, "For a Cosmopolitical Philology: Lessons from Science Studies," *SubStance: A Review of Theory and Criticism* 30, no. 3 (2001): 101–19.
2 Paulson discusses ways in which literary studies could benefit from Latour's works as well as those of Haraway and Stengers in *Literary Culture in a World Transformed: A Future for the Humanities* (Ithaca: Cornell University Press, 2001), in particular in chapter three "Becoming Nonmodern: Learning from Science Studies." He has brought a Latourian nonmodern way of thinking to bear on the study of literature starting from as early as 1995: see "Nous n'avons jamais été dix-neuviémistes, ou l'avenir d'un avant-dernier siècle," *Nineteenth-Century French Studies* 24, no. 1–2 (1995–96): 34–9, and "The Invention of a Non-Modern World," in *Closer to the Wild Heart: Essays on Clarice Lispector*, ed. Cláudia Pazons Alonso and Claire Williams (Oxford: Legenda, 2002), 198–212.
3 See in particular Rita Felski, "Latour and Literary Studies," *PMLA* 130, no. 3 (2015): 737–42; Graham Harman, "Demodernizing the Humanities with Latour," *New Literary History* 47, no. 2–3 (2016): 249–74, and David Alsworth, "Latour and Literature," in *Theory Matters: The Place of Theory in Literary and Cultural Studies Today*, ed. Martin Middeke and Christoph Reinfandt (London: Palgrave, 2016), 305–18.
4 Felski, "Latour and Literary Studies," 738.
5 Ibid.
6 Latour, *We Have Never Been Modern*, trans. Catherine Porter (Cambridge: Harvard University Press, 1999), 47.
7 Ibid., 46–7.
8 Ibid., 13.
9 Ibid., 37.

10 Latour borrows some of this "Constitutional analysis" from Steven Shapin and Simon Schaffer's *Leviathan and the Airpump; Hobbes, Boyle and the Experimental Life* (Princeton: Princeton University Press, 1985).
11 Latour, *We Have Never Been Modern*, 36.
12 Ibid., 37.
13 Ibid.
14 Ibid.
15 Ibid., 40.
16 Ibid., 41.
17 After science studies, anthropology is the second major epistemological model of Latour. We will come back to this model later in our introduction.
18 Latour, *We Have Never Been Modern*, 48.
19 Ibid., 42.
20 Karen Barad uses the term "intra-action" rather than "inter-action" to focus on this mutual Constitution of entangled agencies. She writes: "The notion of *intra-action* (in contrast to the usual 'interaction,' which presumes the prior existence of independent entities/relata) represents a profound conceptual shift" in that it shows that "phenomena are ontologically primitive relations—relations without existing relata." Karen Barad, "Posthumanist Performativity: Toward an Understanding of How Matter Comes to Matter," *Signs: Journal of Women in Culture and Society* 28, no. 3 (2003): 815.
21 Graham Harman, *Prince of Networks: Bruno Latour and Metaphysics* (Melbourne: Re. Press, 2009), 13.
22 Ibid., 14.
23 The expression was coined by Manuel DeLanda in his book *Intensive Science and Virtual Philosophy* (London: Bloomsbury, 2013).
24 Latour shows that this optical model of knowledge makes knowledge itself invisible. In this optical system, the good gaze is one that is immediately transitive and therefore transparent. As such, it implies a conception of science where the scientific process itself is not included and is invisible. Bruno Latour, "A Well-Articulated Primatology: Reflexions of a Fellow Traveller," in *Primate Encounters: Models of Science, Gender, and Society*, ed. Shirley Strum and Linda Fedigan (Chicago: University of Chicago Press, 1997).
25 According to Latour, who borrows the idea from William James, all dualist and optical knowledge is "saltatory" because it is based on the idea that knowledge can be achieved by jumping from a subject's experience to an undefined object.
26 Latour, *We Have Never Been Modern*, 4.
27 Harman, *Prince of Networks*, 76. Original emphasis.
28 Latour also gives a remarkable, and far more detailed, analysis of "circulating reference" in the chapter of the same name "Circulating Reference, Sampling the

Soil in the Amazon Forest," in *Pandora's Hope: Essays on the Reality of Science Studies* (Cambridge: Harvard University Press, 1999), 24–80.

29   Latour, "A Well-Articulated Primatology," 370.
30   Ibid.
31   Ibid.
32   Ibid.
33   Ibid.
34   Felski, "Latour and Literary Studies," 737.
35   See, for example, *We Have Never Been Modern*, 62–5.
36   Graham, "Demodernizing the Humanities with Latour."
37   See chapter 4 of *We Have Never Been Modern* on "Relativism" (91–127).
38   Philippe Descola, *Beyond Nature and Culture*, trans. Janet Lloyd. (Chicago: University of Chicago Press, 2013).
39   See Paulson's enlightening account of this twin birth in *Literary Culture in a World Transformed*.
40   Bruno Latour, "Why Has Critique Run Out of Steam: From Matters of Fact to Matters of Concern," *Critical Inquiry* 30 (2004): 231.
41   Ibid., 230.
42   Ibid., 228.
43   I am paraphrasing Karen Barad's argument in "Posthumanist Performativity."
44   See, for example, Ralph Acampora, "Real Animals? An Enquiry on Behalf of Relational Zoontology," *Human Ecology Review* 8, no. 2 (2001): 73–8.
45   The most vibrant scholarly areas in animal and environmental studies today are those which have indeed bypassed the modern dualist conundrum and are working in the vicinity of Latour, Stengers and Haraway's work—to mention only a few of these nonmodern theorists and practitioners.
46   Rita Felski is one of the first and only critics to have paid serious attention to this question in her *PMLA* essay: "Latour and Literary Studies."
47   Francis Ponge, "L'huître," in *Le Parti-pris des choses* précédé de *Douze petits écrits* et suivi de *Proêmes* (Paris: Gallimard, 1926, 1942, 1948), 43.
48   Francis Ponge, "Le Soleil placé en Abîme," in *Pièces* (Paris: Gallimard, 1961), 157.
49   I am paraphrasing Donna Haraway, who writes "The partners do not precede their relatings" in *When Species Meet* (Minneapolis: University of Minnesota Press, 2008), 17.
50   Felski, "Latour and Literary Studies," 739.
51   I borrow this wonderful formulation from the title of Karen Barad's essay: "Posthumanist Performativity."
52   See the first chapter of Latour's *Pandora's Hope* and Haraway's *When Species Meet*.
53   Haraway, *When Species Meet*, 4.
54   Latour, "A Well-Articulated Primatology," 359.

55 Haraway, *When Species Meet*, 4.
56 Quoted by Felski, "Latour and Literary Studies," 740.
57 Ponge's voluminous criticism is, with a few exceptions (Sydney Levy for example), a perfect illustration of this endless debate between partisans of the primacy of writing and those who take the side of things.
58 Felski, "Latour and Literary Studies," 740.
59 Ibid., 741.
60 I am referring here to "Latour and Literary Studies" and the introduction to the special *New Literary History* issue on Latour and the humanities: "Introduction," *New Literary History* 47, no. 2–3 (2016): 215–29.
61 Bruno Latour, *An Inquiry into Modes of Existence: An Anthropology of the Moderns*, trans. Catherine Porter (Cambridge: Harvard University Press, 2013).
62 Felski, "Latour and Literary Studies," 739.
63 The first categories are found in the *New Literary History* "introduction," the last in "Latour and Literary Studies," 740.
64 Paulson, "For a Cosmopolitical Philology: Lessons from Science Studies," 118.
65 Ibid.
66 The italics are my emphasis. Donna J. Haraway recounts the experiment in *When Species Meet* as follows: "Rowell brings her competent sheep into the yard most days so that she can ask them some more questions while they snack. There, the twenty-two sheep find twenty-three bowls spaced around the yard. That homely twenty-third bowl is the open, the space of what is not yet and may or may not ever be; it is a making available to events; it is asking the sheep and the scientists to be smart in their exchanges by making it possible for something unexpected to happen" (34).

Bibliography

Acampora, Ralph. "Real Animals? An Enquiry on Behalf of Relational Zoontology." *Human Ecology Review* 8, no. 2 (2001): 73–8.

Alsworth, David J. "Latour and Literature." In *Theory Matters: The Place of Theory in Literary and Cultural Studies Today*. Edited by Martin Middeke and Christoph Reinfandt. 305–18. London: Palgrave, 2016.

Barad, Karen. "Posthumanist Performativity: Toward an Understanding of How Matter Comes to Matter." *Signs, Journal of Women in Culture and Society* 28, no. 3 (2003): 801–31.

DeLanda, Manuel. *Intensive Science and Virtual Philosophy*. London: Bloomsbury, 2013.

Descola, Philippe. *Beyond Nature and Culture*. Translated by Janet Lloyd. Chicago: University of Chicago Press, 2013.

Felski, Rita. "Introduction." *New Literary History* 47, no. 2–3 (2016): 215–29.
Felski, Rita. "Latour and Literary Studies." *PMLA* 130, no. 3 (2015): 737–42.
Felski, Rita. *The Limits of Critique*. Chicago: University of Chicago Press, 2015.
Haraway, Donna J. *When Species Meet*. Minneapolis: University of Minnesota Press, 2008.
Harman, Graham. "Demodernizing the Humanities with Latour." *New Literary History* 47, no. 2–3 (2016): 249–74.
Harman, Graham. *Prince of Networks: Bruno Latour and Metaphysics*. Melbourne: Re. Press, 2009.
Latour, Bruno. "An Attempt at a 'Compositionist Manifesto.'" *New Literary History* 41 (2010): 471–90.
Latour, Bruno. *An Inquiry into Modes of Existence: An Anthropology of the Moderns*. Translated by Catherine Porter. Cambridge: Harvard University Press, 2013.
Latour, Bruno. *Pandora's Hope: Essays on the Reality of Science Studies*. Cambridge: Harvard University Press, 1999.
Latour, Bruno. *We Have Never Been Modern*. Translated by Catherine Porter. Cambridge: Harvard University Press, 1999.
Latour, Bruno. "A Well-Articulated Primatology: Reflections of a Fellow-Traveller." In *Primate Encounters: Models of Science, Gender, and Society*. Edited by Shirley C. Strum and Linda M. Fedigan. 357–81. Chicago: University of Chicago Press, 2000.
Latour, Bruno. "Why Has Critique Run Out of Steam?" *Critical Inquiry* 30 (2004): 225–48.
Paulson, William. "For a Cosmopolitical Philology: Lessons from Science Studies." *SubStance* 30, no. 3 (2001): 101–19.
Paulson, William. "The Invention of a Non-Modern World." In *Closer to the Wild Heart: Essays on Clarice Lispector*. Edited by Cláudia Pazons Alonso and Claire Williams. 198–212. Oxford: Legenda, 2002.
Paulson, William. *Literary Culture in a World Transformed: A Future for the Humanities*. Ithaca: Cornell University Press, 2001.
Paulson, William. "Nous n'avons jamais été dix-neuviémistes, ou l'avenir d'un avant-dernier siècle." *Nineteenth-Century French Studies* 24, no. 1–2 (1995–96): 34–9.
Ponge, Francis. *Le Parti-pris des choses* précédé de *Douze petits écrits* et suivi de *Proêmes*. Paris: Gallimard, 1926, 1942, 1948.
Ponge, Francis. "Le Soleil placé en abîme." In *Pièces*. Paris: Gallimard, 1961.
Shapin, Steven, and Simon Schaffer. *Leviathan and the Airpump; Hobbes, Boyle and the Experimental Life*. Princeton: Princeton University Press, 1985.

Part One

Early Modern Tradition from a Latourian Relational Perspective

1

"Nonmodern Humanism": A Relational Reading of Latour and Montaigne

Jan Miernowski

Dla Szymona

The goal of this chapter is to portray Bruno Latour as a humanist. This may seem to be a daring endeavor, both because of the intellectual context within which this task is undertaken and because of the specificity of Latour's thinking. It is widely assumed that we live in a posthuman world. The death of God was closely followed by the death of Man, acknowledged by Sartre right at the end of the Second World War and trumpeted by Foucault in the 1960s.[1] Consequently, the key question with which humanists have wrestled—"What does it mean to be human?"—seems anachronistic. It can also be seen as ethically problematic. Indeed, the specificity, or worse, the superiority of the human being that traditionally is considered to be the foundational claim of humanism, seems outrageous in the era of the Anthropocene.[2] Latour is very vocal in denouncing the process through which we make our planet inhabitable.[3] His ecological thinking and activism stem from his philosophical relationism which is programmatically indifferent to the distinction between humans and nonhumans. Being the "Prince of Networks" that are by definition composed of agents who can be either human, nonhuman, or hybrid, Latour can hardly be suspected of any anthropocentric glorification of Man.[4]

And yet, I would like to claim that Latour's unique way of thinking and writing bears fundamental traits of a humanist practice. Let me insist on the word "practice." Indeed, humanism came to be understood as a doctrine, an "-ism," only recently. The nineteenth century invented humanism as a cultural movement that associated the study of classical literature with a conception of the sovereign Self. Such vision of Man was predicated largely on Kantian philosophy, which, needless to say, was unknown to Renaissance humanists. It is this post-Enlightenment conception of human exceptionalism that came under the fire of postmodern critique.[5] Yet, contrary to nineteenth-century proponents of Kantian *Bildung* and to their twentieth-century critics, Renaissance humanists did not consider Man as a philosophical premise, but rather as the object of an open-ended questioning. This inquiry—*studia humanitatis*—had far-reaching ethical and political implications, but, most importantly, there was at its core a hermeneutical and an oratorical exercise based on the belief that through the exchange of "letters" reality can be changed and people can be made present.

It is in this practical, Renaissance sense, that I would qualify Latour as a humanist. Latour always had a keen interest for the historical period preceding the early seventeenth century for the simple reason that during that time people did not yet claim to be "modern."[6] Before Hobbes and Descartes, Western Europe, along with parts of the world that many still call "underdeveloped," was resolutely "premodern," at least in the eyes of Moderns whose illusion of modernity Latour strives to dispel. The Renaissance did not yet extend the laws of physics to the entire universe; it did not entrench the political communities within national borders. In sum, the "premodern" Renaissance did not complete what Latour calls after Whitehead "the Great Bifurcation," that is, the separation between Nature and Culture, scientific laws and societal rules, the matters of fact and the matters of concern. Latour insists that despite framing the modern mindset, these epistemological dichotomies did not affect the real *modus operandi* of the Moderns. In practice, while claiming the "Great Bifurcation," Moderns never stopped producing hybrids which embodied the displacements, transfers, and translations between what they loudly proclaimed to be "purely natural" on the one hand and "purely manmade" on the other. One of such hybrids is the Anthropocene itself, the beginning of which, according to Latour, should be dated in the first half of the seventeenth century.[7]

There is a great deal of nostalgia in Latour's looking back at "premodern" Renaissance, the blessed era before the hypocritical purisms of Modernity: scientism, nationalism, deism, colonialism, postmodernism (which is just an inverted modernism), etc. "Humanism," understood as a variant of neo-Kantian idealism, is yet another symptom of the nineteenth century's "second Enlightenment." But being nostalgic of the past is one thing, and trying to rethink the present is another. Latour does not advocate the return to premodernity, but rather a leap forward, into "nonmodernism."[8] I would argue that by doing so, Latour acts as a "nonmodern humanist" who revives the practices of the Renaissance humanists.

In order to prove my point, I will propose a few synthetic propositions that characterize the specificity of Renaissance humanist practice and I will demonstrate how Latour revives them in his own work. I would like to insist on the term "revives." Latour's affinity with the Renaissance humanists should be understood in the true spirit of the "Re-naissance" which relied on the realization that Greek and Roman Antiquity belongs to a remote past with which any continuity has been irremediably lost. It is only because Antiquity is a dead, albeit prestigious culture, that it can be reborn in the European fifteenth and sixteenth centuries not as a clone, but as a new, thriving organism. Similarly, Latour's humanist practice is not a mimicry of the philosophical and stylistic idiosyncrasies of Montaigne, Rabelais, or Erasmus, but a fundamentally original intellectual proposition that shares a clearly distinct "air de famille" with ways of thinking and writing of the humanists dead four centuries ago. Latour is not a premodern humanist anachronistically catapulted into post-postmodernity, but a humanist who testifies to our posthuman times and invites us to look into a "nonmodern" future that hopefully will alleviate at least some of the impairments of the Anthropocene. For the sake of brevity, I will focus my demonstration on one of the most programmatic books by Latour—*The Pasteurization of France*[9]—with references to some of his other publications. As an epitome of Renaissance humanism, I will consider Montaigne's *Essays*,[10] while seeking occasional help from other premodern humanists.

Politics: The humanist is not locked up in an ivory tower of scholarship, but, on the contrary, is fully engaged in the public debate.

Machiavelli, seeking solace from the misfortunes of public life in the solitude of his library; Erasmus, portrayed by Holbein, bent over a manuscript in his *studiolo*; Montaigne, laboring on the *Essays* in the tower of his castle after having retired from a judicial position at the court of Bordeaux; etc., we often associate the humanists' *otium* with isolation and indifference to the world around them. Nothing could be more removed from truth. In fact, Renaissance humanists were deeply engaged in the conflicts tearing apart their cities and Europe in general. This is obvious in the case of the *Prince*, which could be seen as an elaborate application for a political position, or with Erasmus's *Querela Pacis*, which was a memorandum for peace sent to the most powerful world leaders in the guise of a bitter-sweet prosopopea. It was also true in the less obvious case of Montaigne's *Essays*, which bear distinct traces of the civil wars during which Montaigne played the role of a diplomatic intermediary between fighting factions.[11]

Like Montaigne in his tower-library, Latour is also surrounded by war. His most recent essay, *Down to Earth: Politics in the New Climate Regime*, maps out the conflicts stirred up by the conjunction of globalization, increased economical inequalities, and climate change in the aftermath of the Cold War. Hence now, fifty years after May 1968, the rise of a new revolutionary spirit throughout Europe, but this time, of a distinctly right-wing orientation.[12] Latour's humanist engagement in politics is a leitmotiv of his scholarship. In the Orwellian year 1984, at the time of the first edition of the *Pasteurization of France*, Latour also had some very pressing concerns. Europe held its breath amidst the Pershing-SS22 missile crisis and under the looming threat of a nuclear conflict. Both the 2017 and the 1984 books share the same anticipation of the worst to come alongside the same glimmer of hope that doom can be averted. This is exactly the same fragile hope that motivates Montaigne's otherwise very gloomy assessment of the war-torn France at the end of the sixteenth century.

But there is another important feature of Latour's thinking that imitates Montaigne's humanist practice: war does not constitute a distinct object of study, and politics is not the field for a discrete disciplinary line of inquiry. Instead, political violence, which imposes by force new relations between things and people, is parallel to other aspects of the human condition—law and our bodily ailments, language and courtship, religion and the pretenses of science, etc. These topics are so closely intermingled that it is hard to tell what is the main argument and what is a digressive example. For instance, in "On Experience," Montaigne invokes the theological quarrels leading to massacres and bloody battles as "purely verbal" disputes. The wars of religion and the deficiency of language are just different instances of our incapacity to empirically grasp reality. In "On Physiognomy," a raid on his castle by some marauders gives Montaigne the opportunity to question the difference between nature and culture: was the mortal danger awaiting the author averted because of the genuine trustfulness of Montaigne's character or thanks to the artfully staged frankness of his facial expression? Similarly, for Latour, reflecting almost twenty years after the first publication of *Pasteurization of France*, war is not simply the historical context in which his book was initially written, but rather a metaphysical risk stemming from the relational nature of reality. War becomes thus a potent epistemological model that allows him to think through the anthropology of science and technology in the same way it is helpful to conceptualize the politics of the day:

> "The war of sciences." I coined this expression then, according to the model of "the wars of religion" [civil wars that took place in France between 1562 and 1598—JM]. My intention was to reference the rapid transformation of a source of peace into the pretext for a scandal, which, at that time, was exemplified by the constant threat of an atomic conflict [...]. The least we can say is that since twenty years ago we have not moved very far from the imbroglios of science and politics. On the contrary, the history has multiplied them abundantly.[13]

Metaphysics: The humanist does not presuppose the superiority of Man, but rather searches for what is human within the marvelous variety of beings.

Politics, sciences, and natural life are closely intertwined in Latour's wartorn universe. Entities as diverse as governmental agencies and strains of bacteria, French colonies in Indochina and colonies of microbes on a Petri dish, scientific associations, and herds of cattle are implicated into the same integrated and ever-changing networks. This attempt to encompass the infinite *varietas* of things is a very humanistic ambition. In the early 1980s, during the last jolts of the Cold War, when Western Europe pondered the choice between being red or dead, that is between the totalitarian annihilation of democratic culture or the self-inflicted nuclear extinction of humankind as an animal species, Latour's opposition to the "Great Bifurcation" of culture and nature was indeed groundbreaking. Soon thereafter, he launched *Politics of Nature*, a book-manifesto fighting on two fronts: on the one hand, against the capitalist exploitation of natural resources in the name of civilizational progress and, on the other, against its mirror image, deep ecology, which dreams of preserving the pristine purity of nature unstained by any trace of human culture.[14] When Latour wondered how we can "bring the sciences into democracy," he did not mean that scientific protocols should be subject to the popular vote, but sought to deny scientists their modern role of gatekeepers between natural facts and cultural values. He wanted them to be integrated into the holistic "parliament of things," alongside other hybrids and under the rule of the new "Constitution" which does not discriminate between human and nonhuman agents.

It is a neo-Kantian, post-Enlightenment illusion to think that humanism consists of assuming the superiority of Man. For Renaissance humanists, being human is not a given, but rather an open question and the object of an unending pursuit. Yes, equality is not a value shaping the premodern *Weltanschauung*. Nonetheless, even if the Renaissance macrocosm is layered hierarchically beginning at unanimated stones and ending at celestial cherubim and seraphim, the place of humans on such an ontological scale is neither stable nor clearly defined. In the eyes of thinkers such as Erasmus, Charles de Bovelles, and Pico della Mirandola, human beings can fulfill their *dignitas* and reach the sublime heights of the spirit, but they can also remain mineralized in a state of insensitive existence. For premodern humanists, the place of the human being in the world has not been set in advance, because humanity is a gradable quality. One may become more or less human, depending on one's free will and the exercise of one's intellect. Consequently, the boundaries between the human and the nonhuman are equally problematic. As evidenced by human–animal and even human–mineral hybrids, admired by the French surgeon humanist Ambroise Paré, God or even Nature, God's playful maiden servant, can at any time reverse hierarchies and obliterate distinctions either in order to convey an important message or to demonstrate its limitless ingenuity.[15]

Latour's "experimental metaphysics" is equally incompatible with anthropocentrism, but it takes Renaissance ontological inventiveness a few steps further in the direction of increased relationality, complicating thus even more the humanist search for what is human.

First, for Latour, contrary to premodern humanists (and a fortiori modern neo-Kantians), there is no such a thing as one Nature composed of creatures that are equipped with a distinct being as such. Latour rejects "mononaturalism" because the existence of one Nature would imply either the exaltation of one ideal and dominant civilization or the acceptance of the multiplicity of incommensurable cultures. Both Eurocentrism and multiculturalism are founded on the bifurcation between one Nature on the one hand and one or many cultures on the other. In order to avoid such modern dualism, Latour invites us to consider the possibility of multiple natures, a multiverse which is not the result of a social construction, but the basis for negotiations in the never-ending process of assembling collectives of humans and nonhumans. Instead of the traditional alternative between mononaturalism composed of stable essences and multiculturalism composed of arbitrary identities, instead of choosing between physical and cultural anthropology, between realism and constructivism, Latour opens the door to a diplomacy of agents, regardless of their human or nonhuman origin. Consequently, Latour does not repeat Terence's and Erasmus's "I am human and nothing human is alien to me," but rather claims: "Nothing that is alien to me is inhuman."[16]

And here comes the second feature of Latour's experimental metaphysics, which both refers to Renaissance and transforms premodern ontology to suit new, nonmodern needs. "Nothing that is alien to me is inhuman" could have been easily understood as the welcoming of alterity in the name of the postmodern lack of any essential meaning. Such interpretation is erroneous because it would lead us back to constructivism and multiculturalism, which, as we have just seen, are for Latour the reverse side of modernism. The point for Latour is to free us from modernist and postmodernist ontologies altogether, because they are both based on the "Great Bifurcation" between one Nature and one or many cultures. In order to do that he rejects essentiality, but at the same time does not leave in its place any ontological void. For Latour, instead of beings as such, reality is composed of "beings-as-other" (*être-en-tant-qu'autre*) and of verifications (*véridictions*) ensuring that minimal requirements are met in order for a "negotiation" between the components of a collective takes place.[17] In such a diversified, dynamic, and interconnected multiverse, human *dignitas* is certainly not, as is the case in Renaissance humanism, the main object of ethical and intellectual pursuit, but, on the other hand it is not entirely irrelevant either.

In fact, Latour revives the humanist questioning of the centrality of Man. Right at the outset of the second part of *Pasteurization of France*, entitled *Irreductions*, Latour states the fundamental principle of his metaphysics: "Everything is the measure of everything else."[18] This aphorism is in fact a reinterpretation of Protagoras's famous sentence, largely quoted in Antiquity: "Man is the measure of all things." In Plato's *Crito* 358e and *Theaetetus* 152a–162a, Protagoras's saying is criticized by Socrates as the embodiment of epistemological relativism to be rejected: no, we cannot say that man is the measure of all things, because it would mean that things do not have an inherent measure of their own and truth would lie in the eyes of each individual beholder. In a typically humanist gesture of imitation, Montaigne rewrites, in his own terms, the critique of Protagoras in a famous fragment of his "Apology of Raymond Sebond," a chapter of the *Essays* which plays a key role in the Renaissance revival of Ancient skepticism:

> Truly Protagoras was telling us some good ones, making man the measure of all things, who never even knew his own. If it is not he, his dignity will not permit another creature to have this advantage. Now, he being in himself so

contradictory, and one judgment incessantly subverting another, that favorable proposition was just a joke which led us necessarily to conclude the nullity of the compass and the compasser.[19]

Montaigne is clearly not interested in defending Plato's transcendent ideas; epistemological relativism is not his target, but rather his ally in his massive attack against the pretenses of human reason. According to Montaigne, truth is ungraspable because of its relativity—what is true on this side of the mountains is false on the other (II, 12, 531 [579])—yet the cause of such impotence of our cognition is not only epistemological but also metaphysical. We cannot secure the object of our perception because reality is in constant flux. We cannot grasp the being, we can only see the becoming.[20] By mocking Protagoras, Montaigne displays his self-irony, which is so quintessentially humanistic. He not only targets anthropocentric vanity, but doubts the pursuit of humanness which underlies the humanistic project itself. Neither humans nor any other creature can be the golden standard for other things in this world. How can we therefore know ourselves? In other words, how can we fulfill the fundamental requirement of humanism engraved on the temple of Apollo at Delphi?

Latour's experimental metaphysics is as corrosive as Montaigne's skepticism. And, again, the key to what may seem—erroneously—just an epistemological constructivism and relativism is to be found at the metaphysical level. What proves that a given product that works in Paris is equally efficient in Ouagadougou? Well, to prove it would require a lab to make in situ the necessary analyses. Once the laboratory study is completed, Latour can reiterate the question for another location, a bit further away.[21] Is such stubborn questioning an attempt to suggest that there is no universal law that governs reality or, worse, that there is no reality but only our constructed vision of it? Neither one nor the other. The value of Latour's questioning lies in the constantly reiterated and never-ending process of proving, probing, and trying. This is exactly what Montaigne does in his *Essays*, the title of which does not mean a collection of texts belonging to the genre of essay—a genre that did not exist at the moment of the publication of the book—but precisely a series of constantly reiterated trials, tests, and experiments.

This is why "everything is the measure of everything else." Not only Man as an ontological given is nowhere to be found, no more than "Nature" and "Society" are.[22] The meaning of Latour's reinterpretation of Protagoras is in fact very Montaignian: nothing can be reduced to anything other (for instance to Man); nothing can be not-reduced to anything other (universal relativity should not become a universal standard of a higher level); but everything has to be probed, inspected, and measured by and against other things.²³ There are no stable forms of things, but only their probing by other things (*épreuves*), that recall on the metaphysical plane what Montaigne does at the epistemological and discursive level, namely the "essaying" of his and his reader's judgment. In other words, if Latour remains agnostic about what is human and what is nonhuman, like Montaigne was skeptical in the same respect, it does not mean that he denies existence to the human being lost among the cyborgs and chimeras of posthumanism. It means that by following Montaigne's example, Latour intends to probe or "essay" reality. And, in turn, he probes and essays the process of probing and essaying itself, in a constant pursuit of knowledge never to be attained. As Latour puts it, "Nothing is known—only realized" (*On ne sait rien mais on réalise*) and to "realize" is not so much to attain a higher consciousness of reality—as any Enlightenment would want it to be—but rather to make the components of networks more real by testing their resistance.²⁴

Exegesis: The humanist is not so much a philosopher as a philologist.

Most importantly, this process of essaying reality is discursive in nature, with the important caveat that discursivity cannot be separated from ontology. Indeed, for Latour, like for Renaissance humanists, to think is to read, and to read is to be and to act. Conversely, to be and to act is to perform a speech act which is always a reading, an interpretation, a translation of someone's discourse, which Erasmus called *sermo* and Latour calls a "proposition," an "enunciation" (be it verbal or not).²⁵ In other words, both for the premodern and for the nonmodern humanists, to be a thinker is to be a reader and a translator.²⁶

To illustrate the discursive nature of relations between agents, to see these relations as translations, let us go back to the case study of the *Pasteurization of France*. As we said, Latour's 1984 book is overshadowed by the very real possibility of a nuclear conflict. War is also the master metaphor of scientific discovery and specifically of Pasteur's fight to establish bacteriology as a discipline of learning in the late nineteenth century. The choice of such a militaristic metaphor in order to conceptualize scientific inquiry should not be surprising given what we know about Latour's metaphysics: "There are neither wholes nor parts. Neither is there harmony, composition, integration, or system [...]. How something holds together is determined on the field of battle."²⁷ Relations between agents forming the collectives are conflictual, because nobody entirely agrees with anybody else, nothing can be harmonized for good with anything, and all is subject to negotiations. Here again Latour is inspired by premodernity, since the reference for his ontological diplomacy is one of the foundational events for Renaissance geopolitics, namely the talks conducted by Henri VIII and Francis I at the Cloth of Gold in 1520, at the dawn of the bloody sixteenth century, when Erasmus published his *Querela Pacis*.[28]

Moreover, the metaphor of the "war of sciences" is not only justified by Latour's experimental metaphysics, but also by the specific political situation in which Pasteur's discoveries took place. Just as Latour's book on Pasteur is written in anticipation of a probable nuclear confrontation, Pasteur's research occurred during the intermission between the disastrous defeat of France in the 1870 war against Prussia and the imminent First World War. Not surprisingly, Latour's entire narration of Pasteur's accomplishments is punctuated with militaristic vocabulary: like Napoleon, Pasteur is portrayed as a commander-in-chief; his scientific advances are seen by his contemporaries and described by Latour as stages of a military campaign, during which Pasteur has to fight many battles against adversarial forces such as evasive microorganisms and conservative scientific associations.

But most importantly, the war metaphor is intertextual and metadiscursive. War is an image dictated by the main intertext of Latour's book, Tolstoï's masterpiece that inspired the initial title of the monograph: *Microbes: War and Peace*. Like any Renaissance humanist, Latour sees reality through the lenses of canonic readings and speculates about the world by interpreting the texts handed down by illustrious classics. For instance, if Pasteur is the Napoleon of bacteriology, it is not because he is the exceptional genius who invents a brilliant strategy and singlehandedly implements it on the battlefield. Pasteur is just a front man for a whole crowd of human and nonhuman agents like Tolstoï's Napoleon is one of the agents of a complex network composed of soldiers, supplies, horses, weapons, topography, weather, epidemics, etc., who, through conflicts, negotiations, and miscommunications move reality from one stage to another.[29] The mediation of reality by a literary text means therefore that the figure of Napoleon that models Latour's image of Pasteur is not the French emperor himself, not the historical man, but rather the fictional character constructed by the Russian novelist. Such intertextual mediation is characteristic for a humanist approach to historical reality. For instance, Montaigne considers Socrates as his main ethical model, but at the same time acknowledges that this sublime archetype of virtue is accessible only as a literary figure in Plato's dialogs.[30] Both the nonmodern and the premodern humanists read the classics in order to understand reality. They need to be philologists in order to be philosophers.

Like Montaigne, who catches the echoes of Socrates's words scattered in Ancient texts, knowing well that he will never hear the tone of Socrates's own voice, Latour follows Pasteur's scientific career as it is reflected in the testimonies of the scientist's contemporaries. Consequently, Latour's book is in fact an extensive exegesis of some major scientific periodicals of the late nineteenth and early twentieth centuries: *La Revue scientifique*, *Les Annales de l'Institut Pasteur*, and *Le Concours medical*. Thanks to a meticulous analysis of the style of these articles, Latour can follow the progress of Pasteur's ideas among health professionals and the French public at large. He can see the change between the loose rhetoric of the "hygienists" who preceded Pasteur in the search for the causes of contagious diseases among humans and animals on the one hand, and the "spare, nervous, rapid style" of the Pasteurians on the other.[31] This stylistic modification is in fact a change in the style of action. A scientific article published by Pasteurians is, in Latour's words, a "war machine" cutting through the frontlines of different forces—human and nonhuman, political, and biological—that are implicated in the fight against the epidemics. To illustrate this fight, Latour chooses an article published by a collaborator of Pasteur on the development of the bubonic plague in Hong Kong. Thanks to a detailed close reading punctuated by numerous quotations from the scientific text, Latour shows how the author installs his field laboratory on a hospital grounds in Hong Kong, how he studies the colonies of microbes in relation to the colonial geopolitics of Indochina, how he carefully displaces the problem from its social space into the secure confines of his laboratory, from the urban context of China slams onto the sterile glass plate where the microbes can be visualized and conceptually circumscribed:

> It is all there. We can see the centers on the map of China; we can see the poor classes in their hovels; we can see the tumors on the armpits of the sick; we can see the dead rats in the houses of the whites; but even better, we can see the curds along the wall of the tube [...] the colonies under the microscope.[32]

The key concept in Latour's exegesis of the article is "displacement." It means both the change of location and the translation of meaning. One of the factors in the success of Pasteurians was their physical mobility: teams of researchers went to the areas affected by epidemics, brought in organic samples to the field laboratories, transported bacterial cultures to the central hub in Paris, spread the results through specialized publications, while entertaining dynamic exchanges with the affected populations as well as with the political authorities. However, besides such physical mobility, "displacement" refers mainly to a semantic transfer. Latour shows that what the Pasteurians succeed in doing—contrary for instance to the physiological school led by Claude Bernard—was not only to relocate biological samples, but most importantly to displace the whole problem of illness from the terrain it affected into the confines of the laboratory where the pathogenic agents could be isolated, visualized, studied and where a proper antidote could be produced.[33] Latour is able to properly acknowledge such semiotic translation of illness to the laboratory, thanks to his relational metaphysics, according to which all the relationships between agents in a network are, in one way or another, a kind of speech act, and every transfer of meaning among agents composing the collectives is an unfaithful translation.

> An actant can gain strength only by associating with others. Thus it speaks in their names. Why don't the others speak for themselves? Because they are mute; because they have been silenced; because they became inaudible by talking at the same time. Thus, someone interprets them and speaks in their place. But who? Who speaks? Them or it? *Traditore-traduttore*.[34]

There is no simple cause and effect relation, no simple communication of information (something Latour calls the "double-click"[35]), but rather a laborious process of composing with reality, always at a cost. There is no faithful commentary, but rather piling up of annotations, one upon another.[36] Latour's philological approach to metaphysics clearly refers to Montaigne's lament over the proliferation of discourse at the expense of substance: "It is more of a job to interpret the interpretations than to interpret the things, and there are more books about books than about any other subject: we do nothing but write glosses about each other."[37]

The need for never-ending commentaries and interpretations is dictated by Latour's metaphysics in which nothing can be "reduced" to anything; all is a relation and every relation is a negotiation. Moreover, if every relation between agents is, at the end of the day, a kind of speech act, conversely, every interpretation (*interpréter*) is a trade-off, an exchange (*inter-prêter*).[38] There is no difference between language and reality; the quarrel between the nominalists and the realists has no sense in the grand scheme of constantly renewed displacements and translations.

Rhetoric: The humanist is not content with mere words, but cultivates eloquence in order to change reality.

Since, for a humanist, to think is to read, and to read is to act, the correlate of exegesis in humanist practice is rhetoric conceived not as vain and deceptive verbosity, but as action in the world.[39] Similarly, for Latour, the agents who compose networks trans-late (*inter-prêtent*) each other, and by doing so, they inter-act. The discursive embodiment of Latour's interactive relationism is the metaphor. Etymologically a metaphor is, precisely, a transfer or a displacement. Therefore, this figure of style epitomizes Latour's vision of reality which is made of physical and semantic displacements. However, there is one thing to keep in mind: since in Latour's metaphysics all relationships between the components of collectives are unfaithful translations, since the style of writing is identical with the style of acting (and vice versa), metaphors are not simply linguistic niceties added to some kind of substantial reality. Reality is, at its very core, metaphoric, and metaphors are real. In other words, there is no inherent difference between figurative and literal meaning:

> Since nothing is reducible or irreducible to anything else [...] thus, there are no clear ways of distinguishing literal from *figurative* meanings. Every group of words may be dirty, exact, metaphorical, allegorical, technical, correct, or far-fetched.[40]

The traditional distinction between literal and figurative meanings presupposes a difference between being as such and a more or less direct discourse about such being. But such a distinction is possible only within the metaphysical framework of the "Great Bifurcation" promoted by the Moderns. The dualism between literal and figurative meanings is incompatible with Latour's experimental metaphysics, where every being is a being-as-other and where discourse does not represent reality in a mimetic sense, but rather re-presents it, makes it present as representative in a negotiation. Since discourse does not speak literally or figuratively about reality, but rather is a mediation between agents, metaphor is just the way elements of relationships act together. War is the historical reality surrounding Pasteur's scientific work, but it is also the form of discourse that expresses the progress of Pasteur's research and his advances among the scientific community. At the same time, war is the master model of thought provided by Tolstoï's novel and, correlatively, the stylistic pattern of Latour's monograph on Pasteur. Finally (the Cold) War is also the reality in which Latour composes his book on Pasteur. From the point of view of a dualist metaphysics this succession of propositions alternates literal and metaphorical meanings of the word "war," but from Latour's point of view such distinction does not matter.

What does matter, however, is the constant search for a new language that would allow us to escape the compartmentalization of words between disciplines of learning. Such linguistic segregations reflect only the "Great Bifurcation" between Nature and Science, literal and figurative senses, and, subsequently, further specialization of terminologies. Latour negates these divisions by translating words and realities. Hence, the metaphoric creativity of Latour's style, which constantly transposes the usual meanings of common vocabulary in order to better grasp the relational character of beings, to tie more firmly the components of the networks he brings to light: "Though there is no proper or figurative meaning, it is possible to appropriate a word, reduce its meanings and alliances, and link it firmly to the service of another."[41] The more he tries to solidify his terminology, adding glossaries to his books and punctuating his texts with cross-references, the more he needs to test new metaphors. Latour's dissatisfaction with the terminology of existing disciplines (*les termes de la tribu*) reminds us of Montaigne's search for a new language that would avoid the illusion of a positive or negative knowledge.[42] Both Latour and Montaigne want to avoid dichotomist choices dictated by the rule of non-contradiction. Yet Latour goes one step further than Montaigne. The Renaissance humanist's primary concern is epistemological and only secondarily ontological. Montaigne looks for a language that would embody the skeptic unending quest. Such Pyrrhonist perpetual movement of thought mirrors in turn the perpetual fluctuation and vicissitude of things. In Latour's case, however, the pursuit of a language indifferent to "tribal" loyalties of disciplines of learning as well as the proliferation of metaphoric transpositions constitute the metaphysical project in itself. There is no distinction between saying, thinking, being, and acting.

Equally useless would be the distinction between discourse and metadiscourse, since there is a continuity of negotiations, translations, and displacements between Pasteur's laboratory research, the Pasteurians rhetorical campaign in their scientific publications, Latour's exegesis of these documents, and finally the interpretations of all the above by the readers of Latour's books. Pasteurians translate the work of their predecessors, the hygienists, by making the microbes visible. Latour, in turn, displaces slightly the work of the Pasteurians, by highlighting the specificity of their style of writing and action, that is, by showing that they were able to make visible the microbes that the hygienists were not able to put in the spotlight. Finally, Latour exposes his own approach to the study of science. There are no differences between all these stages: "I have spoken of the Pasteurians as they spoke of their microbes."[43] The Pasteurians speak about microbes; similarly, Latour speaks about the Pasteurians; and, one may add, Latour speaks about the work accomplished by the Pasteurians like he speaks about his own work. Latour thus takes place in the unending sequence of commentaries and translations, and he acknowledges this fact, by commenting on his own intellectual action and his own style of writing. Such self-consciousness and constant return on one's own practice are also the essence of Montaigne's method. When the Renaissance humanist deplores the profusion of glosses, he targets in fact his own propensity to comment upon his own text: "How often and perhaps how stupidly have I extended my book to make it speak of itself?"[44]

The piling up of commentaries and auto-commentaries, metaphors and metadiscursive metaphors has direct consequences for Latour's style. One of the manifestations of such metadiscursivity is the frequent use of pastiche in Latour's prose. For instance, when Latour writes in his *Irreductions*: "Monades are born free and complete [...], and everywhere they are in chains," he rewrites the incipit of *The Social Contrat* (1762) by Rousseau: "Man is born free, and everywhere he is in chains."[45] The substitution of "monad" for Rousseau's "Man" is not the sign of particular allegiance to Leibniz, like the alternative use of "entelechy" to designate an agent of a network in other fragments of the book is not a tribute to Aristotle. Both philosophical terms are metaphors through which Latour tries to express the propensity of each agent to achieve a state of actuality and self-sufficiency in the relations that tie it to other agents of a network.[46] And here comes the flip of the coin: each monad-entelechy tries to translate the input from other monads-entelechies on its own terms, while remaining at the same time closely dependent on its relations with other agents. This interdependence is expressed through the rewriting of Rousseau's well-known sentence: each monad is enchained to other monads. Of course, such interconnectivity is not, as it is for Rousseau, the curse of social enslavement, but rather the quintessence of Latour's metaphysics of "beings-as-others." This is why, Latour can say, this time through a pastiche of the famous line from Sartre's *No Exit*: "The principle of reality is other people."[47]

Contrary to Sartre, the "others" are not hell, but reality to be probed for its resistance to any reduction. Most importantly, these Latourian "others" are in fact not "other" in the Sartrian sense of this epithet, but rather quite similarly real, since they are also part of the same network and are equally enmeshed in constant translations. Contrary to Sartre's world, Latour's multiverse cannot offer any external, falsely comforting mirror to the gaze of the Self who would prefer to give up the freedom of his or her existence. In Latour's metaphysics Sartrian "others" are simply the reality itself, because the issue is not the alienation of the Self by some bourgeois ideologies, but a world which does not offer any "view from nowhere."[48] Since Latour rejects the modernist "Great Bifurcation" in Nature and Culture, Science and Society, literal and figurative senses, reality and its interpretation, there is no difference between immanence and transcendence.

Theology: The humanist is not indifferent to the matters of faith; on the contrary, belief is the humanist's primary concern.

For Latour, transcendence is not opposed to immanence, because transcendence is immanent. Latour's transcendence is the alterity of the "beings-as-others." Among such beings is also God him- or herself. Latour's God is not the patriarchal figure breathing the spirit into Creation and looking at a globe from above.[49] Nor is God identical to Nature, for the simple reason that, according to Latour, there is no Nature as such. Both the infinitely transcendent God of the mystics and the totally immanent God of the pantheists are excluded. "The great Pan is dead," Latour repeats after Rabelais and Plutarch.[50] For Renaissance humanists, this sentence meant the twilight of pagan gods and ancient oracles. Under the allegorical garment of classical mythology, it meant also that the divine All voluntarily becomes Nothing through the sacrifice of Christ on the cross, the ultimate act of love as Marguerite de Navarre so beautifully sang in her poetry. For Latour, the death of Pan is quite the opposite. It is the absence of the total explication, the impossibility of perfect translation, the unattainability of ultimate salvation. Such absolute is nowhere to be found, because if it were, it would be precisely the expression of pure Nothingness. Such Nothingness would turn All into What Remains (*le Reste*), and since nobody is content with what remains, people would rather want to have it all.

> Because nothing is by itself either reducible or irreducible [...], this absolute force [God—JM] is also the absolutely pure expression of nothingness. [...] This force is the pure nothingness, the mere thought of which transforms all in *What*

Remains; since nobody wants just to keep what remains, this force, conversely, becomes *All*. To avoid the panic of reduction, we must always say: "What is left is all [...]. The great Pan is dead."[51]

This parody of Christian mysticism stems from Latour's rejection of the "Great Bifurcation" whose most radical expression is the dialectic of All and Nothing. Yet Latour's parody of Christian mysticism does not imply indifference to theological questions. It only means that, in conformity with the Catholic tradition that he claims alongside his Burgundian roots, Latour does not shy from mixing the sacred and the profane. In a quite unorthodox way, we must say, Latour ties up gods and things into hybrids that he calls "factishes." He awaits the response that the Earth will give to the destruction caused by humans and fosters a new kind of "animism." At its center, we find Gaïa, which is not a new-age deity representing the environment as opposed to the polluting humanity, but a key agent of a network comprising, among other things, marine currents and fracking industry companies, governments, and endangered species, all "animated" by their respective agencies.[52]

Latour asks us to feel Gaïa's tremors and trust her voice. Like any Renaissance humanist, he is less concerned about speculative theology and more preoccupied with the pragmatics of faith. Like his premodern predecessors, he clearly understands that religion is a historical phenomenon. Erasmus and his disciples accused scholasticism of forging an Aristotelian God, who was completely alien to the Christ of the Gospels. Latour blames the Moderns for putting Science in the role of a transcendent deity.[53] Like Laplace stating that God is a useless hypothesis, Latour considers faith in Science as superfluous. Yet this parodic reversal of nineteenth-century scientism does not mean that faith itself is to be discarded. Latour negates the existence of Science, like an atheist denies existence to God; yet, it does not mean that he is irreligious. It only means that opting for a purely spiritual religion would be as destructive for religious practice as striving for a scientist Science would be for scientific thinking. Montaigne, who criticized the Protestants for disincarnating the Christian creed, knew it all too well.

But how to vivify the letter, how to bring back the spirit to the churches emptied by modern secularization? This requires the right "conditions of felicity." Like "I do" binds two lovers only when uttered in specific circumstances consecrated by traditions, institutions, mores, etc., similarly the act of faith is a speech act that can, in Latour's words, "fabricate" God when performed in the right tone of voice, at the right moment, in the right place. This "fabrication" of

God is not an outrageous idolatry, but the calling for the presence of the other. Latour makes us realize that ultimately the existence of God hinges on human speech, like human relationships depend on felicitous words.[54] But words can make God present for humans, nonhumans, or hybrids only if these words are infused with trust. This is the opening premise of Montaigne's *Essays*: "This book was written in good faith, reader." Good faith, faith in God, trust in thy neighbor, friendship, and love—all the rainbow colors of belief become reality when, and if they are incarnated, made present through the exchange of words in a dialog. This is the fundamental humanist practice that Latour proposes for nonmodernity to enact.

Notes

1 Jean-Paul Sartre, "La fin de la guerre," *Les Temps Modernes* 1, no. 1 (1945): 163–7. See the televized interview by Pierre Dumayet with Michel Foucault in 1966. I would like to thank Ullrich Langer and Caitlin Yocco-Locascio for their suggestions regarding the form of this text.

2 Regarding the important distinction between *homo* and *anthropos*, see Phillip J. Usher, "Untranslating the Anthropocene," *Diacritics* 44, no. 3 (2016): 56–77.

3 Bruno Latour, *Où atterrir? Comment s'orienter en politique?* (Paris: La Découverte, 2017). Translated by Catherine Porter as *Down to Earth: Politics in the New Climatic Regime* (Cambridge: Polity Press, 2018).

4 Graham Harman, *Prince of Networks: Bruno Latour and Metaphysics* (Melbourne: re.press, 2009).

5 Michel Foucault, *Aesthetics, Method, and Epistemology. Essential Works of Foucault. 1954–1984*, ed. Paul Rabinow and James D. Faubion. Vol. 2 (New York: The New Press, 1999), 264.

6 See for instance Latour's conclusion of *Cogitamus. Six lettres sur les humanités scientifiques* (Paris: La Découverte, 2010), 217–18: "If we feel to be so close to the 16th century, it is because it has all the necessary ingredients of the sciences that would follow, except for the idea of a unified nature [...]. Of course, we will never come back to the 16th century—which is a good thing—but I think I share with many people the feeling that we live at the end of a long parenthesis, which started during that era. [trans. JM]." See also Latour's *Nous n'avons jamais été modernes. Essai d'anthropologie symétrique* (Paris: La Découverte, 1991). Translated by Catherine Porter as *We Have Never Been Modern* (Cambridge: Harvard University Press, 1993).

7 Latour chooses this date because the reforestation of the American continent that followed the massive decline of the Native American population decreased the amount of CO_2 to a level that would serve as a benchmark for its subsequent continuous increase that followed until today. See especially the sixth conference in *Face à Gaïa. Huit conférences sur le nouveau régime climatique* (Paris: La Découverte, 2015). Translated by Catherine Porter as *Facing Gaia: Eight Lectures on the New Climatic Regime* (Cambridge: Polity Press, 2017). See also Stephen Toulmin, *Cosmopolis: The Hidden Agenda of Modernity* (Chicago: Chicago University Press, 1990).

8 Bruno Latour, "Why Has Critique Run Out of Steam? From Matters of Fact to Matters of Concern," *Critical Inquiry* 30, no. 2 (2004): 227, note 4.

9 The original French edition is *Pasteur: guerre et paix des microbes*, suivi de *Irréductions* (Paris: La Découverte, [1984] 2001). I quote from *The Pasteurization of France*, trans. Alan Sheridan and John Law (Cambridge: Harvard University Press, 1988).

10 First published in 1580, constantly amplified until the death of the author and the first posthumous edition in 1595. All my references come from Michel de Montaigne, *The Complete Works. Essays, Travel Journal, Letters*, trans. Donald M. Frame, with an introduction by Stuart Hampshire (New York: Everyman's Library, 2003) with page numbers from the French edition provided in brackets. *Essais*, éd. Pierre Villey et Verdun-Louis Saulnier (Paris: Presses Universitaires de France, 1965).

11 George Hoffmann, *Montaigne's Career* (Oxford: Clarendon Press, 1998); Philippe Desan, *Montaigne. Une biographie politique* (Paris: Odile Jacob, 2014).

12 See the editorial by Latour "Après Mai 1968, 'la revolution conservatrice,'" in *Le Monde*, May 5, 2018.

13 Translation mine, from *Pasteur*, Preface to the 2001 edition.

14 Bruno Latour, *Politiques de la nature. Comment faire entrer les sciences en démocratie* (Paris: La Découverte, 1999). Translated by Catherine Porter as *Politics of Nature: How to Bring the Sciences into Democracy* (Cambridge: Harvard University Press, 2004).

15 Ambroise Paré, *Des monstres et prodiges* (1573). Contrary to Davide Tarizzo's assessment of premodern metaphysics, I think that for Renaissance humanists, humanness is not a natural form in search for a place on the *scala naturae*, but rather, in Montaigne's words, a quest for a "forme maîtresse." See Davide Tarizzo, *Life. A Modern Invention* (Minneapolis: University of Minnesota Press, 2018), 106–8.

16 Latour, *Politiques de la nature*, chaps 1 and 5, particularly pp. 46 sq and 275–85. See Isabelle Stengers, "The Curse of Tolerance," in *Cosmopolitics II*, trans. Robert Bononno (Minneapolis: University of Minnesota Press, 2010), 303–11.

17 Bruno Latour, *Enquête sur les modes d'existence. Une anthropologie des Modernes* (Paris: La Découverte 2012), chap. 7. Translated by Catherine Porter as *An Inquiry into Modes of Existence: An Anthropology of the Moderns* (Cambridge: Harvard University Press, 2013).
18 *Irreductions* 1.1.4, *The Pasteurization*, 158 [I modify the English translation in order to conform it to the original].
19 Montaigne, II, 12, 508 [557].
20 Montaigne, III, 2, 740 [804–5].
21 *Irreductions*, 4.5.7.1, in *The Pasteurization*, 226.
22 *The Pasteurization*, 148.
23 *Irreductions*, 1.1.3, in *The Pasteurization*, 158.
24 *Irreductions*, 1.1.5.4, and 1.1.5: "Whatever Resists Trials Is Real," in *The Pasteurization*, 158–9.
25 Latour uses the term "proposition" in the *Politics of Nature*, and the term of "enunciation" in *Enquête sur les modes d'existence*, 371–2.
26 For an accessible exposition of the concept of "translation," see Bruno Latour, *Cogitamus*, 26 sq. The notion of "translation" refers back to Michel Serres's *Hermès III: La Traduction* (Paris: Minuit, 1974).
27 *Irreductions*, 1.2.3.1, in *The Pasteurization*, 164.
28 Ibid.
29 *The Pasteurization*, 13–22.
30 Montaigne, "Of Physiognomy," III, 12.
31 *The Pasteurization*, 19–20, 94–100.
32 Ibid., 98.
33 Ibid., 60–2.
34 *Irreductions*, 1.1.9, in *The Pasteurization*, 160.
35 *Enquête*, 103.
36 *Irreductions*, 2.1.5, in *The Pasteurization*, 178.
37 Montaigne, III, 13, 996 [1069].
38 *Irreductions*, 1.2.12, in *The Pasteurization*, 167.
39 Therefore to think is to write: Bruno Latour, "Life among Conceptual Characters," *New Literary History* 47 (2016): 463–76.
40 *Irreductions*, 2.2.2, in *The Pasteurization*, 181.
41 *Irreductions*, 2.3.2, in *The Pasteurization*, 182.
42 Montaigne, II, 12, 476 [527].
43 *The Pasteurization*, 148.
44 Montaigne, III, 13, 997 [1069].
45 *Irreductions*, 1.5.1, scolia, in *The Pasteurization*, 174. It is important to note that *Irreductions* as a whole is a pastiche of Spinoza's *Theological-Political Treatise*.
46 *Irreductions*, 1.2.8 to which the section 1.5.1 refers the reader.

47 *Irreductions*, 1.2.7, in *The Pasteurization*, 166.
48 For the critique of such a philosophical external perspectivism, see Thomas Nagel, *The View from Nowhere* (Oxford: Oxford University Press, 1986) and Markus Gabriel, *Warum es die Welt nicht gibt* (Berlin: Ullstein Verlag, 2013).
49 Charles de Bovelles, *In hoc volumine continentur ... De Nihilo ...* (Paris: Henri Estienne, 1510), 63r.
50 François Rabelais, *Quart Livre* (Paris: POL, 1993), chap. XXVIII.
51 *Irreductions*, 1.4.6.1, in *The Pasteurization*, 173 [I modify the English translation in order to conform it to the original]; *Cogitamus*, 218.
52 Bruno Latour, *On the Modern Cult of the Factish Gods* (Durham: Duke University Press, 2010) and *Facing Gaïa*.
53 *The Pasteurization*, 13, 213–14.
54 Bruno Latour, *Jubiler ou les tourments de la parole religieuse* (Paris: Les Empêcheurs de tourner en rond, 2002), especially pp. 62–4 and 167. Translated by Julie Rose as *Rejoicing or the Torments of Religious Speech* (Cambridge: Polity, 2013).

Bibliography

Bovelles, Charles de. *In hoc volumine continentur ... De Nihilo ....* Paris: Henri Estienne, 1510.
Desan, Philippe. *Montaigne. Une biographie politique.* Paris: Odile Jacob, 2014.
Foucault, Michel. *Aesthetics, Method, and Epistemology. Essential Works of Foucault. 1954–1984.* Edited by Paul Rabinow and James D. Faubion. Vol. 2. New York: The New Press, 1998.
Gabriel, Markus. *Warum es die Welt nicht gibt.* Berlin: Ullstein Verlag, 2013.
Harman, Graham. *Prince of Networks: Bruno Latour and Metaphysics.* Melbourne: re.press, 2009.
Hoffmann, George. *Montaigne's Career.* Oxford: Clarendon Press, 1998.
Latour, Bruno. "Après Mai 1968, 'la révolution conservatrice.'" *Le Monde.* May 5, 2018.
Latour, Bruno. *Cogitamus. Six lettres sur les humanités scientifiques.* Paris: La Découverte, 2010.
Latour, Bruno. *Enquête sur les modes d'existence. Une anthropologie des Modernes.* Paris: La Découverte, 2012. Translated by Catherine Porter as *An Inquiry into Modes of Existence: An Anthropology of the Moderns.* Cambridge: Harvard University Press, 2013.
Latour, Bruno. *Face à Gaïa: Huit conférences sur le nouveau régime climatique.* Paris: La Découverte, 2015. Translated by Catherine Porter as *Facing Gaia: Eight Lectures on the New Climatic Regime.* Cambridge: Polity Press, 2017.

Latour, Bruno. *Jubiler ou les tourments de la parole religieuse.* Paris: Les Empêcheurs de tourner en rond, 2002. Translated by Julie Rose as *Rejoicing or the Torments of Religious Speech.* Cambridge: Polity, 2013.

Latour, Bruno. "Life among Conceptual Characters." *New Literary History* 47 (2016): 463–76.

Latour, Bruno. *Nous n'avons jamais été modernes. Essai d'anthropologie symétrique.* Paris: La Découverte, 1991. Translated by Catherine Porter as *We Have Never Been Modern.* Cambridge: Harvard University Press, 1993.

Latour, Bruno. *On the Modern Cult of the Factish Gods.* Durham: Duke University Press, 2010.

Latour, Bruno. *Où atterrir? Comment s'orienter en politique?* Paris: La Découverte, 2017. Translated by Catherine Porter as *Down to Earth: Politics in the New Climatic Regime.* Cambridge: Polity Press, 2018.

Latour, Bruno. *Pasteur: guerre et paix des microbes,* suivi de *Irréductions.* Paris: La Découverte, [1984] 2001. Translated by Alan Sheridan and John Law as *The Pasteurization of France.* Cambridge: Harvard University Press, 1988.

Latour, Bruno. *Politiques de la nature. Comment faire entrer les sciences en démocratie.* Paris: La Découverte, 1999. Translated by Catherine Porter as *Politics of Nature: How to Bring the Sciences into Democracy.* Cambridge: Harvard University Press, 2004.

Latour, Bruno. "Why Has Critique Run Out of Steam? From Matters of Fact to Matters of Concern." *Critical Inquiry* 30, no. 2 (2004): 225–48.

Montaigne, Michel de. *Essais.* Edited by Pierre Villey and Verdun-Louis Saulnier. Paris: Presses Universitaires de France: 1965. Translated by Donald M. Frame as *The Complete Works. Essays, Travel Journal, Letters.* New York: Everyman's Library, 2003.

Nagel, Thomas. *The View from Nowhere.* Oxford: Oxford University Press, 1986.

Rabelais, François. *Quart Livre.* Paris: P.O.L., 1993.

Sartre, Jean-Paul. "La fin de la guerre." *Les Temps Modernes* 1, no. 1 (1945): 163–7.

Serres, Michel. *Hermès III: La Traduction.* Paris: Minuit, 1974.

Stengers, Isabelle. "The Curse of Tolerance." In *Cosmopolitics II.* Translated by Robert Bononno. 303–11. Minneapolis: University of Minnesota Press, 2010.

Tarizzo, Davide. *Life. A Modern Invention.* Minneapolis: University of Minnesota Press, 2018.

Toulmin, Stephen. *Cosmopolis: The Hidden Agenda of Modernity.* Chicago: Chicago University Press, 1990.

Usher, Phillip J. "Untranslating the Anthropocene." *Diacritics* 44, no. 3 (2016): 56–77.

2

Practices of Early Modern Orientalism: A Latourian Perspective

Oumelbanine Zhiri

Introduction

For those who study Orientalism, the shadow of Edward Said's seminal book still looms very large. His definitions of Orientalism have been particularly dominant, undoubtedly illuminating important aspects of the field of Orientalism, but also obscuring crucial elements and narrowing the appreciation of the practices, entanglements, and connections that constituted the discipline, especially when it was created in the early modern period. Bruno Latour's insights, his investigations of networks and associations of different actors, and his explorations of the meaning of modernity will help counter these deficiencies and expand the understanding of Oriental studies and their place in the history of culture.

For Said, Orientalism is "a way of coming to terms with the Orient that is based on the Orient's special place in European Western experience."[1] This general definition is soon specified in three narrower descriptions. First, it is the academic discipline to which belongs anyone "who teaches, writes about, or researches the Orient."[2] Although still prevalent when Said first published his book in 1978, this designation has now been superseded by Said's newer definitions: "Orientalism is a style of thought based upon an ontological and epistemological distinction made between 'the Orient' and (most of the time) 'the Occident.'"[3] This extremely broadly defined Orientalism "can accommodate Aeschylus, say, and Victor Hugo, Dante and Karl Marx."[4] Finally, according to the third definition, Orientalism is more historically and materially defined than either of the other two. Taking the late eighteenth century as a very roughly defined starting point Orientalism can be discussed and analyzed as the corporate institution for dealing with the Orient—dealing with it by making statements about it, authorizing views of it, describing it, by teaching it, settling it, ruling over it: in short Orientalism as a Western style for dominating, restructuring, and having authority over the Orient.[5]

Said, drawing on Michel Foucault and Antonio Gramsci, defines this Orientalism as a hegemonic discourse. The Orientalism that many have in mind when using the word in the wake of post-colonial studies is really a mix of the second and third definitions offered by Said, combining the timelessness of an Orientalism that includes any Western text that establishes a distinction with the Orient, and the political motivation of the imperial Orientalism of the nineteenth century and beyond, or Orientalism as an "imperialist tradition."[6]

This confusion is authorized by Said's lack of clarity when he tries to pinpoint the beginnings of modern Orientalism, as a form distinct from the premodern version. He insists that modern Orientalism came to be in the last decades of the eighteenth century, and cites more than once the invasion of Egypt by Napoléon Bonaparte as a decisive origin of modern Orientalism. However, Said also sees as a crucial epistemological break the publication in 1697 of the *Bibliothèque Orientale* by the Frenchman Barthélemy d'Herbelot, an encyclopedia that imposed "a disciplinary order" upon its material, the Orient—an interpretation that ignores that d'Herbelot was clearly inspired by Ottoman examples, especially the scholar Kâtip Çelebi (1609–57), who compiled a still authoritative Arabic-language comprehensive bibliography of Islamic culture, "large parts of which are directly incorporated into the *Bibliothèque*."[7]

However, Said is looking as much for continuities as for ruptures, and insists that modern Orientalism re-purposed inherited structures, as well as a "prodigious cultural repertoire"[8] of images and fantasies. He thus tends to promote a remarkably authoritative teleological view of the relations between East and West. As a result, Said's immensely influential book led many readers to understand Orientalism as a historically enduring and politically motivated stereotyping of the Orient, rather than a phenomenon flourishing solely in the context of modern imperialism. He thus imposed the centrality of modern European empire in shaping the understanding of earlier cultural phenomena. This collapse of historical development is articulated with the view of Orientalism as a pure imposition of power knowledge by the West on the

East, and, as a consequence, with the representation of East and West as a rigid binary. This might explain why, in the words of one of Said's most perceptive commentators, "at the present moment, at least in literary studies, attention to Orientalism seems to have reverted more or less exclusively to the form of cataloguing representations of this or that social collective in this or that body of Western literature."[9]

Mufti himself proposes a different and quite stimulating way of understanding Said's contribution in order to explore the modern field of world literature. Much can also be gained by looking anew on early modern Orientalism as a field of knowledge, by sidestepping as much as possible a teleological stance, and by setting aside the broad terms of East and West. Following a more localized approach, as well as relying on the relational philosophy of Bruno Latour, will help identify and analyze the practices and processes of some episodes of early modern Orientalism, rather than focusing solely on the images they have produced. For that task, the word Orientalism will be used mainly in the first sense mentioned by Said, the sense that was prevalent before he proposed such a drastic and tremendously successful transformation of the concept; it will mean Oriental studies, the scholarly study of the Orient, its languages and its cultures. By highlighting networks and entanglements, this study will help disrupt the East/West rigid binary that has confined too many studies of Orientalism to imagology and the analysis of representations. By looking anew at the birth of the field at the threshold of modern times, and by following the lead of Latour who famously questioned whether Westerners have ever been modern, it will challenge some assumptions built in Europeans' self-image as opposed to their Others, including the Orientals, assumptions that have informed a modern view of Orientalism.

An important way to counter this view is to highlight that Orientalism in its formative early modern period was constructed not only by Westerners, but also by Easterners; many Orientals collaborated with European scholars, teaching them languages and cultures, helping them locate and obtain texts and artifacts. Some were also important writers in their own right, and all deserve to be studied beyond the role of shadowy "informants" to which they are usually still confined. The European Orientalists and their Oriental collaborators inhabited a liminal space in which learned people from East and West were able to work together. They were connected through complex networks that need to be explored. This will allow us to offer a new perspective on the history of Orientalism, supplementing and correcting the more traditional post-colonial approach that has been largely privileged since Edward Said helped found this field of critical studies. These networks and entanglements will be better understood, thanks to a relational approach influenced by Latour. His celebrated ANT—actor network theory—a method designed to examine and "trace associations, translations and negotiations"[10] between different actors, will assist in understanding how these actors and networks helped constitute the contact zone between Europe and its Islamic neighbors. This effort to bypass the stark antinomy between East and West will be bolstered by the reliance on Bruno Latour's reflection of the nature and reality of modernity especially as it relates to scientific inquiry, as will be made clear below. The exploration of an episode in the history of Orientalism set in a specific time and place, Morocco in the early seventeenth century, and the unpacking of its meaning, and most importantly, of its silences, will demonstrate how such an approach can help better account for its import, and more broadly on the significance of early modern Oriental studies.

West Meets East, Orientalism Meets the Orient

Thomas Le Gendre, a rich trader from Rouen, sojourned in Morocco between 1618 and 1625, a country in which he and his family had commercial interests. In 1665, he wrote a memoir of that time. His text was published anonymously in 1670, probably at the request of merchants who were interested in founding a commercial society in Morocco. Among others, it memorialized a remarkable event that occurred when an embassy sent by the government of the Dutch Republic was received by the sultan Mûlay Zaydân:

> On the year 1622, came to Marrakesh an ambassador of the Gentlemen of the States,[11] a squire of the Prince of Orange, and a disciple of Erpenius, professor of Oriental and foreign languages in Leiden, both with presents that were very pleasing to the king Zaydân, but mostly the one from Erpenius, which was an atlas and a New Testament in Arabic; and the eunuchs told us that the king would not stop reading the New Testament. As the ambassador was annoyed to not have been authorized to leave, he was advised to present the king with a petition or request, which was written by this disciple of Erpenius, whose name is Golius, in the Arabic language, and in a Christian style. The king was very much stunned by the beauty of the request, by the writing as well as by the style that was extraordinary in that land. He called immediately for his *talips* or secretaries, and showed them the request, which they admired. He

asked for the ambassador and asked him who wrote it. He answered that it was Golius, a student sent by Erpenius. The king asked to meet him and spoke with him in Arabic. The student answered in Spanish that he understood very well all that His Majesty was telling him, but that he could not answer him in the same language, because his throat would not help him, because one speaks with the throat as well as with the tongue; and the king, who understood Spanish, liked his answer. He responded favorably to the request and gave the ambassador the authorization to return. And today, this Golius is in Leiden, professor of Oriental and foreign languages in the stead of Erpenius, who is now dead.[12]

This anecdote stages an encounter between East and West that doubles as a meeting between knowledge and power, in which three characters play a crucial role: Thomas Erpenius (1584–1624) was since 1613 professor of Oriental languages at Leiden University; his student and friend Jacobus Golius (1596–1667), the central protagonist in this story, accompanied the Dutch embassy that spent two years in Morocco between 1622 and 1624, and would later replace Erpenius after his death as holder of the chair in Oriental languages;[13] the sultan Mûlay Zaydân (d. 1627), from the Saadi dynasty, is mostly a spectator to Golius's prowess as a translator and as a quick-witted interlocutor.

Le Gendre knew that, years after his Moroccan mission, Jacobus Golius had become a distinguished scholar, famous throughout Europe as a specialist of Oriental languages and cultures. At the time of his writing, the prestige of Orientalism as a field of knowledge was high enough even among trading communities to warrant the inclusion of this story. This anecdote would travel beyond these circles, though, and would have an interesting afterlife in the annals of European scholarship: through a citation by an erudite librarian in 1675,[14] it was incorporated in re-editions of widely read encyclopedias, such as the *Grand dictionnaire* by Louis Moreri and the *Dictionnaire historique et critique* by Pierre Bayle, in the entries devoted to Golius. This success tells us that this story, and its representation of an encounter between the European scholar and the Moroccan sultan, between East and West, between knowledge and power, resonated with readers of the time. This anecdote is indeed deserving of a careful unpacking in order to reveal its richness, through what it says, and also what it does not say. An analysis of explicit statements will help better understand how Orientalist knowledge was perceived in Europe in the second half of the seventeenth century; an examination of the silences will suggest new avenues for the study of the field.

Remarkably, Jacobus Golius is the only representative of the Dutch embassy to be named in the text. Even the head of the mission, the Ambassador Albert Ruyl, remains anonymous, while Golius's mentor, Thomas Erpenius, who was not part of the delegation, is mentioned by name. This choice suggests that for Le Gendre, there are two encounters happening at the time, and one is more important than the other: the unnamed Ruyl represents the Dutch Republic, but this political audience pales in comparison to the other meeting happening simultaneously. Indeed, in this telling, Golius is not a mere employee of the ambassador. He is himself an envoy, sent by Erpenius, and offering on his behalf to the sultan two books as presents (including the Arabic New Testament that Erpenius himself had published in Leiden in 1616). In Le Gendre's tale, the main meeting that day did not occur between two countries (Morocco and the Dutch Republic), but between the kingdom of Morocco and another type of power, the European Republic of Letters. Merely mentioning the presents sent by the Dutch government and focusing on Erpenius's gifts to the sultan, Le Gendre thus indicates that Erpenius himself exercises a sort of dominion that enables him to address the sultan as an equal, like the Gentlemen of the States. The domain in which he is a leading figure is the realm of the mind, where learning, intellect, and wit allow one to exert a vast influence, well beyond what his degree of actual wealth and power would warrant.

Furthermore, in this encounter, the West, through the learned Golius, is able to demonstrate to the Orient that it had acquired the tools to know its ways and was able to master its culture: the command of Arabic he displayed in his letter provoked the surprise and the admiration of the sultan and his entourage of professional writers and secretaries. Even his lack of proficiency in speaking Arabic is turned to his advantage when he finds a clever way to excuse this shortcoming. No wonder other citizens of the Republic of Letters, such as Colomiès and the revisers of Moreri's and Bayle's encyclopedic dictionaries, were taken by that story. It promotes a flattering image of their own power as intellectuals and as Europeans who could master other cultures.

This analysis suggests that this story could be read in a classic Saidian light as the imposition of European power on the Oriental Other, and the work of the Orientalist as revealed in this episode could be seen as an example of a Foucauldian power–knowledge nexus, made all the more visible by its very attempt to cover its working; the dream of a Republic of Letters independent of politics would be revealed as an ideological fantasy, in dire need of debunking, especially in light of the fact that the scholar was in the service of the state, at a time of European colonial expansion. This reading has its merits and is supported by other elements in the documents that record the Dutch mission in Morocco.

One can point out, however, that this post-colonial theoretical framework, although useful to an extent, imposes limitations on our understanding of the complex cultural processes called Orientalism. The least is not that this view is largely based on the representations of East and West as rigidly opposed categories. Adding to the body of work that catalogs images of the Orient in Western literature, for example, in the analysis of Le Gendre's account, clearly has its value. But maybe other approaches can help explore early modern intercultural relations without projecting on them the framework imposed by the imperial Europe of the nineteenth century and the ways in which it produced its Others. One aspect distinguishes it from the more modern version: Orientalism as it is represented in Le Gendre's story is not yet secularized, as is made clear by the allusion to the New Testament, the Arabic edition of which was one of Thomas Erpenius's great scholarly achievements. The vision of the Others of Europe, especially its Islamic neighbors, was at that time still structured by an explicitly religious vision, and thus is not to be assimilated to the modern Orientalism which "consists of those Western knowledge practices in the modern era whose emergence made possible for the first time the notion of a single world as a space populated by distinct civilizational complexes, each in possession of its own tradition, the unique expression of its own forms of national 'genius.'"[15]

The Location of Orientalism

Still sustained by an explicitly religious understanding of difference, Le Gendre's representation of European Orientalism is also supported by erasures that significantly frame its meaning and deserve further examination. One major silence concerns the significance of the location in which the anecdote happened. In Le Gendre's account, Morocco is purely the stage in which the European Orientalist deploys his learning, the theater in which he could display his mastery of Oriental learning. This view of Orientalism considers only its results, and completely erases the processes and practices that contributed to build it. The analysis of this deletion puts Orientalism in a decidedly different light. The fact was that, before being the stage on which Jacobus Golius could demonstrate his prowess as an Orientalist, Morocco was the site in which he was working at obtaining the tools needed to perfect his knowledge of Arabic and

Oriental culture. During his time there, he was busy broadening and deepening his knowledge of Arab culture and language, and was seeking to obtain manuscripts for his collection, that would become very well-known among European Arabists. Most importantly, he was in this endeavor collaborating with a local scholar, the Morisco Ahmad al-Hajarî, who would help him find texts and sometime copy them for him. Hajarî will become a remarkable writer in his own right, and he is a crucial figure in the cultural networks that linked Europe and North Africa in the early modern period. His career can also shed a different light on the field of Orientalism, by exploring its extension beyond the European Republic of Letters.

Ahmad ibn al-Qâsim al-Hajarî Afuqay, also known as Diego Bejarano, was a Morisco born in Spain around 1570, and, as a crypto-Muslim, he knew Arabic from childhood. He also mastered Spanish so well that he could pass as an Old Christian. In 1599, he escaped to join the "land of the Muslims" and resided for decades in Marrakesh, capital of the Sa'di dynasty who ruled over Morocco. He was close to the court, and he attached his fate and career to Mûlay Zaydân (r. 1603–27), for whom he worked as a translator of diplomatic documents as well as European scholarly texts, mostly of astronomy and geography. Later, Hajarî was also in the employ of Zaydân's sons. One major turning point in his life occurred in 1609 when the Spanish Crown expelled the Morisco population. When the French ship captains who were transporting some of them to Morocco in 1611 robbed them, the Moriscos complained to Mûlay Zaydan, who authorized Hajarî to represent them. He traveled to France to seek retribution on their behalf, and then to the Dutch Republic in 1613. Around 1634, he left Marrakesh for the pilgrimage to Mecca. After some time spent in Egypt, where he wrote his travel account, and then its abbreviated version, entitled *The Supporter of Religion*, he settled in Tunisia, where he continued to work as translator and author, and where he probably lived until his death, sometime after 1640. In Morocco, Tunisia, Egypt, and Europe, he maintained contact with influential scholars, as he memorialized in his autobiographical writings.[16] Most notably, Hajarî collaborated with famed European students of Arabic, including the French physician Étienne Hubert, who had spent a year in the service of Mûlay Zaydân's father, Ahmad al-Mansûr. Through him, he met Thomas Erpenius, to whom he brought crucial help in his study of Arabic, in France, and later in the Netherlands. Just a few months after their collaboration ended, Erpenius published his extremely influential *Grammatica Arabica* (1613), which remained the standard text for learning Arabic in Europe well into the nineteenth century. There can be no doubt that

Erpenius counseled his student Golius to get in touch with Hajarî in Morocco. Their collaboration was fruitful not only for the Dutch scholar, but also for Hajarî himself, as shown in a letter he wrote to Golius, asking for his help: knowing that Golius owned a book of astronomy, Hajarî asked him to have it translated into one of the two languages he mastered, Spanish or Arabic.[17] The association between Hajarî and Golius was a two-way street.

However, the prevalent tendency of scholarship is to situate Golius and Hajarî in discrete cultures, with only barely meaningful connections: Golius as a member of the European Republic of Letters, as a founding father of early modern Oriental Studies, as an early representative of Enlightenment, whose years spent in Morocco and the Levant, and whose copious interactions with scholars of these regions were just the inert means through which he acquired mastery over Oriental culture; and Hajarî as a simple informant, one intermediary among others who happened to work with many influential Orientalists, but whose work and career should be entirely understood as part of another territory, that of Islamic civilization, or even more narrowly, that of the Morisco subculture. This view leaves little room to the idea that they might belong to the same liminal space between civilizations that would give meaning to their interaction and association, and that is populated by other figures, as well as objects, manuscripts, and knowledge practices that circulated in that space. Understanding it would be helped by the notion of contact zone advanced by Mary Louise Pratt, which "invoke the spatial and temporal copresence of subjects previously separated by geographic and historical disjunctures, and whose trajectories now intersect."[18] Adopting the notion of network and the actor network theory enables to explore the processes that constitute this contact zone, and that connect Hajarî and Golius, through a commitment to understand them empirically. This will allow us to go beyond mere imagology and abstract oppositions.

In this space, Hajarî would be afforded as much agency and importance as Golius. Rather than being a mere informant, who transmitted to Golius and other Orientalists a knowledge (of language, manuscripts, copyists) that was only given meaning when Europeans made it a part of Orientalism, Hajarî will appear as an actor who participated in the production of a transcultural Orientalist knowledge, and whose own work as translator and writer was informed by his connections to Golius and others. Here the distinction established by Latour between intermediary and mediator will reveal its usefulness: for the classic view of Orientalism, these Eastern informants are mere intermediaries who transport "meaning or force without transformation" and who thus can be forgotten (as indeed they often are). A renewed approach will see them as mediators who "transform, translate, distort, and modify the meaning or the elements they are supposed to carry."[19] From this perspective, the presence of these mediators modifies the meaning of Orientalism as a field, and their contribution needs to be reassessed.

This is what Le Gendre's anecdote ignores, erasing the dynamics of knowledge production and obliterating the networks and mediations that made it possible. A character like Hajarî has no place in his succinct representation of Orientalism. The study of European Orientalism has long suffered from such omissions, with the many natives of Oriental countries, including Moriscos or Maronites from the Levant, merchants or ambassadors, captives or adventurers, who played a crucial role in its development being mostly deleted from the history of the field, or often appearing only as shadowy figures in footnotes, and more rarely in a few short paragraphs. Although very valuable work is increasingly making them better known,[20] more is still needed to describe and analyze their contribution, and more importantly, to map out how their role could alter the way the field itself has to be understood.

If in Le Gendre's story, and in much of the studies on Orientalism, East and West are stable categories, the reality of the workings of Oriental studies and of the practices that Golius and Hajarî were actually engaging in reveals a messier, more complex picture. It shows that Hajarî was indeed the collaborator and informant of Golius, but also that Golius could in turn be the collaborator and informant of Hajarî. Golius traveled to Morocco (and later in his career to the Levant and Turkey) to obtain manuscripts, and Hajarî during his time in Europe was in all likelihood acquiring some of the texts of geography and astronomy and objects such as the terrestrial and celestial spheres he was studying as cultural translator for the sultan.[21] This suggests how much can be gained by approaching Orientalism more as a cultural formation born of the circulation in the space between civilizations, rather than a field located solely in one of these ensembles, and the meaning of which resides entirely in an imposition of imperial power/knowledge, even before the onset of modern imperialism.

Expanding its understanding and seeing it as an entanglement of relations and associations would allow us to account for many elements in its history that have too often been disassembled, leading to the elision of important features of its history, especially in the early modern period. A Latourian framework, which seeks to resist the temptation of establishing rigid separations between fields of learning and modes of knowing, can bring a lot to this project. Other elements of

Latour's work, especially on the meaning of modernity, will also help illuminate neglected dimensions of Orientalism in the seventeenth century.

Orientalism between Humanities and Technology

The oversight of the role of scholars from the Arab and Ottoman lands in the construction of early modern Orientalism is only one way in which the space of circulation and contact between civilizations have been drastically narrowed down. Another of Thomas Le Gendre's silences is as remarkable and leads to the erasure of other networks and hybrids. The reader of Thomas Le Gendre's account would not know that Jacobus Golius did not officially participate in the Dutch embassy as a specialist of Arabic; he was sent to accompany Albert Ruyl in his capacity as an engineer. His work as an Arabist (e.g., when he translated Ruyl's request addressed to Mûlay Zaydân) was secondary to this qualification. Golius indeed will obtain the chair of mathematics in Leiden University in 1629 (after taking the chair of Oriental languages in 1625). Although he undoubtedly sought his appointment to the Moroccan delegation at least partly in order to augment his knowledge of Arabic, and his collection of Oriental manuscripts, his work as a specialist of Oriental studies was not the official reason of his participation—contrary to his role in the later diplomatic mission to the Levant and Turkey; when he accompanied the eastern Mediterranean embassy, his "journey had the official purpose of acquiring better knowledge of the 'Oriental languages', profitable in his 'service' of Leiden University."[22] The embassy to Morocco was about the sultan's ill-fated project to build a port on the Atlantic coast of his country, for which he enlisted the help and expertise of his Dutch allies. As the engineer accompanying the mission, Golius authored on July 24, 1624 in the Hague the technical report concluding to the lack of feasibility of Mûlay Zaydân's plan of building this harbor.[23]

However, establishing a strict separation between philology and science in Golius's career would be a mistake. In fact, his interest in the study of Arabic stemmed originally from his mathematical research, as he wanted to be able to read some Greek texts that only survived in Arabic translation, and to study the contributions of scholars writing in Arabic. More generally speaking, the early modern period did not make the strict distinction between science and philology that will become familiar in the nineteenth century, as has been shown with respect to Golius's career.[24] In sum, Le Gendre's account keeps silent about Golius's connection with local scholars, and about the entanglement of the humanities and the sciences in Golius's career. The two erasures intersect, so to speak. Ahmad al-Hajarî, who played such an important role in helping Golius further his knowledge of Arabic culture in Morocco, was himself very much interested in sciences and technology, both out of personal interest (as he revealed in the autobiography he authored in Egypt), and as translator for Mûlay Zaydân, as well as in his later years when he translated from the Spanish a treatise on gunnery written by a fellow Morisco. Scholars from East and West were often interested in the Other's scientific accomplishments, as evidenced by their translations and their efforts to acquire scientific books and instruments.

The Entangled Practices of Early Modern Orientalism

Both these elements (the networks established between European and Oriental scholars, and the entanglement of science and humanities) are overlooked by Le Gendre, and thus his account deprives early modern Orientalism of important dimensions. These two erasures have been to a great extent a common feature in the study and understanding of Orientalism in the following centuries. This field is still understood solely as a humanistic field, mainly comprised of literary and cultural representations and of philological studies, and mostly deprived of its scientific and technological dimensions.

Latour's analyses and categories offer ways to assess anew the history of early modern Orientalism without conflating it with later formations. Going back to the ambiguities of the historical account presented in *Orientalism*, Said, at the same time, searched for the moment of epistemological break that would clearly distinguish between premodern and modern Orientalism, and asserted somewhat confusingly defined continuities between the two periods. This abstruseness resulted in the promotion of a teleological approach, which finds in imperial modern Orientalism the retrospective meaning of earlier representations of the East in Europe. On the other hand, when Latour rejects the notion of Foucauldian self-contained epistemes in favor of the notion of a "past" that "is not surpassed but revisited, repeated, surrounded, protected, recombined, reinterpreted and reshuffled,"[25] he allows the frustrating search for the moment in which the modern decisively breaks with the premodern to cease. He also opens up the possibility to "think temporal interdependency without telos, movement without supersession."[26] To study early-seventeenth-century Orientalism will not mean to reconstruct images and representations, and to implicitly or explicitly interpret them as precursors of later views. Rather, the goal will be to assess the associations and connections, the practices and processes, the people and the objects, that are constitutive of Orientalism at that moment in time—and that could help understand other versions of Orientalism differently situated in time or space.

Questioning the separation between the premodern and the modern opens for another way of using Latour's thinking, and especially what is arguably his most important book, *We Have Never Been Modern*. Some of its insights can help navigate the difficulties of assessing the relations between East and West through the prism of Orientalism. Latour describes the Constitution of the modern world, through the separation or purification of the two different realms of nature and culture (or the nonhumans and the humans), an instance of which can be found in the assessment of Golius's career as early as in Le Gendre's account, where his scientific work is ignored, in favor of highlighting his philological and rhetorical prowess in Arabic. This view is not just a characteristic of modern Orientalism, as opposed to its premodern version, but should rather be understood as a modern way of looking at Orientalism itself. The moderns view Orientalism not as the connective networks of Orientals and Westerners, of scientific and literary studies, based on the collection of manuscripts and of cultural and natural objects, that its practices show it to largely be, but as a more narrowly conceived pursuit, only interested in the representation of the languages, cultures, and societies of the East. As a consequence, the interest of early modern Orientalists in the scientific achievements of the Orient is mostly occulted.

This aspect is essential in the sense that modern Orientalism (or the moderns' view of Orientalism) is but one instance of the West's self-assessment as modern. Modernity constructs the nonmoderns (or premoderns, including the European past) at the same time that it constructs itself. This double enterprise is parallel to the production of Easterners as well as Westerners by Orientalism, in Edward Said's view—or, in Bruno Latour's terminology, the modern West is based on the work of purification, the divide between nature and culture, which is paralleled by a "second partition—an external one this time—through which the moderns have set themselves apart from the premoderns."[27]

When looking at the relations between East and West, many studies are dominated by the overarching idea of East being premodern, and West being modern, with the general tendency to explain the lack of modernity of the East by the notion of decline, especially of Islamic civilization, which still plagues studies of its history and cultures. What is undermined by Bruno Latour's innovation is the "existence of the great epistemological divide, separating us from our past or from the pre-moderns."[28] Moreover, basing the distinction West/East, or more generally, West/Rest, on modernity, means basing it on science. Indeed, science is a crucial feature of modernity's self-assessment; it is an essential part of the West's definition of itself; it is what makes it modern, that is Western. This implies that science cannot be an attribute of nonmodern societies, and that Orientalism has to erase its own forays into Oriental science. This is why the issue of technology and science has to play a strategic role in the effort to find ways to reassess the history of Orientalism. Methodologically, the insights of the history of science are important for this task, especially when it comes to the early modern period, which witnessed the founding feature of European self-concept of modernity, the Scientific Revolution, a peculiarly resistant narrative and mythology:

> It is a genuine mythology, which means it expresses in condensed and sometimes emblematic forms themes too deep to be unsettled by mere facts, however plentiful and persuasive. The Scientific Revolution is a myth about the inevitable rise to global domination of the West, whose cultural superiority is inferred from its cultivation of the values of inquiry that, unfettered by religion or tradition, allegedly produced the sixteenth- and seventeenth-century "breakthrough to modern science", which holds both proponents and opponents in its thrall.[29]

This persistent notion of a modernity gap between West and East has arguably played a crucial role in the tendency to not seriously account for the transcultural collaborative work that went into the production of Orientalism, especially in the domain of sciences.

To sum up, a renewed perspective on early modern Orientalism can be devised by adopting some of Latour's insights, thanks to which one can bypass the rigid binaries and teleological conceptions that still dominate the field to a great extent. This perspective will help study the Orientalists and their Oriental collaborators on a same level, without ignoring the contribution of the latter. The analysis of the networks they traced in the early modern cultures will also restore the importance of the role of the sciences and of technology in the development of the field. Such a study would situate Golius and Hajarî, the Orientalist and his Maghribî interlocutor, in the same cultural landscape, the liminal zone in which Oriental Studies flourished, and will allow to entertain and explore the notion that Orientalism is not merely located in the West, but also at different sites in the East, and in networks connecting East and West. This assessment could end up substantially modifying our understanding of Orientalism itself.

Notes

1 Edward W. Said, *Orientalism: Western Conceptions of the Orient*, reprint with a new preface (London: Penguin Books, 2003), 1.
2 Ibid.
3 Ibid., 2.
4 Ibid., 3.
5 Ibid.
6 Ibid., 15.
7 Alexander Bevilacqua, *The Republic of Arabic Letters. Islam and the European Enlightenment* (Cambridge: Harvard University Press, 2018), 118.
8 Said, *Orientalism*, 63.
9 Aamir Mufti, *Forget English! Orientalisms and World Literatures* (Cambridge: Harvard University Press, 2016), 23.
10 Anders Blok and Torben Elgaard Jensen, *Bruno Latour: Hybrid Thoughts in a Hybrid World* (New York: Routledge, 2011), 23.
11 The States General (*Staten-Generaal*), assembly of the provincial states of the Netherlands.
12 "En l'année 1622, vint à Maroc un ambassadeur de Messieurs des Estats, un escuyer du prince d'Orange, & un disciple de Harpinius, professeur ès langues orientales et etrangeres à Leyden, tous deux avec des presens qui furent bien agreables au roi Mouley Zidant, mais principalement celuy d'Harpinius, qui estoit un atlas et un Nouveau Testament en arabe; & il nous fut rapporté par les eunuques que le Roy ne cessoit de lire dans le Nouveau Testament. Or comme l'Ambassadeur s'ennuyoit de ce qu'on ne luy donnoit point son expedition, il fut conseillé de presenter au Roy une peticion ou requeste, laquelle fut faite par ce disciple d'Harpinius, nommé Golius, en écriture et langue arabesque, & en stile chrestien. Ce roy demeura estonné de la beauté de cette requeste, tant pour l'écriture que pour le stile extraordinaire en ce païs-là. Il manda aussitost ses talips ou écrivains, leur montra cette requeste qu'ils admirerent. Il fit venir l'Ambassadeur, auquel il demanda qui l'avoit faite. Il luy répondit que c'étoit Golius, disciple et envoyé d'Harpinius. Le Roy le voulut voir, luy parla en arabe. Ce disciple répondit en espagnol qu'il entendoit fort bien tout de ce que Sa Majesté luy disoit, mais qu'il ne pouvoit luy répondre en la mesme langue, parce que la gorge ne luy aidoit point (car il faut autan parler de la gorge que de la langue); ce que le Roy, qui entendoit bien l'espagnol, trouva fort bon; & accordant les fins de la requeste, fit donner à l'Ambassadeur les expeditions pour son retour. Et aujourd'huy ce Golius est à Leyden, professeur ès langues orientales & étrangeres, au lieu et place d'Harpinius, qui est mort," in *Sources Inédites de l'Histoire du Maroc*, Série Saadienne, Archives et bibliothèques de

France, vol. 3, ed. Henry de Castries (Paris: Ernest Leroux, 1911), 731–2.
13 On Erpenius and Golius, see Arnoud Vrolijk and Richard van Leeuwen, *Arabic Studies in the Netherlands. A Short History in Portraits, 1580–1950*, trans. Alastair Hamilton (Leiden-Boston: Brill, 2014), 31–48. On Golius, see also Jan Loop, *Johann Heinrich Hottinger. Arabic and Islamic Studies in the Seventeenth Century* (Oxford: Oxford University Press, 2013), 14 and sq.
14 Paul Colomiès, *Mélanges historiques* (Orange: 1675), 75–8.
15 Mufti, *Forget English!*, 24.
16 Ahmad ibn Qâsim al-Hajarî, *The Supporter of Religion against the Infidels*, rev. edn., translation and presentation P. S. van Koningsveld, Q. al-Samarrai, and G. A. Wiegers (Madrid: CSIC, 2015).
17 J. J. Witkam, "The Leiden Manuscript of the '*Kitâb al-Musta'înî*,'" in *Ibn Baklarish's Book of Simples: Medical Remedies between Three Faiths in Twelfth-Century Spain*, ed. Charles Burnett (London: Arcadian Library; Oxford: Oxford University Press, 2008), 80.
18 Mary Louise Pratt, *Imperial Eyes: Travel Writing and Transculturation* (London: Routledge, 1992), 7.
19 Bruno Latour, *Reassembling the Social. An Introduction to Actor-Network-Theory* (Oxford: Oxford University Press, 2005), 39.
20 To mention just a few of these studies, see Nasser Gemayel, *Les Échanges culturels entre les Maronites et l'Europe*. 2 vols. (Beirut: Y. & Ph. Gemayel, 1984); Alastair Hamilton, "An Egyptian Traveller in the Republic of Letters: Josephus Barbatus or Abudacnus the Copt," *Journal of the Warburg and Courtauld Institutes* 57 (1994): 123–50; Bernard Heyberger (ed.), *Orientalisme, science et controverse. Abraham Ecchellensis (1605–1664)* (Turnhout: Brepols, 2010); Jan Schmidt, "An Ostrich Egg for Golius: The John Rylands Library MS Persian 913 and the History of the Early Modern Contacts between the Dutch Republic and the Islamic World," in *The Joys of Philology: Studies in Ottoman Literature, History and Orientalism (1500–1923)*, vol. 2. Istanbul: Isis Press, 2002, and "Between Author and Library Shelf," in *The Republic of Letters and the Levant*, ed. Alastair Hamilton, Maurits H. van den Boogert, and Bart Westerweel, 27–51 (Leiden: Brill, 2005); G. A. Wiegers, "Moriscos and Arabic Studies in Europe," *al-Qantara* 31, no. 2 (2010): 587–610.
21 Oumelbanine Zhiri, "The Task of the Morisco Translator in the Early Modern Maghrib," *Expressions maghrébines* 15, no. 1 (2016): 11–27.
22 Schmidt, *The Joys of Philology*, 31. On Golius's sojourn in the Levant, see Schmidt "Between Author and Library Shelf."
23 *Sources Inédites de l'Histoire du Maroc*, Série Saadienne, Archives et bibliothèques des Pays-Bas, vol. 3 (Paris: Ernest Leroux—La Haye, Martinus Nijhoff, 1912), 571–85.
24 Fokko van Dijksterhuis, "The Mutual Making of Sciences and Humanities:

Willebrord Snellius, Jacob Golius and the Early Modern Entanglement of Mathematics and Philology," in *The Making of the Humanities. Volume II—From Early Modern to Modern Disciplines*, ed. Rens Bod, Jaap Maat, and Thijs Weststeijn, 73–92 (Amsterdam: Amsterdam University Press, 2012).

25 Bruno Latour, *We Have Never Been Modern*, trans. Catherine Porter (Cambridge: Harvard University Press, 1993), 75.
26 Rita Felski, *The Limits of Critique* (Chicago: University of Chicago Press, 2015), 158.
27 Latour, *We Have Never Been Modern*, 99.
28 Blok et al., *Bruno Latour: Hybrid Thoughts*, 72.
29 Katherine Park and Lorraine Daston, "Introduction: The Age of the New," in rev. edn. of *The Cambridge History of Science*. vol. 3, *Early Modern Science*, ed. Katherine Park and Lorraine Daston (New York: Cambridge University Press, 2008), 15.

Bibliography

Bevilacqua, Alexander. *The Republic of Arabic Letters. Islam and the European Enlightenment*. Cambridge: Harvard University Press, 2018.

Blok, Anders, and Torben Elgaard Jensen. *Bruno Latour: Hybrid Thoughts in a Hybrid World*. New York: Routledge, 2011.

Colomiès, Paul. *Mélanges historiques*. Orange, 1675.

Dijksterhuis, Fokko Jan. "The Mutual Making of Sciences and Humanities: Willebrord Snellius, Jacob Golius and the Early Modern Entanglement of Mathematics and Philology." In *The Making of the Humanities. Volume II—From Early Modern to Modern Disciplines*. Edited by Rens Bod, Jaap Maat, and Thijs Weststeijn, 73–92. Amsterdam: Amsterdam University Press, 2012.

Felski, Rita. *The Limits of Critique*. Chicago: University of Chicago Press, 2015.

Gemayel, Nasser. *Les Échanges culturels entre les Maronites et l'Europe*. 2 vols. Beirut: Y. & Ph. Gemayel, 1984.

al-Hajarî, Ahmad ibn Qâsim (1997 *The Supporter of Religion against the Infidels*). Revised edition, translation, and presentation by P. S. van Koningsveld, Q. al-Samarrai, and G. A. Wiegers. Madrid: CSIC, 2015.

Hamilton, Alastair. "An Egyptian Traveller in the Republic of Letters: Josephus Barbatus or Abudacnus the Copt." *Journal of the Warburg and Courtauld Institutes* 57 (1994): 123–50.

Heyberger, Bernard (ed.). *Orientalisme, science et controverse. Abraham Ecchellensis (1605–1664)*. Turnhout: Brepols, 2010.

Latour, Bruno. *Reassembling the Social: An Introduction to Actor-Network-Theory*. Oxford: Oxford University Press, 2005.

Latour, Bruno. *We Have Never Been Modern*. Translated by Catherine Porter. Cambridge: Harvard University Press, 1993.

Loop, Jan. *Johann Heinrich Hottinger. Arabic and Islamic Studies in the Seventeenth Century*. Oxford: Oxford University Press, 2013.

Mufti, Aamir. *Forget English! Orientalisms and World Literatures*. Cambridge: Harvard University Press, 2016.

Park, Katherine, and Lorraine Daston. "Introduction: The Age of the New." In revised edition of *The Cambridge History of Science*. Vol. 3, *Early Modern Science*. 1–17. Edited by Katherine Park and Lorraine Daston. New York: Cambridge University Press, 2008.

Pratt, Mary Louise. *Imperial Eyes: Travel Writing and Transculturation*. London: Routledge, 1992.

Said, Edward W. *Orientalism: Western Conceptions of the Orient*. Reprint with a new preface. London: Penguin Books, 2003.

Schmidt, Jan. "Between Author and Library Shelf." In *The Republic of Letters and the Levant*. Edited by Alastair Hamilton, Maurits H. van den Boogert, and Bart Westerweel. 27–51. Leiden: Brill, 2005.

Schmidt, Jan. "An Ostrich Egg for Golius: the John Rylands Library MS Persian 913 and the History of the Early Modern Contacts between the Dutch Republic and the Islamic World." In *The Joys of Philology: Studies in Ottoman Literature, History and Orientalism (1500–1923)*. Vol. 2, 9–74. Istanbul: Isis Press, 2002.

Sources Inédites de l'Histoire du Maroc, Série Saadienne, Archives et bibliothèques de France. Edited by Henry de Castries. Vol. 3. Paris: Ernest Leroux, 1911.

Sources Inédites de l'Histoire du Maroc, Série Saadienne, Archives et bibliothèques des Pays- Bas. Edited by Henry de Castries. Vol. 3. Paris: Ernest Leroux—The Hague, Martinus Nijhoff, 1912.

Vrolijk, Arnoud and Richard van Leeuwen. *Arabic Studies in the Netherlands. A Short History in Portraits, 1580–1950*. Translated by Alastair Hamilton. Leiden-Boston: Brill, 2014.

Wiegers, G. A. "Moriscos and Arabic Studies in Europe." *al-Qantara* 31, no. 2 (2010): 587–610.

Witkam, J. J. "The Leiden Manuscript of the '*Kitâb al-Mustaʿînî*'." In *Ibn Baklarish's Book of Simples: Medical Remedies between Three Faiths in Twelfth-Century Spain*. Edited by Charles Burnett. 75–94. London: Arcadian Library; Oxford: Oxford University Press, 2008.

Zhiri, Oumelbanine. "The Task of the Morisco Translator in the Early Modern Maghreb." *Expressions maghrébines* 15, no. 1 (2016): 11–27.

Part Two

Reassessing Literary and Political Modernity with Latour

3

Nonmodern Flaubert

William Paulson

"*I am no more modern than I am ancient …*"
    Gustave Flaubert to Louise Colet, August 26, 1846 (*Letters*)

"*Thus he would declare in his booming voice that the modern does not exist …*"
    Émile Zola, *Les Romanciers naturalistes*

Has literature ever been modern? In the usual terms, of course—and, arguably, never more so than in the novels and pronouncements of Gustave Flaubert. But if "we have never been modern," in Bruno Latour's phrase, then perhaps not.[1] Not even in *Madame Bovary*, that touchstone of literary modernity?

In Latour's account of a modernity founded on the triumph of natural science, the moderns claim to have figured out how to strip away the accretions of culture from our knowledge of nature so as to purify the latter; they can then differentiate themselves from premoderns, whom they accuse of mixing nature and culture together and thereby obscuring the specificity of both. By the same token, modern Western society, as the proud titleholder to science, modernity, and critical reason, relegates all other societies to a premodern or archaic status—sometimes romanticized or otherwise recuperated as desirable or authentic, but always incommensurable with the standards and dynamism of the modern Western ascendancy.

Yet these acts of self-definition and self-distinction via the separation of Nature and Society are only a single half of what Latour calls the "modern Constitution," the implicit fundamental law according to which modernity carries out its science and its politics. Alongside the official separation of the natural and the social comes the ever more extensive hybridization of nonhumans and humans, their weaving together in ever longer and more complex networks. Nature and society, in this account, are not foundations or essences but constructions, the products of doing natural and social science. The modern world enlarges, extends, and develops sociotechnical hybrids on an unprecedented scale, binding nonhumans and humans ever more inextricably together in its practices while distinguishing between them ever more rigorously as objects of knowledge. It thus continues to be nonmodern, not unlike its putatively premodern "predecessor."

Literary modernity is not self-evidently the modernity questioned by Latour, but it is by no means unrelated. Our current (or, in the digital age, residual) sense of literature as a category and institution arguably dates from the late eighteenth to the early nineteenth centuries—to the era, that is, of modern ascendency. But many figures of then-emerging literary culture defined themselves and their mission in opposition to this ascendency, so that in some respects literature acquired the status of antimodern protest or premodern residue. Literary "modernity" as such, and especially the various (and diverse) movements designated by terms such as *modernism* and *modernismo*, is generally understood as a somewhat later development, in some respects a (modern) rejection of literary antimodernism or of continuity with a premodern past, in other respects a sharpening or formalization of literature's dissidence from economically and technically dominant modernity.

We cannot, then, translate between Latour's analysis and the literary field merely on the basis of *modern-* words in the latter, not even if we limit ourselves to Flaubert and his interpreters. We need to begin with conceptual analogies and historical confluences. The notion that science provides true knowledge of nature corresponds to an instrumental and representational view of language— the view that Michel Foucault described as that of the classical *épistemè* (late seventeenth and eighteenth centuries)[2] and that Roland Barthes ascribed to what he called the *bourgeois writing* of roughly the same period.[3]

Yet this modern ideal of a transparent language reliably capable of transmitting content was not really identified with literature, or even with the bellettristic genres that preceded the unitary concept of literature as such. The mathematician and *Encyclopédie* co-editor Jean le Rond d'Alembert saw the ascendency of Newtonian science, a predominantly mathematical mode of knowing that, in his view, had relegated previous philosophies to a premodern realm of error, as having reduced the scope for imaginative cultural production. The theorists of "general grammar" and representation who accused the similitudes and resemblances characteristic of earlier writing of being premodern were generally not literary in orientation, though their strictures are paralleled by the rejection of Renaissance writing and aesthetics by poet-critics such as Malherbe and Boileau.

Despite an ideal of representational clarity and certain compatibilities with the representational project of modern science, the dominant forms of written expression in the seventeenth and eighteenth centuries also owed much to the traditions of rhetoric, whose origins lay in oratory and other oral genres. The literary scholar and media theorist Walter J. Ong described this era as one of *rhetorical culture*—"oral culture shrouded in writing"—characterized, in particular, by rules of poetic diction and by a hierarchy of genres with their attendant styles. In the nineteenth century, these rules and hierarchies became the object of a critique that is modern in the Latourian sense: for having conflated content and form, rhetorical culture came to seem premodern, a literary Old Regime from which writers and critics could escape by techniques of separation and purification.

Claiming to strip away the ornamentation of rhetoric and the misleading seductions of resemblance so as to enable language to serve as an instrument of representation, moderns accused premoderns of having let convention, eloquence, high style, and other properties of language itself become confused with the ideas, feelings, and things to be represented. Get rid of the artifices of neoclassical genres and diction, the romantics said, and real individuality, emotion, and thought will come through. The invention of aesthetics as an autonomous discipline and the doctrine of art for art were among the most obvious moments of a purification process that created the aesthetic/poetic/formalistic end of a modern polarity between art and life, or form and content. Modern literature came to require originality of form, self-purification from the suspicion of subservience either to content or to previous models and forms of writing. The formalist valorization of literary writing as such, of the *writtenness* of literature, could be said to correspond, *mutatis mutandis*, to the social-scientific turn of the modern critique, in which representations of nature are denounced as being purely social and/or cultural constructions: here language and literary form are said to be the cause, literary content or subject matter the effect.

The French critic Jean Paulhan described the dominant stance of modern literary criticism (roughly, from Romanticism to his own early twentieth century) as that of *terror*, by which he meant a demand or requirement for purity. Paulhan's *Les Fleurs de Tarbes ou la terreur dans les lettres*, published in 1941, is as close to a nonmodern manifesto as literary criticism has ever come.[4] Its surprising title contains the germ of its argument: in the town of Tarbes, a sign indicates that one may not enter the public park while carrying flowers.[5] This rule is presumed to enable the enforcement of a ban on cutting flowers in the park.[6] Similarly, the critical condemnation of the flowers of rhetoric—cliché and conventional ornament—is supposed to guarantee literary originality. By critical *terror*, then, Paulhan designates the accusation that writers who use commonplaces or clichés thereby abdicate their autonomy and succumb to what he calls the *power of words*. Terror's indictment amounts to a demand for innovation and purity—a demand that has, indeed, been crucial to literature in the modern era, ever since romanticism's rejection of poetic diction, stable genres, and neoclassical rhetoric.

This is a *modern* accusation in the Latourian sense. Just as moderns accuse *premoderns* or so-called traditional cultures of mixing up the natural and the cultural, of having *beliefs* about nature that are distorted by culture instead of *knowledge* of nature purified from its influence, so terrorists accuse those who use rhetoric and clichés of mixing up thought and word, whether by letting language shape their ideas or by allowing the autonomy of their writing to be profaned by the vulgar business of representing reality. But just as Latour argues that moderns never really escape the hybrid networks joining humans and nonhumans, Paulhan contends that literature never escapes rhetoric and commonplaces. A wiser rule for the garden would be to require all visitors to carry flowers.[7]

Latour also displaces the modern schema of denunciation by arguing that nature and culture, object and subject, are not foundational realities but carefully constructed idealizations, end points refined (at considerable cost) from a continuum of actually existing entities. Paulhan offers a comparable treatment of language and thought: "Language and thought ... are not so much things given to us as they are things we extract *by artifice* from a 'chaos'; they are more like a manufactured object than a tree or a stone."[8] Like Latour, Paulhan rejects the subject–object dualism of modern philosophy, which both attribute to Descartes.[9] The dualisms of mind and body and of living and inert matter are, for Paulhan, of a piece with the binary of idea and word, or signified and signifier.[10]

Paulhan calls into question both the poetic/formalist and the realist/naturalist poles of literary modernity, and indeed points to a fundamental kinship between the two. The demand for pure originality, he writes, while most commonly expressed as a requirement of formal novelty or of attention to language as such, often turns out to be equivalent to a demand for transparency, spontaneity, and freedom from the deformations of any conventional language. Each new literary school, insistent on its formal novelty and its refusal of all earlier styles and rhetorics, also claims to reveal new literary contents or objects that "the previous schools took it upon themselves to hide beneath words."[11]

Paulhan thus shows how these opposite imperatives of modern literature have in common a reliance upon separation and purification: of truth from rhetoric, of content from form or genre, of the new from the inherited. It is no paradox that the literary modernity of the mid-nineteenth century simultaneously gives rise to realism and parnassianism, then naturalism and symbolism—and to corresponding tendencies within the work of Flaubert, who appears to be an exemplary modern in two opposing ways: documentary, quasi-scientific realist and high priest of art and style.

These two major lines of argument for Flaubert as paradigmatic modern writer, realist and formalist, all but contradict each other and thereby recall the tension between the acceptance of the term *modern* in the general and aesthetic fields—a tension that might better be described as a kind of displacement, and which is often registered by a shift in terms from modern to modernist or modernism, with the more general noun *modernity* available to both senses.

The argument for Flaubert as realist has its origin in the journalistic criticism of Flaubert's own time, both favorable and derogatory, perhaps epitomized by Sainte-Beuve's "Flaubert holds the pen as others hold the scalpel" and the famous caricature of Flaubert performing an autopsy on Emma Bovary. On this view, Flaubert was a disenchanter of the world, denying his readers the consolations of idealism and the comforts of decorum (the antimodern accusation against him) so as to extend a spirit of scientific analysis and critical demystification into the sphere of *belles-lettres* (which justified him in the eyes of his modern partisans). Following Sainte-Beuve's qualified endorsement, this realist literary modernism was championed by Zola, who saw in Flaubert the first serious practitioner of a scientific outlook in the novel. Indeed he described *Madame Bovary* as having inaugurated what Thomas Kuhn, writing about science almost a century later, would call a paradigm: "The code of the new art was now written. […] All that remained, for each novelist, was to follow the route laid out, while affirming his particular temperament and trying to make personal discoveries."[12] Just as for Kuhn the great paradigm of the scientific paradigm, Newton's formulation of the laws of motion, makes the everyday work of "normal science" possible for the first time, so for Zola *Madame Bovary* sets the parameters within which what we might call the "normal modern novel" will be written. (Roland Barthes echoes Zola's attribution of paradigm status to Flaubert, though he does so to the detriment of naturalism and socialist realism, which he accuses of falling into the rut of a conventional, prefabricated literariness by following Flaubert's writing as a model rather than as an exemplary instance of innovation.)[13]

Zola was himself a modern who was convinced that Flaubert had been a great initiator of the novel's modernity, but who knew that Flaubert refused this role. At the same time, Zola rejected Flaubert's own formalist claims, which he correctly saw to be a one-sided account of the older writer's work. With only a bit of exaggeration, one could say that Zola saw through (and denounced) Flaubert's claim to be purely interested in style, but felt that Flaubert failed to make or sustain what would have been (according to Zola) his justified claim to having modernized the novel by focusing it rigorously on the real. Zola acknowledged Flaubert's formal contribution, but interpreted it as that of having solved the problem of novelistic form once and for all.

The second (and more influential) construction of Flaubert as modern writer makes of him a formalist, a champion of literary autonomy and of the primacy of the text itself as work of art. The first major exponent of this view is arguably Henry James; others associated with it would include Proust and the practitioners and theorists of the *nouveau roman* and structuralism, such as Alain Robbe-Grillet, Nathalie Sarraute, and Barthes. Because this approach has been the most influential, at least in our own time, in constructing Flaubert's literary modernity, I will focus in some detail on its critical readings of Flaubert, notably those of Nathalie Sarraute and Mario Vargas Llosa.

The title of Sarraute's article "Flaubert le précurseur" has helped make it the canonical statement from this group, although it is in part a critique of the overly facile assumption that Flaubert is the great institutor of modernity because he is the great and uncompromising literary formalist, "the first for whom form played a predominant role."[14] Analyzing Flaubert's style, however, Sarraute finds it wanting. Since his works are almost entirely descriptive, readers will respond by forming images out of the messy material of their own reminiscences. The images we see in our minds when we read Flaubert are like "paintings of dubious quality."[15] Flaubert thus fails Sarraute's first test of artistic purity.

Sarraute nonetheless saves Flaubert for modernism and formalism on two counts. First, he is the author of one true masterpiece, *Madame Bovary*. Why only this novel? Sarraute multiplies her own modernist distinctions and commitments to purification: in *Bovary* Flaubert innovates by portraying something new, *inauthenticity*, and for this purpose his otherwise dubious imagery and glacial stylistic beauty are well adapted, creating a new literary object or subject matter, the *inauthentic*. Clichés are explicitly denounced as such in *Bovary* and are thus artistically redeemed. "Appearances are unmasked, and the opening through which they are exposed changes this beautiful form of dubious quality into an art form."[16] Moreover, Sarraute adds in a quasi-contemporaneous lecture on Flaubert, Emma's sentiments are copies of "degraded literary forms," so that in calling attention to her seduction by literature Flaubert calls attention to literature as such and makes it the context of his own work, thereby reinforcing the autonomy of literature.[17]

This is, indeed, one of the common *idées reçues* about *Madame Bovary*: that *reading* and the false seductions of literature constitute a uniquely privileged theme of the novel. Emma's story, or Gustave's critical achievement, on this reading, is fundamentally about the dangers of reading in a naive way that encourages identification with characters, projecting oneself into events, desiring the surroundings and objects described in books. It is thus a novel about literature.

Yet despite the obvious importance of books and reading in the production of desire, especially imitative or mimetic desire, *Madame Bovary* does not really give books and reading a unique or special place, set apart from other forms of activity, of imagination, of participation in society. The novel instead places reading alongside various other forms of sensory and social experience. Young Emma encounters painted plates with explanatory legends,[18] the perfumes and images accompanying the Mass, metaphors in sermons, the sensations of confession,[19] love-songs of the last century,[20] and fashion magazines.[21] Objects and sensations, no less than readings—the confessional, perfumes, dishes, "the distant sound of some late hackney cab still rolling along the Boulevards,"[22] a riding habit, reserved seats at the Rouen Opera—inspire Emma's imitative desire.

This novel's world, in other words, is tremendously material, but a material world invested with social meaning. The contrast of city and countryside, no less than books, is a device—one might almost say a technology—for imagining and desiring. The same can be said about the Catholic religion, in the coming together of its spiritual and sensory dimensions, about fashion as embodied in both the clothes and the magazines, or about the lifestyles of the rich and noble—the Vaubyessard Château, its occupants, and their possessions function in the same way for Emma as do novels, magazines, cities, or well-cut clothes.[23]

Emma's situation and modes of desire are thus strongly linked to the entire network of techniques, mediation, communication, and commerce that we find in the novel, which are very much those of the nineteenth century: printed books and lending libraries, of course, but also fashion magazines and the newspaper; the city, the countryside, and the vehicles that go between them; the architecture and rituals of the Church; the political technology of county fair speeches and prizes; neighborly proximity and surveillance of comings and goings in the village; touring opera companies; and so forth. Books and literature are important, but not in a transcendent or even marked way: simply in proportion to their relatively large place in the early-nineteenth-century mediasphere as experienced by a provincial French girl on the fringes of the middle class. Far from producing a modernist or postmodernist foregrounding of literature, then, *Madame Bovary* shows us a nonmodern, hybrid world of socialized and meaningful objects.

Sarraute's second argument hinges on one of the most famous passages from all of Flaubert's letters, his wish to write a "book about nothing":

> What seems beautiful to me, what I should like to write, is a book about nothing, a book dependent on nothing external, which would be held together by the internal strength of its style, just as the earth, suspended in the void, depends on nothing external for its support; a book which would have almost no subject, or at least in which the subject would be almost invisible, if such a thing is possible.[24]

With this statement, Sarraute contends, Flaubert "foretold, even invoked, the literature of the future," an "abstract art" no longer burdened with plot and character.[25] What ultimately matters to her is not whether Flaubert was already modern, but that he was a modernizer. "Are these not the goals," she continues, "toward which the modern novel tends? And this being so, can there be any doubt that Flaubert was its precursor?"[26]

Sarraute is representative and not idiosyncratic in hanging the case for a modernist Flaubert on the *livre sur rien*. In 1962 the influential Swiss critic Jean Rousset entitled a chapter of his book *Forme et signification* "*Madame Bovary* ou le livre sur rien," thereby suggesting that Flaubert's first published novel already realized his ideal of a book sustained only by its style. Like Sarraute, he places Flaubert in a narrative of modernization: "He is the first in date of the non-figurative novelists."[27] To be sure, Rousset concedes that "the subject—and the psychology—of *Madame Bovary* certainly still play their part, albeit a muted one, in the concert of the novel, which could not exist without them. Yet," he then continues, "we have the right, and perhaps the duty, to ignore them."[28] In other words, we ought to modernize Flaubert, stressing what unites him with the then-current *nouveau roman* of the 1950s and 1960s while setting aside what once linked him with Balzac and other predecessors.

The critical overvaluation of the *livre sur rien* is thus itself a characteristically modern gesture. The remark is taken as a crucial, even defining moment on the assumption that it is among the most *advanced* of Flaubert's many statements on literature, and that there is a progressive history of aesthetics in which advancement is a good thing. We claim to know that formalism is more advanced than realism, internal poetics more progressive than the assemblage and processing of documentary material, and from this vantage point we choose from Flaubert the places in which he got these things right. But what has happened to this teleological vector now that the contemporary novel is embodied not by Nathalie Sarraute and John Barth but by Virginie Despentes and Karl Ove Knausgard?

The *livre sur rien* passage, almost unique in the surviving correspondence, occurs in a letter to Louise Colet written on January 16, 1852, about four months after Flaubert began writing *Bovary*. Gustave was responding to what he called Louise's "excessive enthusiasm" for some parts of his unpublished *L'Education sentimentale* (1843–5), which she had read in manuscript. Louise had particularly liked the reflections on art in the chapters recounting the development of the character Jules as a writer. These chapters stand alone within Flaubert's fiction in their serious presentation of aesthetic ideas; he replies to Colet that he could now improve on them, but won't, strongly implying that he no longer approves of the explicit self-portraiture they amount to. He then explains what he regards as the novel's failure by describing himself as containing two writers or writing personalities; this passage, too, is famous and much commented:

> There are in me, literarily speaking, two distinct persons: one who is infatuated with bombast, lyricism, eagle flights, sonorities of phrase and lofty ideas; and another who digs and burrows into the truth as deeply as he can, who likes to treat a humble fact as respectfully as a big one, who would like to make you feel almost *physically* the things he reproduces; that one likes to laugh, and enjoys the animal side of man.[29]

So far, so modern: subjectivity and objectivity, mind and matter, form and content. But then Flaubert adds that "*L'Education sentimentale* was, unbeknownst to me, an attempt to fuse these two tendencies of my mind"[30] *Unbeknownst to me*: like a good Latourian modern, we might say, Flaubert was making a subject/object hybrid without realizing or acknowledging it. He finished his book but now considers the fusion to have been a failure because it did not accomplish the necessary work of mediation: "The causes are shown, the results also, but the linkage of cause to effect is not. That is the book's vice."[31]

The early *Sentimental Education* was one attempt, he continues; *La Tentation de Saint-Antoine* was another, wholly on the lyric end of the polarity, and it was an even worse failure, pearls without a string. *Bovary* is to be a third try: this time, he writes, he must succeed or throw himself out the window. Presumably, according to the logic of the argument Flaubert is making, *Bovary* is an attempt to get the balance right by means of both a material, down-to-earth subject *and* unsparing pursuit of stylistic effect. But in the place of this sort of comment on his novel-in-progress, which would seem to be the logical next step, Flaubert, caught between an uncongenial project and an open window, suddenly shifts course: "What seems beautiful to me, what I should like to write, is a book about nothing." As Mario Vargas Llosa pointedly noted when criticizing Sarraute's reading in his book on *Madame Bovary*, the *livre sur rien* is a fantasized substitute for the novel at hand, perhaps a hypothetical revenge of the lyrical fellow in Flaubert over his materialistic counterpart.[32] Having presented the idea and image of the book about nothing, Flaubert proceeds to interpret it as a culmination of a progressive story, akin to Michelet's account of universal history, of the dematerialization of art, its emancipation from such constraints as the material weightiness of Egyptian sculpture and the fixed forms of poetic genres. "I believe the future of Art lies in this direction."[33]

Yet the daydream of a *livre sur rien* remains a very particular, even transitory moment in Flaubert's thinking and writing. After this letter, Flaubert will return constantly to his preoccupation with style, to his pride of craftsmanship as a maker of sentences; he will often let his "lyrical fellow" be his spokesman, or tell us that the lyrical one is dearer to his heart than the other guy, the materialist—but in spite of this he will barely come back to the *livre sur rien* as an aesthetic ideal, thereby making a distinction between his personal predilection for the subjective pole of writing and his conviction, albeit a reluctant one, that the objective and material pole is just as necessary to the integrity of his literary art.

In rejecting Sarraute's interpretation of the *livre sur rien*, and in certain other aspects of his extensive and impassioned treatment of *Madame Bovary*, Mario Vargas Llosa stresses the inclusive and nondualistic character of Flaubert's writing and his thoughts about literature. Not surprisingly, however, for someone publishing in his essay in 1975, he retains a strong commitment to modernity and literary autonomy. He attempts to subsume Flaubert's novelistic materiality into the formalism of nothingness by constructing it as specifically *fictional* and *antirealistic*. Vargas Llosa is wonderfully attentive to the things of the novel, but he also tries to integrate this attention into his depiction of Flaubert as a formalist precursor of avant-gardes. In this he writes as a representative Latourian modern, insisting on purity and distinctions so as to deny the networked hybridization he explores and extends.

To reconcile the novel's materiality and its project of achieving autonomy on the plane of language and style, he argues that the object world of *Madame Bovary* is uniquely produced by its language, thereby confirming the aesthetic autonomy of that language and thus of the novel. In so doing, however, he makes the quintessentially modern mistake of believing only in the top half of what Latour calls the modern Constitution, that is, believing that humans and nonhumans really are essentially separate. This enables him to portray Flaubert as a counterfactual literary artificer:

> This descriptive frenzy is not an end in itself but a procedure the narrator uses to destroy reality and re-create it as a different reality. The verbal substance that swallows up innumerable real facts does something more insidious than enumerating the properties of men and things; the intent behind it is to render all these heterogeneous ingredients that have been wrested from life homogeneous by endowing them with properties that are its own—those of language itself, formal properties. The materiality of the fictional world is the result of an adulteration, perpetrated by language, of objects, persons, sentiments, actions, thoughts, and even words. *In the fictional reality the boundaries separating them fall; applied with a particular bias to men and things, the descriptive system of the novel produces that marvelous inversion whereby in Emma Bovary's world, contrary to what is the case in the reader's world, emotions and ideas appear to have corporeality, color, taste; and objects seem to possess a mysterious intimacy, a mind.*[34]

This reading depends on an extremely strong but unstated premise: namely, that outside the fiction, there are *real* boundaries separating objects from emotions and ideas, so that the latter can never "appear to have corporeality, color, taste" and the former can never "seem to possess a mysterious intimacy, a mind." But are mind and matter truly so separate in "real life"? The top, official half of Latour's modern Constitution says yes, but the bottom half is one long work of extending and complicating their inextricable mixture. And when we turn to Vargas Llosa's own analyses of "Things Humanized"[35] and "Human Beings Turned into Things,"[36] what we find are not forms of perception unique to *Madame Bovary*, or even to the language of fiction: we encounter things that come with social and cultural meanings, human bodies perceived in concrete, even fragmented materiality, and human thoughts and feelings expressed through material metaphors. Such is "Emma Bovary's world"—but is there anyone for whom it is otherwise? Tail coats and frock coats signify higher social position than dress smocks—at the Bovary-Rouault wedding just as in the rest of nineteenth-century France.[37] To be sure, Flaubert's prose produces more extended, more carefully articulated metaphors and material counterparts than most of us hit upon in the routine workings of our mind; he places the social meanings of objects in a context that makes them clearer and more intense than they usually are for most of us. Flaubert's literary art, in other words, is real and valuable, but it does not overthrow a (modern) world of absolute dichotomies between the human and the nonhuman so as to produce an autonomous literary modernity in which their hybridization is uniquely possible. Or, we might say, if such is indeed the work carried out by Flaubert's texts, then what he was doing was displaying, in fiction, the lower half of the nonmodern Constitution: he was inventing a fictional version of modernity in which we have never been modern!

I will conclude by arguing directly for the nonmodernity of Flaubert's novelistic aesthetic based on his own statements about his writing (some of which, of course, have already been considered above). His insistence on the unity of form and content is well-known and generally acknowledged even by his most formalistic interpreters. He states flatly that the two terms are abstractions wrongfully drawn out from an inseparable whole: "Until someone comes along and separates for me the form and the substance of a given sentence, I shall continue to maintain that that distinction is meaningless," he writes to Louise Colet in 1846.[38] Flaubert is nonetheless willing to use these terms, especially *form*, in a generally conventional way so as to talk about his understanding of their mutual implication and intrication. Successful form depends on the subject matter, he repeats, writing to Colet, again, in 1853: "One must thoroughly ruminate one's objective before thinking about form, for it will only come out well if we are obsessed by the illusion of the subject."[39] Flaubert repeatedly evokes the necessity of coordinated subject matter via a recurrent metaphor that I've already mentioned in passing, that of the pearls and string of a necklace. He seems to have used this figure for the first time in the letter on the *livre sur rien*. How passionately he had fashioned the pearls of *Saint Antoine*, forgetting only the string![40] "The pearls make up the necklace, but it's the string that makes the necklace," he writes the next year.[41] He returns to the image in December 1875 to tell George Sand that he hasn't yet come up with the subject for a new modern novel: "I'm still lacking the string of the necklace (that is, the main thing)."[42] As much as he enjoyed shaping stylistic pearls, he never thought they would make a work unless strung on the unifying thread of subject matter.

In an 1853 letter in which he said that there are no intrinsically beautiful subjects for literature, Flaubert made his one known return to the idea of a "book about nothing" and in so doing he both clarified its status as fantasized object of desire and reaffirmed the insufficiency of attending purely to verbal form:

> I would like to produce books which would entail only the writing of sentences (if I may put it that way), just as in order to live it is enough to breathe. What I dislike are the tricks inherent in the making of an outline, the arranging of effects, all the underlying calculations—which are, however, Art, for they and they alone account for the stylistic effect.[43]

Flaubert recognized the need for that part of the work of writing that he did not like, and that many of his more opinionated pronouncements neglect or even seem to exclude. In the nonmodern poetics of the novel he articulates here, any kind of subject, at least potentially, will do—and that is its modern side, the notion of art having been separated from that of intrinsically noble actions and situations—but the shape of the subject matter, its processes, and above all the work of mediation and translation by which it is rendered into words are absolutely crucial, no matter how much the would-be modern writer would love to play only in the verbal element, and that is why this poetics is ultimately nonmodern. As Flaubert was to describe the balance some years later, "a good subject for a novel [...] is a matrix idea, from which all the others derive. An author is not at all free to write this or that. He does not choose his subject. [...] Therein lies the secret of masterpieces—in the concordance of the subject and the author's temperament."[44]

Flaubert repeatedly told his correspondents that *Madame Bovary* was not his kind of book. He wrote that he disliked the subject matter, that he longed to do something grander and more lyrical, in line with his desires. At the same time, he recognized that doing this novel was, in some very profound sense, good for him—that he was a more complete writer for going against his own proclivities. In expressing his dislikes or his preference he often sounds either modern or antimodern, yearning for purely autonomous art or an escape into the past. But when he acknowledges the value of the work he was putting himself through—when he sounds the note of being truly the maker of *Madame Bovary* and not that of being the opiniated Gustave Flaubert—then he comes across as antidualistic and inclusive: as nonmodern. On August 26, 1853 he wrote to Colet that *Bovary* is good for him because it forces him outside of himself and requires enormous effort, whereas if he writes something that he likes, that comes from his lyrical inclinations, he can write quickly and easily but at the price of having it be repetitive and badly conceived.[45] Gustave, in other words, would enjoy being a formalist or an antiquarian, either a modern or an antimodern trying to pass as a premodern, but as the writer of *Bovary* he knows that he had better be something like what we can now call a nonmodern.

A related articulation of Flaubert's nonmodern views can be found in his comments on the Parnassian poet Leconte de Lisle, a contemporary for whom he expressed qualified admiration. Flaubert was impressed by Leconte de Lisle's *Poèmes antiques* (1852) and could identify with his devotion to formal, impersonal beauty and his refusal of both romantic declamation and contemporary vulgarity. While he appreciated Leconte's "purity," presumably his pure devotion to beauty and to his calling as a poet, he objected to his attempt to take refuge in antiquity and in formal beauty: "Art is not just the straightness of lines and polish of surfaces."[46] The modern element was lacking in Leconte, wrote Flaubert, and he explained that by modern he did not mean up-to-date doctrines or feelings, but the energy that comes with living in one's own time: *the contemporary*, we might well translate. "What's lacking in his talent as in his character is the modern side, *color in motion*. With his ideal of noble passions, he doesn't notice that he's drying up, in everyday life, and making himself literarily sterile. The ideal is fertile only if one brings *everything* into it. It's a work of love and not of exclusion."[47] Leconte, he in effect said, was right to want to avoid being merely modern, and he was admirable (and perhaps either truly modern or truly antimodern) in the purity of his devotion to formal beauty, but he was wrong to settle for being an antimodern, a counterfeiter of antiquity rather than someone who would unite ancient ways of being with the energy of life in the present. (It is well to remember that for Latour, antimoderns are disgruntled moderns.)

Flaubert followed the above remark on Leconte with a historical commentary on the ravages of modernization (my term, not his) in French literature. "For two centuries now France has sufficiently trod this path of ascendent *negation*. Nature, frankness, caprice, personality, and even erudition have been more and more eliminated from literature."[48] The reference to "two centuries" identifies the path of negation with French classicism and the Enlightenment. Over many years, Flaubert in his letters expresses admiration and love for writers of the sixteenth century—Rabelais, Ronsard, Montaigne, and Shakespeare—whom he sees as having taken an inclusive and all-encompassing approach to writing, as opposed to purifiers of taste such as Malherbe and Boileau and enlighteners such as Voltaire.[49] Ronsard, he notes approvingly, enjoined poets to study manual trades as sources of metaphors.[50] Flaubert thus sees the seventeenth- and eighteenth-century ideal of representation or transparency, which as I noted above was an early avatar of the modern in language and writing, as limiting and sterilizing. Rejecting that era's critical accusation that the writers of the Renaissance were premodern, mired in resemblances or incapable of clarity and necessary distinctions, Flaubert regards them as the only possible models for writers who would stand outside the limitations of schools and ideals and thus free contemporary French literature and manners from the twin (and highly compatible) straightjackets of neoclassical taste and Revolutionary virtue.[51] He sees his sixteenth-century favorites as the last writers to have avoided the (modern) bane of purification, which he himself works so hard to overcome.[52]

When he felt that he had succeeded in that task, Flaubert would describe what he had done as an overcoming of dualisms and separations—between writing and life, or subject and object. With *Bovary*, he wrote to Colet on July 7, 1853, "I will have made some written real (*du réel écrit*), which is rare."[53] And in what is arguably the most rhapsodic moment in all his letters, he describes the act of writing in terms that both anticipate Latour's concept of "circulating reference"[54] and describe a situation in which no Great Divide separates mind from matter or human from nonhuman:

> it is a delicious thing to write! To be no longer *oneself* but to circulate in the entire creation of which one is speaking. Today, for example, both man and woman, at once lover and mistress, I rode on horseback in a forest, on an autumn afternoon, under yellow leaves, and I was the horses, the leaves, the wind, the words that they said to each other and the red sun that made them almost close their love-drowned eyes.[55]

Notes

1   Bruno Latour, *We Have Never Been Modern*, trans. Catherine Porter (Cambridge: Harvard University Press, 1993).
2   Michel Foucault, *The Order of Things: An Archaeology of the Human Sciences* (New York: Vintage, 1973), 56, 62, 78–124.

3   Roland Barthes, *Writing Degree Zero*, trans. Annette Lavers and Colin Smith (London: Jonathan Cape, 1967), 62–6.
4   Jean Paulhan, *Les Fleurs de Tarbes ou la terreur dans les lettres* (Paris: Gallimard, 1941); *The Flowers of Tarbes or, Terror in Literature*, trans. Michael Syrotinski (Urbana: University of Illinois Press, 2006). For Paulhan's works and all others, I refer to English editions whenever possible and give my own translation when citing from French editions.
5   Paulhan, *The Flowers of Tarbes*, 9.
6   Ibid., 16.
7   Ibid., 93.
8   Paulhan, *Les Fleurs de Tarbes*, 250.
9   Bruno Latour. *Pandora's Hope: Essays on the Reality of Science Studies* (Cambridge: Harvard University Press, 1999), 4–9; Paulhan, *The Flowers of Tarbes*, 34; *Les Fleurs de Tarbes*, 250–3.
10 Paulhan, *The Flowers of Tarbes*, 33.
11 Ibid., 41; see also 12–14, 67, 86.
12 Émile Zola, "Gustave Flaubert," in *Œuvres complètes*, vol. 11. *Les Romanciers naturalistes*, ed. Henri Mitterand (Paris: Cercle du livre précieux, 1968), 97.
13 Barthes, 73–9.
14 Nathalie Sarraute, "Flaubert," trans. Maria Jolas, *Partisan Review* 33, no. 2 (1966): 193.
15 Ibid., 199.
16 Ibid., 205.
17 Sarraute, *Oeuvres complètes*, ed. Jean-Yves Tadié (Paris: Gallimard "Bibliothèque de la Pléiade," 1996), 1649; cf. 1659–60.
18 Flaubert, *Madame Bovary*, trans. Lydia Davis (New York: Penguin, 2010), 30.
19 Ibid., 31.
20 Ibid., 31–2.
21 Ibid., 49.
22 Ibid., 33.
23 Ibid., 42–4, 121.
24 *The Letters of Gustave Flaubert*, ed. and trans. Francis Steegmuller, vol. 1 (Cambridge: Harvard University Press, 1979), 154.
25 Sarraute, "Flaubert," 207, 208.
26 Ibid., 208.
27 Jean Rousset, "*Madame Bovary*: Flaubert's Anti-Novel," trans. Paul de Man, in Flaubert, *Madame Bovary*, ed. Paul de Man (New York: Norton, 1965), 441. ("Flaubert's Anti-Novel" is de Man's translation of "ou le livre sur rien" in Rousset's chapter title.)

28 Ibid.
29 Flaubert, *Letters*, 1: 154. Translation modified.
30 Gustave Flaubert, *Correspondance*, ed. Jean Bruneau, vol. 2 (Paris: Gallimard "Bibliothèque de la Pléiade," 1980), 30.
31 Ibid.
32 Mario Vargas Llosa, *The Perpetual Orgy: Flaubert and Madame Bovary*, trans. Helen Lane (New York: Farrar, Straus, and Giroux, 1986), 39–41.
33 Flaubert, *Letters*, 1: 154.
34 Vargas Llosa, 127–8. Emphasis added.
35 Ibid., 128.
36 Ibid., 133.
37 Ibid., 130–1.
38 Flaubert, *Letters*, 1: 77. Sarraute acknowledged Flaubert's reiterated insistence on the unity of form and content, and even identified this aspect of his thinking with a temporality neither premodern nor modern: "In these ideas, which are based on his genuine experience, he remains a writer for all time." Sarraute, "Flaubert," 207.
39 Flaubert, *Correspondance*, 2: 469.
40 Flaubert, *Letters*, 1: 154.
41 Flaubert, *Correspondance*, 2: 417.
42 Flaubert, *Correspondance*, 4: 997.
43 Flaubert, *Letters*, 1: 189.
44 Flaubert, *Letters*, 2: 20.
45 Flaubert, *Correspondance*, 2: 416.
46 Ibid., 2: 298.
47 Ibid., 2: 514. See also this remark about Leconte de Lisle from July 1853: "He has no instinct for modern life; he lacks heart. By this I do not mean personal or even humanitarian feelings, no—but *heart*, almost in the medical sense of the word" (Flaubert, *Letters*, 1: 193).
48 Flaubert, *Correspondance*, 2: 514.
49 See Flaubert, *Correspondance*, 1: 188–9; 2: 45, 209, 517, 529, 544.
50 Flaubert, *Correspondance*, 2: 545.
51 Ibid., 2: 514.
52 Flaubert's treatment of sixteenth-century writing is echoed by Barthes, who, contrasting it with the strictures and representational project of the seventeenth century, refers to "a language in which ornaments are not yet ritualistic but are in themselves a method of investigation applied to the whole surface of the world … the genuine appearance of many-sidedness, and the euphoria which comes from freedom" (Barthes, 61). See also Stephen Toulmin's argument about modernity's quest for certainty and clarity, with its beginnings in the seventeenth

century, as a "counter-Renaissance" (*Cosmopolis: The Hidden Agenda of Modernity* [Chicago: University of Chicago Press, 1990], 45–137) and Latour's recent commentary on Toulmin (*Facing Gaia: Eight Lectures on the New Climatic Regime*, trans. Catherine Porter [Cambridge: Polity Press, 2017], 185–90). And see also Foucault's remarks to the effect that what he calls modern literature—but that I am calling nonmodern in at least the case of Flaubert—reconnects with a "living being of language [….] that had been forgotten since the sixteenth century" (Foucault, 43–4).

53 Flaubert, *Correspondance*, 2: 376.
54 Latour, *Pandora's Hope*, 69–74.
55 Flaubert, *Letters*, 1: 203. Translation modified.

Bibliography

Barthes, Roland. *Writing Degree Zero*. Translated by Annette Lavers and Colin Smith. London: Jonathan Cape, 1967.

Flaubert, Gustave. *Correspondance*. Edited by Jean Bruneau. 5 vols. Paris: Gallimard "Bibliothèque de la Pléiade," 1973–2007.

Flaubert, Gustave. *The Letters of Gustave Flaubert*. Edited and translated by Francis Steegmuller. 2 vols. Cambridge: Harvard University Press, 1979–82.

Flaubert, Gustave. *Madame Bovary*. Translated by Lydia Davis. New York: Penguin, 2010.

Foucault, Michel. *The Order of Things: An Archaeology of the Human Sciences*. New York: Vintage, 1973.

Latour, Bruno. *Facing Gaia: Eight Lectures on the New Climatic Regime*. Translated by Catherine Porter. Cambridge: Polity Press, 2017.

Latour, Bruno. *Pandora's Hope: Essays on the Reality of Science Studies*. Cambridge: Harvard University Press, 1999.

Latour, Bruno. *We Have Never Been Modern*. Translated by Catherine Porter. Cambridge: Harvard University Press, 1993.

Paulhan, Jean. *Les Fleurs de Tarbes ou La Terreur dans les lettres*. Edited by Jean-Claude Zylberstein. Paris: Gallimard "Folio/Idées," 1990.

Paulhan, Jean. *The Flowers of Tarbes or, Terror in Literature*. Translated by Michael Syrotinski. Urbana: University of Illinois Press, 2006.

Rousset, Jean. "*Madame Bovary*: Flaubert's Anti-Novel." Translated by Paul de Man. In Flaubert, *Madame Bovary*, edited by Paul de Man. 439–57. New York: Norton, 1965.

Sarraute, Nathalie. "Flaubert." Translated by Maria Jolas. *Partisan Review* 33, no. 2 (1966): 193–208.
Sarraute, Nathalie. *Oeuvres complètes*. Edited by Jean-Yves Tadié. Paris: Gallimard "Bibliothèque de la Pléiade," 1996.
Toulmin, Stephen. *Cosmopolis: The Hidden Agenda of Modernity*. Chicago: University of Chicago Press, 1990.
Vargas Llosa, Mario. *The Perpetual Orgy: Flaubert and Madame Bovary*. Translated by Helen Lane. New York: Farrar, Straus, and Giroux, 1986.
Zola, Émile. *Les Romanciers naturalistes*. In *Oeuvres complètes*. Edited by Henri Mitterand. Vol. 11. Paris: Cercle du livre précieux, 1968.

4

Latour, Stengers, and Nonmodern Poetry

Claire Chi-ah Lyu

I

My chapter pays heed to Paulson's call to reflect on how literary studies "fit[s] into a world where nonhuman things matter" and to consider what literary scholars can learn from Latour and Stengers.[1] Paulson asks, "What does modern literature look like if we have never been modern?"[2] I bring his inquiry to bear on poetry to explore what modern poetry and poetic criticism might look like if we have never been modern. I experiment with reorienting poetry from modern purification to nonmodern mediation so as to explore how poetry can relate us to, rather than separate us from, the nonhuman world. Currently in poetic studies, we do not have a way of defining poetry that does not characterize it in terms of purification, that is, one that does not presuppose the Great Divide between Nature and Culture: the model of autonomous discourse that shuns the nonhuman world in its self-referential negativity, and which is predicated on the Great Divide, still has a strong hold on mainstream poetic establishment. Prigent, a contemporary French poet, critic, and theorist, for example, considers that a poem "duplicat[es] [...] the fatal relegation of the world by the word."[3] To this day, we continue to rely on the formalist paradigm of poetry that ensued from the linguistic turn of the second half of the twentieth century and treat language, society, and world as separate entities.

In the twenty-first century, however, we live in an interpretive context that has radically shifted from the time of the linguistic turn. Climate change—by which I mean, with Latour, the global and inevitable imbrication of discourse, politics, and nature (i.e., I am not addressing climate change as a scientific or ecological issue)—forcefully foregrounds the mutual entanglement of humans and the nonhuman material world. The undeniability of human and nonhuman immanence has consequences poetic studies can no longer ignore, especially in regards to the paradigms of purification and transcendence it upholds. This is because the conditions of possibility for these paradigms no longer obtain in the current interpretive context of climate change. This applies for both the traditional form of "trans-ascendence" (e.g., ecstatic aesthetics, human exceptionality) and the deconstructionist version of "trans-descendence" (e.g., trace, *différance*).[4] Indeed, Latour has pointed out that the sublime—the poetic paradigm of transcendent subject par excellence—is no longer possible.[5] The same holds, and this is my chapter's argument, for the modern paradigm of poetry as self-referential negativity. The Latourian nonmodern, I wish to suggest, gives the conceptual and practical means to shift poetry away from the linguistic turn, which is centered exclusively on humans, and to envisage poetry from the perspective of the "nonhuman turn" that is gaining momentum in the larger context of posthuman studies.[6]

What the new interpretive context of climate change challenges most directly in the model of poetic self-referential negativity is the absence of the nonhuman material world and the unconcern toward this absence such an anthropocentric model enacts. Initially called the "poetic function" in Jakobson's structuralist poetics, self-referentiality designates the way in which language draws attention to itself and, in doing so, eschews its referential function. Jakobson is careful to note, however, that self-referentiality becomes dominant in poetry without excluding the other functions: there is no "monopoly," only a "different hierarchical order" between functions, as he puts it.[7] Subsequent theoretical movements (poststructuralism and deconstruction in particular) further nuance the "hierarchical order" of self-referentiality over referentiality. In its mildest formulation, self-referentiality is said to suspend or neutralize the referential world; in its strongest formulation, it is said to negate and annihilate the world. What remains constant across various formulations is the erasure of the nonhuman referential world which is made to recede passively into the background. And it is the thesis of passivity and erasure of the nonhuman world that the new interpretive context of global warming invalidates: we now live in a situation where the world can no longer be discarded because it intrudes on us. "Gaia, the intruder," as Stengers calls it,[8] bursts upon the stage "where she was not anticipated and screws all established relations up, undermining what these relations were all taking for granted."[9] Gaia refuses to be reduced to passive background.[10] It is an agency that responds to us and makes demands on us in a direct rebuke to our negation and unconcern.

Thus, the shift in interpretive context challenges us to find an alternative way of defining poetry: not uniquely as the privileged model of purification and autonomous discourse, but as a hybrid genre that entangles language, thought, body, affect, and the nonhuman material world in a conjoined work of both purification and mediation. Latour makes it clear: the moderns practice both purification and mediation but disconnect the two and acknowledge only the former while making the latter invisible. Reorienting poetry from modern to nonmodern entails attending to poetry's unacknowledged work of mediation to examine how it relates us and situates us with respect to the larger nonhuman material world. In this regard, my chapter envisions the practices of poetic studies in terms of what Paulson calls "cosmopolitical philology" which is "concerned both with itself—its signs, the discursive communities in which it participates at any given place and time—and with its others, the articulated but nonlinguistic and often nonhuman world."[11] How can we conceive poetry as that which mediates between language, humans, and the "nonlinguistic and often nonhuman world"?

II

In recent years, poetry scholars have sought to go beyond the impasse of solipsistic self-referentiality. Collot, for example, combines formalism with phenomenology and psychoanalysis in order to restitute the whole of poetic experience that encompasses language (formalism), world (phenomenology), and subject (psychoanalysis).[12] Ramazani proposes two notions—"transnational poetics" which takes poetry beyond national, cultural, and linguistic containment; and "dialogic poetics" which combines Jakobson's "poetics" with Bakhtin's "dialogic"[13]—in order to conceive poetry as an interactive, rather than an insular, genre that engages with the reality and concerns of various contemporary phenomena of globalization. Acquisto, in turn, redefines poetic self-reflexivity as an inward turn that also moves outward toward the world, bringing productive dynamism rather than aporetic paralysis.[14] These new approaches aim at rendering the hermetic seal of autonomous discourse more porous so as to reconnect language with society and the world. But they do so within the frame of the Great Divide which they do not contest: language remains the exclusive property of human culture, and they start with segregated endpoints which they then proceed to reconnect. As such, they ultimately play into what Latour calls the "parallel traps of naturalization and sociologization" that go hand in hand with autonomization of discourse.[15]

In poetic studies, then, we still consider language as pertaining to referentiality and representation: we put words on the side of Culture and the world on the side of Nature and have words deal with the unbridgeable gap. Language oscillates between the dream of transparent correspondence and the impossibility of correspondence between the two sides; that is, between the perfect referentiality on the one hand and the denial of referentiality in the name of self-referentiality on the other. The "hierarchical order" becomes exclusion; self-referentiality comes to negate referentiality in most radical terms. Prigent's statement that poetic language is "what separates us from the world [...] what always names both the world and the distancing of the world"[16] encapsulates the still enduring modern theoretical tenet: poetry, Prigent writes, "tries to designate the real as a gap";[17] "[p]erhaps [...] it is to this unfillable gap, to this irruption of the negative, and to these alone that the poetic text bears witness."[18] The aporia of naming ("to designate the real as a gap"), thematized as negation ("this irruption of the negative"), becomes the very subject—indeed the only subject—of poetry ("this [...] gap, this irruption of the negative, and these *alone*, to which the poetic text bears witness"). In this solipsistic model, there is nothing but language; world and reality are effects of language. Caught in the contradiction between the dream of perfect naming and the impossibility of naming, poetry can never get out of (human) language and thus can never get to the "nonlinguistic and often nonhuman world."[19]

It is in fields outside of poetic studies (e.g., feminist/gender/queer studies, science studies, posthuman/nonhuman/animal studies) that we find a contestation of the representational model that goes further than a negation and leads to an alternative: conceptualization of language as performative rather than representational. I am interested in the "posthumanist performative" approach to language articulated by Haraway and Barad for their explicit mobilization and inclusion of the nonhuman material world.[20] In the performative view language is not autonomous, transcendent, or uniquely linguistic but immanent to the flow of interaction between all human and nonhuman actors alike. The human world and the nonhuman material world are entangled and co-generative of each other. We move from human exceptionality to flat ontology and from substance philosophy to relationality. For Barad, the performative model constitutes an explicit contestation of "the excessive power granted to language to determine what is real."[21] Haraway speaks of a "material-semiotic technology" that links "meanings and bodies" to generate situational, rather than intrinsic, knowledge of "webbed connections" where location and embodiment, not transcendence, are key.[22] The performative model of language in Barad and Haraway refuses to accept the Great Divide: it stays in the middle ground of nature-culture—away from the endpoints of Nature vs. Culture—where matter and materiality are not passive but acquire agency.[23]

What interests me most in this performative model is that it enables us, as Barad writes, to "shift the focus from questions of correspondence between description and reality to matters of practices, doings, and actions."[24] Put otherwise, it shifts us from mimesis to *poiesis*. The performative model brings us back to poetry in its etymological sense of making. And it does so not by espousing the anti-mimetic stance of structuralism, post-structuralism, and deconstruction, but by way of an alternate reconfiguring of language, human, and the nonhuman material world in an ongoing, dynamic, co-creative entanglement: what Barad calls "intra-action" in contradistinction to "inter-action" which "presumes the prior existence of independent entities/relata."[25] It thus gives us a model for articulating a performative, as opposed to a representational, concept of naming. The "posthumanist performative" naming, then, enables us to conceive a nonmodern *poiesis* that takes into account the nonhuman world to which it grants full agency. In other words, it offers a model of nonmodern poetry where, to quote Latour, "words finally carry the worlds."[26] It is thus for poetic and political reasons that I wish to argue for a performative model of poetry that is inclusive of the nonhuman material world as an alternative to representationalism that perpetuates the Great Divide.

III

What does it mean to shift our conceptualization of language from representational to performative? How do we do so? And what does this mean for poetic studies? What would a nonmodern performative practice of criticism look like? I explore these questions by taking up, as do Collot, Ramazani, and Acquisto, the thesis of self-referentiality that presumably grants to poetry a status that is "absolutely modern" (Rimbaud) and "exception[al]" (Mallarmé). I focus on the correlated issue of negativity which designates more specifically the radical denial of referentiality by way of self-referentiality. I thus reformulate my initial question (what might modern poetry and poetic criticism look like if we have never been modern?) as: what would happen to the modern conceptualization of poetry as self-referential negativity if we were to take the new interpretive context of climate change seriously, as I think we must? In other words, how can we orient poetry away from negativity/mimesis and toward performativity/*poiesis*? And I add a corollary question: how would we approach Mallarmé, the consecrated modern poet of self-referential negativity, in nonmodern performative terms?

I proceed in two steps by pairing two modern figures, Blanchot and Mallarmé, with two nonmodern thinkers, Stengers and Latour. First, I attend to the conceptualization of poetic language by juxtaposing two approaches to naming: the modern, representational model Blanchot elaborates in "Literature and the Right to Death"[27] (which I read as a kind of Modern Constitution for poetry); and the nonmodern, performative model Stengers proposes in her talk "Gaia, the Urgency to Think (and Feel)."[28] I pay particular heed to the status of the nonhuman material world in the two models. What kind of relation to the nonhuman material world do they allow? Do they make the work of mediation visible or invisible? Second, I experiment with a nonmodern performative style of poetic criticism. I consider side by side an exemplary work of modern self-referential negativity—Mallarmé's poem "A Throw of Dice Will Never Abolish Chance"—and a nonmodern performance art piece: Latour's collaborative theatrical production *Gaia Global Circus* together with the keynote speech Latour delivered at the symposium entitled "Seeing/Sounding/Sensing."[29] I suggest that Latour's *Gaia Global Circus* can be read as performing Mallarmé's "A Throw of Dice" in the sense of *poiesis*. Coincidentally, both Stengers's and Latour's talks took place in September 2014, one year before the 2015 United Nations Framework Convention on Climate Change in Paris. Their reflections situate themselves explicitly in relation to climate change. I have chosen these works (rather than their published versions in book format) to underscore the situatedness and performativity of their thinking that is shared with an audience through embodied presence and voice in a specific location and time.[30]

IV

I focus on the act of naming for three reasons. First, it constitutes the quintessence of language conceived as representation. The poet (or man) is the one who names the (usually) nonhuman world (or a nonmale entity) in Western religion (e.g., Genesis), poetry (e.g., Dante), and philosophy (e.g., Heidegger) alike.[31] Thus conceived, naming is tethered to the idea of truth understood as correspondence and is an act of abstract cognition from a distance. Second, it indicates what relation obtains between the humans who name and the nonhuman material world that is named. Third, in its specifically modern incarnation, naming emphasizes the materiality of language which is coterminous with self-referentiality and maintains an ambiguous relation with the materiality of the nonhuman world: it is part of, but also stands apart from, the referential material world.

How do these three characteristics of representational naming play themselves out in Blanchot? Blanchot inherits faithfully from the Western tradition of the "poet as namer": he places naming at the heart of poetry but in order to carve out a distinctly modern kind of naming in the manner of the Modern Constitution Latour lays out in *We Have Never Been Modern*;[32] that is, playing on the conjoined, yet separated, pairings of transcendence and immanence that leave out the middle ground where "everything happens by way of mediation, translation and networks."[33] I'd like to look more closely at how Blanchot enacts the Modern Constitution and renders the middle invisible. First, he introduces a radical difference between "civilized" naming and "primitive" naming:

> We cannot do anything with an object that has no name. The primitive man knows that the possession of words gives him mastery over things, but for him the relationship between words and the world is so close that the manipulations of language is as difficult and as fraught with peril as contact with living beings: the name has not emerged from the thing, it is the inside of the thing which has been dangerously brought out into the open and yet it is still the hidden depths of the thing; the thing has therefore not yet been named. The more closely man becomes attached to a civilization, the more he can manipulate words with innocence and composure ["*sang-froid*"]. Is it that words have lost all relation to what they designate? But this absence of relation is not a defect, and if it is a defect, this defect is the only thing that gives language its full value, so that of all languages the most perfect is the language of mathematics, which is spoken ["*qui se parle*"] in a rigorous way and to which no entity corresponds.[34]

The premodern man lives in a state of immanence where language and world are inextricably bound ("the relationship between words and the world is so close"; "the name has not emerged from the thing"); he attends to hybrids of nature-culture with overwhelming receptivity ("fraught with peril" suggests affect, awe). By contrast, the modern man lives in transcendence where nature, language, and subject are separate ("words have lost all relation to what they designate"; "this absence of relation"): words are detached objects he handles with disaffection ("composure" ["*sang-froid*"]). Blanchot radicalizes the difference between premodern naming and modern naming by making them into two opposing endpoints. The language of the premoderns becomes a non-language (it does not name: "the thing has therefore not yet been named"), while the language of the moderns tends toward the ideal language of mathematics which achieves perfect negativity through infinite subtraction ("to which no entity corresponds") and perfect self-referentiality ("*qui se parle*" ["which is spoken"])[35]. Blanchot makes the premodern hybrids and the relation of mediation invisible by relegating them to the unconceptualized and unconceptualizable limit of non-language.

Second, he puts poetic language under the sign of Adam's naming in a way that crosses out God. Following Kojève's interpretation of language as conceptual, abstract negation in Hegel, Blanchot provocatively likens poetry's naming of the world to a murder. He projects poetic language back to the moment in Genesis when Adam names the animals and contends that, in naming the animals, Adam kills them. And for Blanchot, poetic language "recalls the first name which would be the murder Hegel speaks of":[36]

> Hegel [...] writes: "Adam's first act, which made him master of the animals, was to give them names, that is, he annihilated them in their existence (as existing creatures)."* Hegel means that from that moment on, the cat ceased to be a uniquely real cat and becomes an idea as well. The meaning of speech, then, requires that before any word is spoken, there must be a sort of immense hecatomb, a preliminary flood plunging all of creation into a total sea. God had created living things, but man had to annihilate them.[37]

Thus, Blanchot claims the radically distinct nature of modern poetic naming by severing it from the premodern version on the one hand, and by placing it between two ideal limits on the other: Adam's language and mathematical language. And in both, the nonhuman material world becomes abstracted to two limit states: pure Nature—freshly created by God in the absence of man—in the case of Adam's (murderous) language, and pure matter or extension—the de-animated Cartesian *res extensa* dominated by man—in the case of mathematical language. Modern poetic language names only these two extreme, purified versions of the world and keeps them out of reach.

Third, Blanchot transfers materiality, reality, and presence from the referential world to language. He speaks of "the materiality of language" where "everything physical takes precedence: rhythm, weight, mass, shape."[38] Language becomes an opaque, impenetrable object that bars access to the referential world: the "real presence and material affirmation of language give it the ability to suspend and dismiss the world."[39] But Blanchot is quick to point out the paradox: as language "tak[es] on a tangible quality" it "becomes a thing" itself;[40] "it is a written thing, a bit of bark, a sliver of rock, a fragment of clay in which the reality of the earth continues to exist."[41] Rather than to turn us away from things, the self-referential material words paradoxically connect us to the referential material world. The materiality of language is thus the site of both discontinuity and continuity between self-referential words and the referential world. Blanchot speaks of this ambiguity in terms of the "two slopes" of literature that are impossible to segregate: when we read literature, we might think we are on the side of the referential world, but before we know it we slip to the side of self-referentiality. And the converse holds as well: we might think we are on the side of self-referentiality but soon enough we glide to the side of the referential world.[42] "Literature is divided between these two slopes. The problem is that even though they are apparently incompatible, they do not lead toward distinctly different works or goals, and that an art which purports to follow one slope is already on the other."[43] Words, Blanchot writes, are "monsters of two faces, one being reality, physical presence, and the other meaning, ideal absence."[44] Purification and mediation become inevitably entangled, yet remain mutually exclusive of each other.

Blanchot's account of poetic language is modern in the Latourian sense in that he qualifies the conjunction between purification and mediation (or continuity and discontinuity) ultimately as a "contradiction," an "imposture."[45] Purification, or the ability to distinguish, is the norm with respect to which mediation, or the inability to distinguishes, is deemed to be even a "treachery."[46] Blanchot identifies a "powerful trickery, a mysterious bad faith that allows [literature] to play everything both ways,"[47] attesting to what Latour rightly sees as the "prodigious efficacy" of the moderns.[48] In more general terms, Blanchot's model of poetic language is modern because it keeps the endpoints separate. There is oscillation between them but the middle ground between the two endpoints remains invisible, unconceptualized, and impossible: it is a "contradiction." It is modern also in that it maintains the Great Divide and remains asymmetrical. It may grant material presence to words and have them become things; it may have words escape the grasp of the rational subject and weaken human agency, but it does not, for all that, share agency with the nonhuman material world in a symmetrical way. The strictly human, linguistic model of language does not enable us to address the "nonlinguistic and often nonhuman world."[49]

V

Gaia, however, is the middle ground: she is a hybrid that mediates in the middle. If modern poetry names only the two purified extreme versions of the world, then Gaia is what modern poetry cannot name. The intrusion of Gaia reveals the limit of the modern paradigm of poetic language. Gaia demands to be named, but not through naming conceived as negation or unconcern. How can we reconceptualize naming so as to be able to name Gaia responsively? This is an urgent question the new interpretive context of global warming brings to the fore and from which there is no escape. Indeed, Latour writes that climate change literally shifts the ground we stand on ("each of us is feeling the ground slip away beneath our feet"[50]) and that even *"the very notion of soil is changing."*[51]

> *Under* the ground of private property, of land grabs, of the exploitation of territories, *another ground*, another earth, another soil has begun to stir, to quake, to be moved. A sort of earthquake, if you like, that led the pioneers to say: "Watch out, nothing will be as it was before; you are going to have to pay dearly for the return of the Earth, the outburst of powers that had been tame until now."[52]

Bursting out on us, Gaia, in Latour and Stengers, is neither ideal nature nor inert matter. No longer passive in the face of our disregard, she is a mighty actor that resists and threatens humans. It is impossible not to address Gaia and impossible thus not to address poetry's incapacity to name Gaia. How can poetry name Gaia? How can it reclaim naming? Can we envisage a naming that mediates rather than purifies? I'd like to advance that reclaiming naming as mediation (as opposed to purification) entails shifting from the modern, representationalist model of naming to a nonmodern, performative model of naming.

Stengers can help us do so. In her talk "Gaia, the Urgency to Think (and Feel)," Stengers proposes a perfect example of a nonmodern performative model of naming. Echoing closely Latour's proposal to move away from the mode of negative critique,[53] Stengers describes naming as "add[ing] reality to" rather than "subtract[ing] reality from" what we name.[54] "Mattering" is how Stengers defines the reality we add when naming.[55] Naming obtains when what we name comes to matter; to name is "to protect and care" for what we name[56] and simultaneously to "become aware, not reflexively or theoretically but affectively."[57] Moreover, naming, for Stengers, is a "pragmatic business" that "giv[es] to what is named the power to induce thinking and feeling in a particular way."[58] In contradistinction to modern naming, here, both the namer and the named have agency, and this redistribution of agency in mutual responsiveness makes naming a matter not of cognition or reflexivity, and certainly not of self-reflexivity or self-referentiality, but of receptivity and sensitivity that engage us in a "metamorphic (rather than a representational) relation" to the world—or a performative relation, we might say.[59]

Stengers's additive, "metamorphic," and performative naming thus constitutes a direct rebuke to Blanchot's subtractive and representational model. As the reference to Hegel and Kojève shows, modern naming is an act of conceptual abstraction and subtractive purification: "murder" indexes the passage to the realm of transcendent ideals and the casting away of the concrete, the real, the material, the bodily, and the empirical. Stengers, however, orients naming and language toward mediation. "Mattering," as opposed to "murdering," specifies the dynamic entanglement of language, materiality, body, and affect. Stengers brings language out of transcendent isolation and situates it in the middle ground of quasi-objects and quasi-subjects that are "simultaneously real, discursive, and social."[60]

The fundamental difference between Stengers's additive, affective naming and Blanchot's subtractive, negative one is that the former is a pragmatic, reciprocal, and thus a performative engagement, whereas the latter is an ideal, transcendent, one-way act of cognition from a distance.[61] Stengers's immanent pragmatism, aligned with Barad's "posthumanist performativity," leads to what Haraway calls "situated knowledges."[62] Naming, for Stengers, performs situated thinking in response to the pressing question "How can a culture as educated as ours be so oblivious, so reckless, in its relations to the animate earth?"[63] Stengers's responsive naming, then, situates itself with respect to the history of human destruction of the earth of which climate change is the latest/last incarnation. In a move of extraordinary intellectual rigor, she writes: "As a European modern philosopher, I try to think as situated by the world destroying process which started on the European grounds, with enclosures, the destruction of the commons."[64] Gaia solicits a "commitment" on our part to "resist all great philosophical tales which, often without a second thought, ratify [...] destruction in the name of reason or progress—the commitment to think and feel what we call reason and progress together with devastation and expropriation."[65] Stengers situates herself on the European soil and does so with an awareness that "[her] own practice and tradition situate [her] on one side of the divide" (the side of the colonizers) and that "many other peoples and societies have undergone such a world destroying intrusion."[66] Naming, then, consists of learning to think and feel with people who are not white, European, or male, and, moreover, to have their experiences matter to us and to "give them the power to situate us."[67] For Stengers, Gaia is "a provocative name for the challenge specifically addressed to us" to resist the tale of Western human exceptionality.[68] Thus, naming Gaia entails first and foremost letting go of the subject/object divide that conceives naming as abstract cognition from a distance; it means redistributing agency more symmetrically between humans and the nonhuman world and attending to the common middle ground, the "contact zone," as Haraway calls it, where humans and the nonhuman world co-create one another.[69]

VI

Where does reorienting poetic naming from modern negativity to nonmodern performativity lead us? What new possibility might this open for approaching Mallarmé, in particular in the new interpretive context of global warming? I would like to attempt a *rapprochement* between Latour, the thinker of the nonmodern, and Mallarmé, the quintessential poet of the modern, who is celebrated for his poetics of self-referential negativity. I'd like to consider Mallarmé's "A Throw of Dice Will Never Abolish Chance" (which is one of the consecrated exemplars of modern negativity) in tandem with *Gaia Global Circus* (which is a collaborative theatrical production Latour designed with a team of artists and scientists to address the issue of global warming) to explore what possibilities might emerge from the contact zone.[70]

Mallarmé is the central figure on which modern theorists base their concept of poetic self-referential negativity. Derrida writes that words in Mallarmé are "cut off [...] from all meaning [...] and all referent" and "finally refer only to their own game, and never really move toward anything else,"[71] specifying that in the Mallarméan "act of naming, the direct relationship to the thing, is [...] suspended."[72] Blanchot's example for naming as murder—"For me to be able to say, 'This woman', I must somehow take her flesh and blood reality away from her, cause her to be absent, annihilate her"[73]—refers specifically to Mallarmé's famous pronouncement "I say: a flower! [...] absent from all bouquets."[74] Among all of Mallarmé's works, "A Throw of Dice" is most emblematic of modern poetry.[75] It contains ruptured sentences, dispersed words, irregular fonts, and, most importantly, an unusual presence of the blank space—or *le blanc*—which "strikes first" as Mallarmé underscores in his preface.[76] The blank space is ordinarily the inert, discarded background we leave out when we read. In "A Throw of Dice," however, it intrudes and disrupts our reading and, in doing so, makes itself visible and becomes part of the reading. Mallarméan scholarship has read the blank space mostly as the space of negativity and absence whereby language disengages from the world. Derrida reads *les blancs* as the free play of signifiers, the "textuality of the text," and *différance*.[77] "A Throw of Dice" and its blank space stand for the autonomous discourse, purified of nature and society.

As for Latour's collaborative theatrical production *Gaia Global Circus*, I came across it through the keynote speech he gave at the MIT symposium "Seeing/Sounding/Sensing." Latour included parts of the video-taped performance of the play to give an example of artwork addressing the question "How do we make ourselves sensitive to Gaia?"[78] It is a question arising from the puzzling disconnect Latour finds between "the importance of what is at stake and the narrow repertory of emotions and senses with which we try to grasp these questions."[79] Moving away from the style of political manifesto or moralizing didacticism which fails to reach climate skeptics, Latour and his team of artists and scientists aim to address climate change by way of the shared aesthetic experience a play affords. They transpose their question across different interpretive contexts through a double translation: the initial question "how do we make ourselves sensitive to Gaia?" becomes first "why is it so difficult to make yourself sensitive to this new situation?"; then "how do we cope with a new time [and] space in a completely different medium?"[80] In other words, the question of our relation to Gaia becomes a question of our relation to earth as a ground that is shifting which, in the context of theatrical production, becomes an issue of background and décor. Accordingly, the team produces a play where the décor changes and moves around: they devise a canopy with a large white sail and suspend it on top of the stage with helium balloons and attach it also to the actors by threads. This setup enables the white canopy—the inert décor that ought to stay in the background—to move in an unpredictable fashion in response to the movements of the actors and the helium balloons which are affected by the temperature and the air pressure of the room which, in turn, depend on the degree of animation of the audience, and so on. During the play, the canopy rises up or comes down, moves to the back or the front of the stage, disturbing actors and audience alike, so much so that it soon becomes the main protagonist of the play. Different video images of the earth are projected onto the moving canopy which serves as the screen, the décor, the sky, the cloud, the climate, and the nonhuman actor to which human actors and audience are forced to pay attention. Sensitive to its environment while rendering everyone *sensitive* toward it, the canopy is an aesthetic rendering of Gaia.

Gaia Global Circus exemplifies two things. First, it enacts Stengers's conceptualization of a pragmatic, immanent naming where nonhuman and human actors become mutually attentive and responsive to one another. It constitutes a nonmodern performative as elaborated by Latour, Barad, and Haraway. And as to the second: I must admit that the minute I saw the white canopy, I thought of Mallarmé's blank space in his poem "A Throw of Dice": it was as if Latour's white mobile sheet were translating and performing Mallarmé's *blanc*. This moving *blanc* brought all the white surfaces in Mallarmé's work and life to the foreground for me: the white sail of his boat on which he loved to sail; the eggshells, fans, and envelops on which he wrote haiku like "poems" he sent as gifts to family and friends; the satiny fabric with which he enveloped women in the fashion journal he wrote singlehandedly under pseudonyms such as Miss Satin (which echoes the initials *S*téphane *M*allarmé); and so on. Canopy-screen-paper-page-sail-satin-egg shells-fan-envelop—in my mind, all of Mallarmé's *blancs* began to entangle with one another, defying the scholarly divide between pure poetic writings and mere circumstantial writings. Indeed, what is Mallarmé's *blanc* if not the poetic articulation of the question of the shifting ground Latour's *Gaia Global Circus* addresses? The blank space invading the textual space, the white page striking us more than the words, form disrupting content, all enact the movement of the shifting ground—background irrupting into the foreground—that reactivates all relations to inflect them in unexpected and newly significant ways. Might the shifting ground constitute a common ground between Latour and Mallarmé? Might it be the middle ground that enables us to connect the nonmodern and the modern, mimesis and *poiesis*, words and the world?

Valéry, the first one to have seen the page proofs of "A Throw of Dice," wrote that Mallarmé has elevated "*a page to the power of the starry night sky!*"[81] At the end of this chapter—when the purifying modern scholar in me (still reticent of the immanent mingling of transcendent *blancs*) is finally making room for the nonmodern in me—I would like to propose bringing "A Throw of Dice" Valery enshrined in celestial transcendence "down to earth." And I imagine Latour projecting the pages of "A Throw of Dice" onto the canopy of *Gaia Global Circus* where the modern and the nonmodern would come together, even if momentarily. On that common ground, language and poetry would no longer represent or purify the world; instead, they would perform and mediate the world. And on that immanent ground, poetry might no longer stand for the disengaged unconcern for the world; instead, it may lead to what really matters to us: to the nonhuman material world that is near and real and with which we are already deeply entangled. A nonmodern performative approach to modern poetry, then, highlights the participatory nature of our reading practice.[82] It invites us to learn to respond to the possibility of being entangled in the messy middle ground of discourse-nature-society a poem makes available to us; to actualize the relational vitality of mediation; and to practice a democratic language of the parliament of things.

Notes

1 William Paulson, "For a Cosmopolitical Philology: Lessons from Science Studies," *SubStance* 30, no. 3 (2001): 101. See also his book, *Literary Culture in a World Transformed: A Future for the Humanities* (Ithaca: Cornell University Press, 2001).
2 Paulson, "For a Cosmopolitical Philology," 103.
3 Christian Prigent, *L'Incontenable: Essais* (Paris: POL, 2004), 13. My translation. Thus in poetic criticism, to read a poem is to read it as an autonomous linguistic structure that has nothing to do with, and even negates, the world it refers to, the one who wrote it, and even the one who reads it.
4 Jean-Marie Schaeffer makes a case against aesthetic as well as human transcendence from a philosophical point of view in *Adieu à l'esthétique* (Sesto San Giovanni: Mimésis, 2016), *L'Expérience esthétique* (Paris: Gallimard, 2015), and *La Fin de l'exception humaine* (Paris: Gallimard, 2007).
5 "Life among Conceptual Characters: A Letter to Conclude the Special Issue of *New Literary History* on 'Recomposing the Humanities with Bruno Latour,'" *New Literary History* 47, no. 2–3 (2016): 475–6.
6 See *The Nonhuman Turn*, ed. Richard Grusin (Minneapolis: University of Minnesota Press, 2015). For a discussion of the relation between the posthuman, nonhuman, and the nonmodern, see Bruce Clarke, "The Nonhuman," in *The Cambridge Companion to Literature and the Posthuman*, ed. Bruce Clarke and Manuela Rossini (London: Cambridge University Press, 2016), 141–52. On the subject of Latour and the humanities, see the special issue "Recomposing the Humanities—with Bruno Latour" of *New Literary History*.
7 Roman Jakobson, "Closing Statement: Linguistics and Poetics," in *Style in Language*, ed. Thomas A. Sebeok (Cambridge: MIT Press, 1960), 353.

8   Gaia is a term Stengers and Latour borrow from Lovelock and Margulis to designate the world that returns. Clarke examines the process of this borrowing in "Rethinking Gaia: Stengers, Latour, Margulis," *Theory, Culture & Society* 34, no. 4 (2017): 3–26.
9   Isabelle Stengers, "Gaia: The Urgency to Think (and Feel)," 5. It is a paper she presented at the International Colloquium "The Thousand Names of Gaia: From the Anthropocene to the Age of the Earth." Rio de Janeiro, September 15–19, 2014. https://osmilnomesdegaia.files.wordpress.com/2014/11/isabelle-stengers.pdf, downloaded from https://osmilnomesdegaia.eco.br (accessed January 15, 2019).
10 To be more precise, Gaia denotes not so much the nonhuman material world in itself but the inextricable imbrication of humans and the nonhuman material world: it is the middle ground where mediation takes place.
11 Paulson, "Cosmopolitical Philology," 117. Isabelle Stengers develops her notion of "cosmopolitics," in *Cosmopolitics*, trans. Robert Bononno, 2 vols. (Minneapolis: University of Minnesota Press, 2010–11).
12 Michel Collot, *La Poésie moderne et la structure d'horizon* (Paris: PUF, 1989).
13 Jahan Ramazani, *A Transnational Poetics* (Chicago: University of Chicago Press, 2009), especially chapter 2; *Poetry and Its Others: News, Prayer, Song, and the Dialogue of Genres* (Chicago: University of Chicago Press, 2014), 7–8.
14 Joseph Acquisto, *Poetry's Knowing Ignorance* (New York: Bloomsbury, 2019).
15 Bruno Latour. *We Have Never Been Modern*, trans. Catherine Porter. (Cambridge: Harvard University Press, 1993), 64.
16 Prigent, *L'Incontenable*, 11. My translation.
17 Ibid., 17.
18 Ibid., 23.
19 Paulson, "Cosmopolitical Philology," 117. See also Goeffrey Galt Harpham, *Language Alone: The Critical Fetish of Modernity* (New York: Routledge, 2002).
20 The expression is Karen Barad's: see "Posthumanist Performativity: Toward an Understanding of How Matter Comes to Matter." *Signs: Journal of Women in Culture and Society* 28, no. 3 (2003): 801–31; *Meeting the Universe Halfway: Quantum Physics and the Entanglement of Matter and Meaning* (Durham: Duke University Press, 2007), 135. This is not to say that (poetic) theory has overlooked the performative view of language, but it is treated, again, within the confines of the Great Divide. For Derrida's take on speech act theory, see Jacques Derrida, *Limited Inc*, ed. Gerald Graff, trans. Jeffrey Mehlman and Samuel Weber (Evanston: Northwestern University Press, 1988).
21 Barad, "Posthumanist Performativity," 802. For a comparison between performative and the representational models of language from a sociological perspective, see Ester Baringa, "A Performative View of Language—Methodological

Considerations and Consequences for the Study of Culture," *Forum: Qualitative Social Research* 10, no. 1 (2009). Art. 24. http://nbn-resolving.de/urn:nbn:de:0114-fqs0901244. (accessed January 15, 2019).

22 Donna Haraway, "Situated Knowledges: The Science Question in Feminism and the Privilege of Partial Perspective," *Feminist Studies* 14, no. 3 (1999): 585.
23 Jane Bennett also approaches materiality in nonmodern terms in *Vibrant Matter: A Political Ecology of Things* (Durham: Duke University Press, 2010).
24 Barad, *Meeting the Universe*, 135.
25 Barad, "Posthumanist Performativity," 815. Original emphasis.
26 Bruno Latour, "How to Talk About the Body? The Normative Dimension of Science Studies," *Body & Society* 10, no. 2–3 (2004): 210.
27 Maurice Blanchot, "Literature and the Right to Death," trans. Lydia Davis, in *The Work of Fire*, trans. Charlotte Mandell (Stanford: Stanford University Press, 1995), 300–44. I mean the general referential/representational framework that includes all the variants of a-/anti-/self-referentiality.
28 See Stengers, "Gaia: The Urgency to Think (and Feel)."
29 Bruno Latour, Keynote address, SEEING/SOUNDING/SENSING: A symposium hosted by the MIT Center for Art, Science & Technology (CAST)—September 26–27, 2014. See video of keynote address: https://arts.mit.edu/cast/symposia/seeing-sounding-sensing/#keynote-bruno-latour (accessed January 15, 2019). Transcript of keynote address: http://rtlln1kraz3heqyqi5ac19ce-wpengine.netdna-ssl.com/wp-content/uploads/2014/12/Symposium2014_Video-3.pdf (accessed January 15, 2019).
30 The expanded book versions are: Isabelle Stengers, *In Catastrophic Times: Resisting the Coming Barbarism*, trans. Andrew Goffey (Lüneburg, Germany: Open Humanities Press, 2015); Bruno Latour, *Facing Gaia: Eight Lectures on the New Climatic Regime*, trans. Catherine Porter (Cambridge: Polity Press, 2017).
31 Walter Benjamin writes that man is the name giver—who inherits the power to name from God—and that poetry is "partly, if not solely, founded on the name language of man" in "On Language as Such and on the Language of Man," in *Reflections: Essays, Aphorisms, Autobiographical Writings*, ed. Peter Demetz, trans. Edmund Jephcott (New York: Schocken, 1978), 330.
32 Latour, *We Have Never Been Modern*, 13–48.
33 Ibid., 37.
34 Blanchot, "Literature and the Right to Death," 322. Barthes drives home the radical rupture between classical poetry versus modern poetry in "Is There Any Poetic Writing?" in *Writing Degree Zero*, trans. Annette Laver and Colin Smith (New York: Hill and Wang, 1968), 41–52.

35 The French "*qui se parle*" has a reflexive dimension that is lost in the English translation "which is spoken."
36 Blanchot, 326.
37 Ibid., 322–3. The asterisk refers to the note in which Blanchot acknowledges his debt to Kojève and Hegel. The note reads: "A. Kojève, in his *Introduction to the Reading of Hegel*, interpreting a passage from the *Phenomenology*, demonstrates in a remarkable way how for Hegel comprehension was equivalent to murder."
38 Ibid., 327.
39 Maurice Blanchot, "The Myth of Mallarmé," in *The Work of Fire*, trans. Charlotte Mandell (Stanford: Stanford University Press, 1995), 37.
40 Ibid.
41 Blanchot, "Literature and the Right to Death," 327–8.
42 Ibid., 332.
43 Ibid.
44 Ibid., 341.
45 Blanchot, "The Myth of Mallarmé," 32, 41.
46 Blanchot, "Literature and the Right to Death," 333.
47 Ibid., 338.
48 Latour, *We Have Never Been Modern*, 35. We see here the resemblance between Blanchot's account of literary language and the one Jean Paulhan elaborates in *The Flowers of Tarbes, or, Terror in Literature*, trans. Michael Syrotinski (Champaign: University of Illinois Press, 2006). "Literature and the Right to Death" is partially a response to Paulhan's work. See Paulson's wonderful reading of Paulhan's book which is "as close to a nonmodern manifesto as literary criticism has even come" ("Cosmopolitical Philology," 104).
49 Paulson, "Cosmopolitical Philology," 117. For a comprehensive treatment of the materiality of language from a larger perspective, see David Bleich, *The Materiality of Language: Gender, Politics, and the University* (Bloomington: Indiana University Press, 2013).
50 Bruno Latour, *Down to Earth: Politics in the New Climatic Regime*, trans. Catherine Porter (Cambridge: Polity, 2018), 5.
51 Ibid., 4. Original emphasis.
52 Ibid., 17. Original emphasis.
53 Bruno Latour, "Why Has Critique Run Out of Steam? From Matters of Fact to Matters of Concern," *Critical Inquiry* 30, no. 2 (2004): 225–48.
54 Stengers, "Gaia: The Urgency to Think (and Feel)," 3–4.
55 Ibid.
56 Ibid., 3.
57 Ibid., 7.

58 Ibid., 1.
59 Isabelle Stengers, "Reclaiming Animism," *e-flux journal* 36 (2012): 4, downloaded from https://www.dropbox.com/s/ppphccmhlyqyz8v/Stengers_Reclaiming%20 Animism.pdf?dl=0 (accessed January 15, 2019).
60 Latour, *We Have Never Been Modern*, 64.
61 Latour also makes use of the distinction additive/subtractive when proposing the model of articulation as opposed to statement in "How to Talk About the Body," *Body & Society* 10, no. 2–3 (2004): 206–14.
62 See Haraway, "Situated Knowledges."
63 Stengers, "Reclaiming Animism," 6.
64 Stengers, "Gaia: The Urgency to Think (and Feel)," 6
65 Ibid.
66 Ibid., 5.
67 Ibid., 6.
68 Ibid., 5.
69 Donna J. Haraway, *When Species Meet* (Minneapolis: University of Minnesota Press, 2008), 35.
70 Stéphane Mallarmé, "A Throw of Dice Will Never Abolish Chance," in *Œuvres complètes*, ed. Bertrand Marchal, vol. 1 (Paris: Gallimard [Pléiade], 1998), 363–87; Bruno Latour, "Dossier Gaia. Compagnie AccenT et Soif Compagnie présentent *Gaïa Global Circus* un projet de Bruno Latour," downloaded from http://www.bruno-latour.fr/sites/default/files/downloads/DOSSIER%20GAIA%20oct%20 2012_3.pdf (accessed January 15, 2019). See also "Gaia Global Circus Teaser," https:// www.youtube.com/watch?v=uMlfgMU6qG0 (accessed January 15, 2019); and the performance of *Gaia Global Circus: Une Tragi-Comédie Climatique* at https:// www.youtube.com/watch?v=8mkNg2nDWmY and http://www.bruno-latour.fr/sites/default/files/downloads/DOSSIER%20GAIA%20oct%202012_3.pdf (accessed January 15, 2019). Materials for the stage can be found in "Gaïa Tragi-comédie climatique et globale …: Matériel pour une écriture de plateau dans le cadre du projet Gaïa Global Circus" at http://www.bruno-latour.fr/sites/default/files/downloads/GAIA-VERSION%2005-11-ssimage_1.pdf (accessed January 15, 2019).
71 Jacques Derrida, "Mallarmé," in *Acts of Literature*, ed. Derek Attridge (New York: Routledge, 1992), 121
72 Ibid., 122. The title of Vincent Kaufmann's book illustrates the direct connection between Mallarmé and modern theory: *La Faute à Mallarmé: L'aventure de la théorie littéraire* (Paris: Seuil, 2011).
73 Blanchot, "Literature and the Right to Death," 322.
74 Stéphane Mallarmé, "Crise de vers," in *Œuvres complètes*, ed. Bertrand Marchal, vol. 2 (Paris: Gallimard [Pléiade], 2003), 213. My translation.

75 The title of R. Howard Bloch's recent book reads: *One Toss of the Dice: The Incredible Story of How a Poem Made Us Modern* (New York: Liveright, 2017).
76 Stéphane Mallarmé, "Observation concerning the poem 'A Throw of Dice Will Never Abolish Chance,'" in *Œuvres completes I*, 391. My translation.
77 Jacques Derrida, "La Double séance," in *La Dissémination* (Paris: Seuil, 1972), 300. My translation.
78 *Gaia Global Circus* has been performed in different venues in both France and the United States.
79 Latour, "Dossier Gaia. Compagnie AccenT et Soif Compagnie présentent *Gaïa Global Circus* un projet de Bruno Latour," 4. My translation.
80 Latour, Keynote address, SEEING/SOUNDING/SENSING.
81 Paul Valéry, "*Le coup de dés*. Lettre au Directeur des *Marges*," in *Œuvres*, ed. Jean Hytier. vol. 1 (Paris: Gallimard [Pléiade], 1957), 626. Original Emphasis. My translation.
82 Several scholars have underscored the participatory nature of reading: Paulson, *Literary Culture in a World Transformed: A Future for the Humanities*; Rita Felski, *Uses of Literature* (Oxford: Blackwell, 2008), "Latour and Literary Studies," *PMLA* 130, no. 3 (2015): 737–42, *The Limits of Critique* (Chicago: University of Chicago Press, 2015); Marielle Macé, *Façons de lire, manières d'être* (Paris: Gallimard, 2011); Heather Love, "Close but Not Deep: Literary Ethics and the Descriptive Turn," *New Literary History* 41, no. 2 (2010): 371–91; Yves Citton, *Lire, interpréter, actualiser: Pourquoi les études littéraires?* (Paris: Amsterdam, 2017).

Bibliography

Acquisto, Joseph. *Poetry's Knowing Ignorance*. New York: Bloomsbury, 2019.

Barad, Karen. *Meeting the Universe Halfway: Quantum Physics and the Entanglement of Matter and Meaning*. Durham: Duke University Press, 2007.

Barad, Karen. "Posthumanist Performativity: Toward an Understanding of How Matter Comes to Matter." *Signs: Journal of Women in Culture and Society* 28, no. 3 (2003): 801–31.

Barinaga, Ester. "A Performative View of Language—Methodological Considerations and Consequences for the Study of Culture." *Forum: Qualitative Social Research* 10, no. 1 (2009). Art. 24. http://nbn-resolving.de/urn:nbn:de:0114-fqs0901244. (accessed January 15, 2019).

Barthes, Roland. "Is There Any Poetic Writing?" In *Writing Degree Zero*. Translated by Annette Laver and Colin Smith. 41–52. New York: Hill and Wang, 1968.

Benjamin, Walter. "On Language as Such and on the Language of Man." In *Reflections: Essays, Aphorisms, Autobiographical Writings*. Edited by Peter Demetz. Translated by Edmund Jephcott. 314–32. New York: Schocken, 1978.

Bennett, Jane. *Vibrant Matter: A Political Ecology of Things*. Durham: Duke University Press, 2010.

Blanchot, Maurice. "Literature and the Right to Death." Translated by Lydia Davis. In *The Work of Fire*. Translated by Charlotte Mandell. 300–44. Stanford: Stanford University Press, 1995.

Blanchot, Maurice. "The Myth of Mallarmé." In *The Work of Fire*. Translated by Charlotte Mandell. 27–42. Stanford: Stanford University Press, 1995.

Bleich, David. *The Materiality of Language: Gender, Politics, and the University*. Bloomington: Indiana University Press, 2013.

Bloch, R. Howard. *One Toss of the Dice: The Incredible Story of How a Poem Made Us Modern*. New York: Liveright, 2017.

Citton, Yves. *Lire, interpréter, actualiser: Pourquoi les études littéraires?* Paris: Amsterdam, 2017.

Clarke, Bruce. "The Nonhuman." In *The Cambridge Companion to Literature and the Posthuman*. Edited by Bruce Clarke and Manuela Rossini. 141–52. London: Cambridge University Press, 2016.

Clarke, Bruce. "Rethinking Gaia: Stengers, Latour, Margulis." *Theory, Culture & Society* 34, no. 4 (2017): 3–26.

Collot, Michel. *La Poésie moderne et la structure d'horizon*. Paris: PUF, 1989.

Derrida, Jacques. "La Double séance." In *La Dissémination*. 214–347. Paris: Seuil, 1972.

Derrida, Jacques. *Limited Inc*. Edited by Gerald Graff. Translated by Jeffrey Mehlman and Samuel Weber. Evanston: Northwestern University Press, 1988.

Derrida, Jacques. "Mallarmé." In *Acts of Literature*. Edited by Derek Attridge. 110–26. New York: Routledge, 1992.

Felski, Rita. "Latour and Literary Studies." *PMLA* 130, no. 3 (2015): 737–42.

Felski, Rita. *The Limits of Critique*. Chicago: University of Chicago Press, 2015.

Felski, Rita. *Uses of Literature*. Oxford: Blackwell, 2008.

Felski, Rita. (ed.). "Recomposing the Humanities—with Bruno Latour." *New Literary History* 47, no. 2–3 (2016).

Grusin, Richard (ed.). *The Nonhuman Turn*. Minneapolis: University of Minnesota Press, 2015.

Haraway, Donna J. "Situated Knowledges: The Science Question in Feminism and the Privilege of Partial Perspective." *Feminist Studies* 14, no. 3 (1988): 575–99.

Haraway, Donna J. *When Species Meet*. Minneapolis: University of Minnesota Press, 2008.

Harpham, Goeffrey Galt. *Language Alone: The Critical Fetish of Modernity*. New York: Routledge, 2002.

Jakobson, Roman. "Closing Statement: Linguistics and Poetics." In *Style in Language*. Edited by Thomas A. Sebeok. 351–77. Cambridge: MIT Press, 1960.

Kaufmann, Vincent. *La Faute à Mallarmé: L' aventure de la théorie littéraire*. Paris: Seuil, 2011.

Latour, Bruno. "Dossier Gaia. Compagnie AccenT et Soif Compagnie présentent *Gaïa Global Circus* un projet de Bruno Latour." http://www.bruno-latour.fr/sites/default/files/downloads/DOSSIER%20GAIA%20oct%202012_3.pdf (accessed January 15, 2019).

Latour, Bruno. *Down to Earth: Politics in the New Climatic Regime*. Translated by Catherine Porter. Cambridge: Polity, 2018.

Latour, Bruno. *Facing Gaia: Eight Lectures on the New Climatic Regime*. Translated by Catherine Porter. Cambridge: Polity Press, 2017.

Latour, Bruno. "Gaia Global Circus Teaser." https://www.youtube.com/watch?v=uMlfgMU6qG0. (accessed January 15, 2019).

Latour, Bruno. *Gaia Global Circus: Une Tragi-Comédie Climatique*. https://www.youtube.com/watch?v=8mkNg2nDWmY and http://www.bruno-latour.fr/sites/default/files/downloads/DOSSIER%20GAIA%20oct%202012_3.pdf (accessed January 15, 2019).

Latour, Bruno. "Gaïa Tragi-comédie climatique et globale …: Matériel pour une écriture de plateau dans le cadre du projet Gaïa Global Circus." http://www.bruno-latour.fr/sites/default/files/downloads/GAIA-VERSION%2005-11-ssimage_1.pdf (accessed January 15, 2019).

Latour, Bruno. "How to Talk About the Body? The Normative Dimension of Science Studies." *Body & Society* 10, no. 2–3 (2004): 205–29.

Latour, Bruno. Keynote address. SEEING/SOUNDING/SENSING: A symposium hosted by the MIT Center for Art, Science & Technology (CAST)—September 26-27, 2014. https://arts.mit.edu/cast/symposia/seeing-sounding-sensing/#keynote-bruno-latour and http://rtlln1kraz3heqyqi5ac19ce-wpengine.netdna-ssl.com/wp-content/uploads/2014/12/Symposium2014_Video-3.pdf (accessed January 15, 2019).

Latour, Bruno. "Life among Conceptual Characters: A Letter to Conclude the Special Issue of *New Literary History* on 'Recomposing the Humanities—with Bruno Latour.'" *New Literary History* 47, no. 2–3 (2016): 475–6.

Latour, Bruno. *We Have Never Been Modern*. Translated by Catherine Porter. Cambridge: Harvard University Press, 1993.

Latour, Bruno. "Why Has Critique Run Out of Steam? From Matters of Fact to Matters of Concern." *Critical Inquiry* 30, no. 2 (2004): 225–48.

Love, Heather. "Close but Not Deep: Literary Ethics and the Descriptive Turn." *New Literary History* 41, no. 2 (2010): 371–91.

Macé, Marielle. *Façons de lire, manières d'être*. Paris: Gallimard, 2011.

Mallarmé, Stéphane. "Crise de vers." In *Œuvres complètes*. Edited by Bertrand Marchal. Vol. 2, 204–13. Paris: Gallimard [Pléiade], 2003.

Mallarmé, Stéphane. "Observation Concerning the Poem 'A Throw of Dice Will Never Abolish Chance.'" In *Œuvres completes*. Edited by Bertrand Marchal. Vol. 1, 391–2. Paris: Gallimard [Pléiade], 1998.

Mallarmé, Stéphane. "A Throw of Dice Will Never Abolish Chance." In *Œuvres complètes*. Edited by Bertrand Marchal. Vol. 1, 363–87. Paris: Gallimard [Pléiade], 1998.

Paulhan, Jean. *The Flowers of Tarbes, or, Terror in Literature*. Translated by Michael Syrotinski. Champaign: University of Illinois Press, 2006.

Paulson, William. "For a Cosmopolitical Philology: Lessons from Science Studies." *SubStance* 30, no. 3 (2001): 101.

Paulson, William. *Literary Culture in a World Transformed: A Future for the Humanities*. Ithaca: Cornell University Press, 2001.

Paulson, William. "Literary Studies in the Twenty-First Century: A Future for the Humanities." *Colloquia Germanica* 35, no. 3-4 (2002): 201–16.

Prigent, Christian. *L'Incontenable: Essais*. Paris: POL, 2004.

Ramazani, Jahan. *Poetry and Its Others: News, Prayer, Song, and the Dialogue of Genres*. Chicago: University of Chicago Press, 2014.

Ramazani, Jahan. *A Transnational Poetics*. Chicago: University of Chicago Press, 2009.

Schaeffer, Jean-Marie. *Adieu à l'esthétique*. Sesto San Giovanni: Mimésis, 2016.

Schaeffer, Jean-Marie. *L'Expérience esthétique*. Paris: Gallimard, 2015.

Schaeffer, Jean-Marie. *La Fin de l'exception humaine*. Paris: Gallimard, 2007.

Stengers, Isabelle. *Cosmopolitics*. Translated by Robert Bononno. 2 vols. Minneapolis: University of Minnesota Press, 2010–11.

Stengers, Isabelle. "Gaia: The Urgency to Think (and Feel)," presented at the International Colloquium "The Thousand Names of Gaia: From the Anthropocene to the Age of the Earth." Rio de Janeiro, September 15–19, 2014. https://osmilnomesdegaia.files.wordpress.com/2014/11/isabelle-stengers.pdf and https://osmilnomesdegaia.eco.br (accessed January 15, 2019).

Stengers, Isabelle. *In Catastrophic Times: Resisting the Coming Barbarism*. Translated by Andrew Goffey. Lüneburg, Germany: Open Humanities Press, 2015.

Stengers, Isabelle. "Reclaiming Animism." *e-flux journal* 36 (2012): 4. https://www.dropbox.com/s/ppphccmhlyqyz8v/Stengers_Reclaiming%20Animism.pdf?dl=0 (accessed January 15, 2019).

Valéry, Paul. "*Le coup de dés*. Lettre au Directeur des *Marges*." In *Œuvres*. Edited by Jean Hytier. Vol. 1, Paris: Gallimard [Pléiade], 1957.

5

Kafka's Whipper and Joyce's Pandybat: Reading Scenes of Discipline with Latour

Gabriel Hankins

How is literature tied to the history of governmental control and disciplinary practices? How is literature related to governmental practices, institutions, even the dreaded "bureaucracy"? The anti-institutionalist positions of Foucault and Althusser on discipline and the state ideology, along with the critical sociology of Pierre Bourdieu, serve as lasting touchstones for political readings in literary studies. Pierre Macherey, D. A. Miller, and their critical descendants transformed the political critique of disciplinary power into an entire literary-critical program, one that Rita Felski has described as a main branch of the culture of "critique," with symptomatic reading as the primary tool and suspicion as the dominant affect.[1] Symptomatic readings of the operation of dominant power hinge on the power of central disciplinary scenes staged within the classroom, courtroom, and jailhouse, in the hailing of the police and the panoptic gaze of the penitentiary: but what if the sites where modern governmental power operates are constructed quite differently from the standard notions of state disciplinary power, at once more pervasive and less determinative? A Latourian political sociology could help us revise our view of the proper sites of political reading, pointing us to the power of paperwork, whips, diagrams, and accounting standards. Latour's reconception of the social gives us new tools to describe disciplinary scenes in the modernist period, in particular, in ways that should transform our readings of familiar modernist political allegories.

This chapter offers a Latourian account of the way institutional power and practice link up with literary and cultural texts, in the service of what we might call the "weak program" in literary studies: a turn away from strong theories of interpretation, ideological determination, and critical affect, and toward the weaker powers of description, reassembly, and tracing the transformative effect of nonhuman agents on the social world. The weak program in modernist studies begins as early as Nietzsche's anti-foundationalist announcement of the "death of the Gods," by Gianni Vattimo's account, and links recent work in queer studies, affect theory, object-oriented approaches to literature, and digital literary studies.[2] Through a re-reading of heightened scenes of disciplinary violence, and through quieter scenes of account books, missing reports, and posted exams, this chapter seeks to develop a new way to read the sites of politics in early-twentieth-century literature. First, a classic modernist disciplinary figure, the Whipper at the center of Kafka's *The Trial*.

Kafka's Whipper

Kafka's parable of the "whipper," one of central narrative pericopes within *The Trial*, concretizes the modernist relation to disciplinary life in a particularly exemplary way. Let us recall: K. is passing from his office at the Bank to the main staircase when he hears "convulsive sighs" behind a door he had always assumed was a lumber-room for excess furniture and supplies. When he opens the door, he sees that he has assumed "correctly":

> Bundles of useless old papers and empty earthenware ink bottles lay in a tumbled heap behind the threshold. But in the room itself stood three men, stooping because of the low ceiling, by the light of a candle stuck on a shelf…. One of the men, who was clearly in authority over the other two and took the eye first, was sheathed in a sort of dark leather garment which left his throat and a good deal of his chest and the whole of his arms bare.[3]

When asked what they are doing, the two men (Franz and Willem) cry out that they are to be flogged because of a complaint lodged against them by K. over the conditions of his own earlier "arrest." K. attempts to intercede on their behalf, even trying to bribe the Whipper with money to let them go. "For in my view they are not guilty," says K., "the guilt lies with the organization. It is the high officials who are guilty."[4] Nevertheless, the Whipper refuses not to perform his duty: "What you say sounds reasonable enough, said the man, but I refused to be bribed. I am here to whip people and whip them I shall."[5] When the whipping begins, "a shriek rose from Franz's throat, single and irrevocable, it did not seem to come from a human being but from some martyred instrument"; K., "beside himself," pushes Franz to the floor, "but even then Franz did not escape his punishment, the birch-rod found him where he was lying, its point swished up and down regularly as he writhed on the floor."[6]

The scene requires us to read it as a parable of disciplinary power, just as the famous "Before the Law" episode obviously points outside the narrative in which it was belatedly inserted. As with the best Kafka parables, the scene is both irreducible and overdetermined, challenging simple hermeneutic apparatuses, asking that we read again that which resists an end to reading. Of the many possible interpretations the story demands and refuses, the most relevant is a lesson about the ambiguity of rule and ruler, of the whip-man and the rod. Who is the agent of the whipping, the "ruler" who "rules"? Who is ultimately responsible for the violence of authority? Certainly not K., who protests against the whipping he has caused; not the whip-man himself, according to his own account.

Other options proliferate, depending on our notions of the political field and philosophical anthropology at work. K. states that the "organization" is the guilty party. Perhaps the agent of the whipping is the governmental process which has also proclaimed K.'s guilt, though everything in the novel demonstrates how contentless that process is. Perhaps the agent is the hidden hand of governmentalized reason, operating through an instrumental ideology which reifies humans through their functionalities, as "martyred instruments" and Whippers; the scene would then serve as an allegorical staging of the inner irrationality of bureaucratic, rationalist administrative modernity. This is what we might call the "classical" sociological reading of the scene. Or else the agent is a divinely ordained Sovereign Authority, whipping humanity because humanity demands to be whipped (following Joseph de Maistre, Wyndham Lewis, and one line of conservative anti-liberal thinking). The Whipper becomes a quasi-theological figure in this line of political theology, "*dio boia*, Hangman God" as Joyce will put it.[7] Yet of course the scene resists both simplified politico-theological and sociological readings, even as it invites them. Adorno remarks in his "Notes on Kafka": "[Kafka's] is a parabolic system the key to which has been stolen: yet any effort to make this fact itself the key is bound to go astray by confounding the abstract thesis of Kafka's work, the obscurity of the existent, with its substance. Each sentence says 'interpret me,' and none will permit it."[8]

We could follow another possibility: the disciplinary power of the scene emerges as a result of the assemblage of hand, leather costume, birch-rod, office closet, and Law, pulled together through a network of unseen but determinative forces, forces concretized in the detritus of office bureaucracy, the "useless old papers and empty earthenware ink bottles."[9] What these waste products of official modernity signify here is exactly the absent presence of the Law itself, not just as sovereign theological power but just as an arrangement of paper, of process, of passages from one legal chamber to another, the rhizomatic connections of the "Kafka-machine" that Deleuze and Guattari diagnose (and which Latour will formalize in his *Making of Law*).[10] The Whipper transforms into his function, just as Franz's voice detaches from the individual: "It did not seem to come from a human being but from some martyred instrument."[11] The union of the theological and scientific in that final metaphor is characteristic of Kafka and also of Latour's analysis of the many modes of being that infuse governmental scenes: social agent, divine authority, the sacrificial suffering of the instrument, all suggest the ways in which disciplinary power has never been "modern" and certainly never fully instrumental.

Kafka is interested here neither in the "agency" of the three men nor in political claims about governmental power (despite K.'s "reasonable" rationalist humanitarianism): Kafka is interested in the "junk rooms" adjoining bureaucratic offices where power is produced and exercised. Significantly, the grammar of the final sentence moves agency and subjecthood explicitly to the "birch-rod" which "found him where he was lying," removing the Whipper from any sense of control: the function of power is the subject here, not its supposed human agents. Power is located with the networks of order, commands, rules, functionaries, law books that rhizomatically articulate to the scene of violence here embodied, as Deleuze and Guattari also argue in their reading of the "Kafka-machine." Disarticulating the networks that produce this scene of power and violence, as Kafka shows us, is both banal and revelatory: room opens upon room, absurdity waits upon reason, the books of the Law are filled with pornography. Significantly, the offices of the Bank, where K.'s office is located, are somehow continuous with the offices of the Court where justice is given and the offices of the Police who enforce it. Kafka's scene thus precisely analyzes the concrete production of governmental power within interlocking chambers we could loosely group under "bureaucratic rationality," while insisting on the specificity of the object life that attends it—a specificity that vivifies rather than reifying the scene, in my reading, connecting paperwork, ink, and candle to the suffering bodies of the ruled. Kafka here concretizes the institutional forms of modernist governance, the offices and paperwork that stand behind state and corporate violence.

The usual term for this form of state power is "bureaucracy," an intriguing hybrid term for new-materialist readers of politics. "Bureaucracy" is notable for being one of few forms of political power named by a structural technology of power rather than after a human agent or class. A "bureau" does of course employ human agents, but the word originally refers to tables, chairs, offices, audience rooms, and metonymically governmental business. Bureaucracy refers to an assemblage of objects and spaces that has taken power: an etymology that Kafka would applaud. John Stuart Mill, among others, inveighed against loss of "free agents" entailed in such rule, which arose across European languages in the eighteenth century: bureaucracy thus stands as the objective non-correlative of an ideal liberal state, even as it merged into the functional definition of liberal rule. Max Weber, famously, made the routinization and procedural rationality of bureaucratic life the central feature of his account of modernity. In sociological accounts after Weber, the bureau tends to be afforded the same routinization claimed for the inner logic of bureaucracy itself. Yet as we see in Kafka's parable, as well as other modernist scenes of institutional life, the object life of bureaucracy can have a fascinating and defamiliarizing radiance, a charisma that belies the disenchantment of an administered world. The *bureau* itself becomes an unexpected agent within modernity, a use which echoes the grammatical form of the latter, just as the development of the rationalized German state, in Cornelia Vismann's view, depends on the development of "files" (*Akten*) as the media technology that would embody and spread bureaucratic rule.[12]

Critics gloss Kafka's governmental fables as dramas of absurdity and meaninglessness of life under bureaucratic, administered modernity, with such scenes as the episode of the Whipper as prime examples. How absurd, to continue to serve one's function despite the request of the accuser for forgiveness, despite the offer of bribery! Yet, as Deleuze and Guattari note, and as Stanley Corngold and others differently show in the case of Kafka's office writings, the process of bureaucratic office functions turns out to be *productive*, meaningful, even fulfilling, if one can accept the laughter occasioned by the Whipper as a kind of hard fulfillment, an obscure bureaucratic joy.[13] Kafka himself was a successful middle manager, we now know, not the desperate artist chained to his desk that he sometimes dramatized in letters: "Writing and office cannot be reconciled, since writing has its center of gravity in depth, whereas the office is on the surface of life. So it goes up and down, and one is bound to be torn asunder in the process."[14] But what if the material surface of life, its rooms and waste papers and books of the Law, is where the productive power of law and the state reside?

Re-reading *The Trial* and other famous modernist depictions of a bureaucratized modern world as rhizomatic explorations of the production of power, territory, law, and spiritual meaning by actor-network assemblages, as in Deleuze and Guattari's "Kafka-machine," suggests a new materialist sociology of the novel of bureaucracy, one that differs sharply from both the classic sociologists and critical sociologists like Bourdieu. Social power, disciplinary power, is in this view always in the process of assembly, and its specific place of assembly is exactly the waiting rooms, side chambers, and junk rooms of modern power where Kafka stages his gestural theater of discipline.

Joyce: A Portrait of the Artist as a Young Institution

Let us move to another key site of discipline for modernist thought, from Robert Musil's *Young Törless* to Jean Vigo's *Zéro de conduite* to Louis Althusser and post-68 theory: the schoolhouse. For Anglophone modernism the central crux here is James Joyce's *A Portrait of the Artist as a Young Man*, and particularly the scene of the "pandybat," another moment of motiveless, malevolent violence:[15]

> —Lazy idle little loafer! cried the prefect of studies. Broke my glasses! An old schoolboy trick! Out with your hand this moment!
>
> Stephen closed his eyes and held out in the air his trembling hand with the palm upwards. He felt the prefect of studies touch it for a moment at the fingers to straighten it and then the swish of the sleeve of the soutane as the pandybat was lifted to strike. A hot burning stinging tingling blow like the loud crack of a broken stick made his trembling hand crumple together like a leaf in the fire: and at the sound and the pain scalding tears were driven into his eyes. His whole body was shaking with fright, his arm was shaking and his crumpled burning livid hand shook like a loose leaf in the air. A cry sprang to his lips, a prayer to be let off. But though the tears scalded his eyes and his limbs quivered with pain and fright he held back the hot tears and the cry that scalded his throat.
>
> —Other hand! shouted the prefect of studies.
>
> Stephen drew back his maimed and quivering right arm and held out his left hand. The soutane sleeve swished again as the pandybat was lifted and a loud crashing sound and a fierce maddening tingling burning pain made his hand shrink together with the palms and fingers in a livid quivering mass. The scalding water burst forth from his eyes and, burning with shame and agony and fear, he drew back his shaking arm in terror and burst out into a whine of pain. His body shook with a palsy of fright and in shame and rage he felt the scalding

cry come from his throat and the scalding tears falling out of his eyes and down his flaming cheeks.

—Kneel down, cried the prefect of studies.

Stephen knelt down quickly pressing his beaten hands to his sides. To think of them beaten and swollen with pain all in a moment made him feel so sorry for them as if they were not his own but someone else's that he felt sorry for.

This classic moment of scholastic violence can be read as a pure eruption of disciplinary power that disrupts modernist *Bildung*, a moment of sacralized violence that sets up Stephen as scapegoat, martyr, and avenger. Disciplinary power here is figured through the arbitrariness of the disciplinary act itself (Stephen has not intentionally broken his glasses); through loss of scopic power thus entailed and the emphasis on a reduced sphere of touch and feeling; and paradoxically through the very disembodiment that then results, as Stephen feels his hands "as if they were not his own but someone else's." Intimate experiences of violence break down the Cartesian boundaries between mind and body, self and experience, as the piling up of adjectival gerunds ("hot burning stinging tingling") emphasizes. As Sarah Cole notes in her reading of the scene, the scene stages the emergence of human language itself, out of the completely closed child's identification with the body of the first blow, then the cry which springs to his lips, a cry that becomes a prayer, a whine, and then a moment of abstract empathy, and a dissociation with his own body that foretells Stephen's later theory of impersonal composition.[16] This passage serves as an origin point for the following modernist narrative, in her view, in its progressive movement from a moment of intimate violence to the distance required to put that violence into language. Sacralized violence—intimated by the swish of the soutane, the theater of the schoolroom, and the priestly scholastic setting—gives way to desacralized description, an overpowering of the brutal force of the "Hangman God" and his institutional agents by the resistant modernist individual whose later "*non serviam*" will finally resolve the play of attraction and resistance to priestly institutions, if not to educational institutionalization itself (Stephen later plays the part of the bored teacher in the "Nestor" episode of *Ulysses*).

The comparison to the scene of disciplinary violence in *The Trial* is instructive: both stage disciplinary violence as disconnected from motive, ground, or procedural logic; both discover an autonomous logic to whipping itself: "I am here to whip people, and whip them I shall."[17] In both cases the individual, subjective experience of being beaten is folded into a larger institutional logic that plays out through the larger work, in the rhizomatic spread of pathways and doorways that lead Stephen and K. through their different disciplinary societies. Here too the specific objects within the scene ramify outwards into corridors, hallways, and topologies of experience that will unfold over the course of the text: the hand, which crumples here like a leaf in the fire, will elsewhere be linked to the discovery of sexual difference ("Eileen had long thin cool white hands too because she was a girl"), the metaphoric power of language ("[Her hands] were like ivory; only soft"), and sectarian identity ("That was the meaning of *Tower of Ivory* but protestants [sic] could not understand it and made fun of it").[18] The "loud crack" of the pandybat will echo again after Stephen's rebellion against his punishment, in the "sound of the cricket bats" that end the first section of his childhood. Stephen's glasses too move from the occasion for violence and implied threat of castration to the symbol of his triumph over the disciplinary arbitrariness of the priests, who must finally apologize, as presaged by the first poetic and Promethean chiasma of the text: "*Pull out his eyes,/ Apologise,/Apologise,/Pull out his eyes.*"[19] This is partly to say that the object life of educational disciplinary forms a sustained counterpoint to the ostensible subject of the modernist bildungsroman as such, the development of the autonomous individual as artist.

The bildungsroman is the preeminent novelistic form of the nineteenth-century novel exactly because it stages the most important political narrative of its time, the emergence of the autonomous liberal individual from his stable social surroundings: a generic form that functions for Nancy Armstrong to ratify the distinctive social myths of liberal individualism, and for Franco Moretti as a symbolic form that mediates the experience of constant change associated with a capitalist modernity.[20] The modernist bildungsroman usually is read as a radicalization of this identification with constant change and continual individualization, as in the changing styles that inflect the chapters of *Portrait*, pointing toward the integration of a rejected social outside into the supreme artistic vision of the rebel iconoclast. The social is posited by the artist (as by the modern "critical" sociologist) as an enclosure to be escaped, the linguistic, religious, and political "nets flung at [the soul of a man] to hold it back from flight. You talk to me of nationality, language, religion. I shall try to fly by those nets."[21] The picture of progressive interiorization and social escape central to liberal individuation is complicated by the scene of violence above, however, which does not at all move simply from outside inward, or from experience to language to the Icarian heights of artistic depiction. By the final paragraph, Stephen is still an incoherent mess of bodily experience, emotional reaction, social awareness, and incoherent outcry: "His body shook with a palsy of fright and in shame and rage he felt the scalding cry come from his throat and the scalding tears falling out of his eyes and down his flaming cheeks." While we tend to read this as a paratactic grammar of the body's intrusion on inner order, the experience of violence here also stages the independent life and willful multiplicity of that collective agent we hypostatize as "body": a smaller, weaker body politic than the disciplinary state which the prefect of studies embodies. Pain, tears, outcries shatter the coherence of the self; rage responds with uncontrollable shaking; shame impinges on the body in the form of the scalding tears and the flaming blush. This blush will return again, in another confrontation with political and disciplinary power, and in another dialog with the politics of disciplinary power.

Much later, in the final chapter of *Portrait*, we see a mirror of this scene, in Stephen's confrontation of the liberal nationalist world order of his childhood, its various avatars and forms of discipline. Liberal world order is no abstraction here, but rather appears through a variety of concretions, apparatuses, tests, and forms of life: not as an enveloping enclosure, net, or panoptic apparatus, as in the modernist metaphors that guide the theorists of discipline, but as a set of threshold and chambers, standards and fashions, ties and life trajectories. In the opening pages of the last chapter of *Portrait*, Stephen Dedalus hears a clock "beating eleven strokes in swift precision." The clock in its precision and universality recalls his schoolmate MacCann, and he laughs to think of him polemicizing for world peace on the corner:

> —Dedalus, you're an antisocial being, wrapped up in yourself. I'm not. I'm a democrat and I'll work and act for social liberty and equality among all classes and sexes in the United States of the Europe of the future.[22]

We later see MacCann preaching almost exactly these sentiments, alongside a picture of Czar Nicolas II. The implicit reference of the last line is to W. T. Stead's *The United States of Europe* (1899), a journalistic and propagandistic volume that also opens with a faintly iconic picture of the Czar. In 1898 Czar Nicolas had made the first overtures for an international peace conference aimed at disarmament and the development of international law, a set of proposal for a pacific anti-imperial world received with suspicion at the time. We note in this opening bit of MacCann's speech that he is a late Victorian social liberal on the model of L. T. Hobhouse, devoted to social liberty, equality, and democracy within a cosmopolitan federation of European states—a liberal fueled by both religious and secular energies. He represents, in the schema of *Portrait*, one of the alternate voices and futurities that Stephen must confront and pass by in order to fulfill his particular artistic vocation.

Joyce stages the following confrontation between Stephen and MacCann, which takes up a surprising number of the following pages, as a play between misrecognition and sympathy, a characteristic Joycean dyad. As Stephen and Cranly (his close friend, confessor, and observer) exit their physics lecture, they see the "propagandist" canvassing for signatures near the door of the lecture hall: "On the table near the door were two photographs in frames and between them a long roll of paper bearing an irregular tail of signatures. MacCann went briskly to and fro among the students."[23] Stephen pauses "irresolutely" near the door and questions Cranly as to the subject of the petition; after learning that it is *"per pax universalis,"* Stephen points to the photograph of the Tsar and says: "He has the face of a besotted Christ." MacCann begins his speech:

> MacCann began to speak with fluent energy of the Tsar's rescript, of Stead, of general disarmament arbitration in cases of international disputes, of the signs of the times, of the new humanity and the new gospel of life which would make it the business of the community to secure as cheaply as possible the greatest possible happiness of the greatest possible number.[24]

MacCann's enthusiastic ideological promiscuity mixes cosmopolitan pacifism, a smattering of the late Victorian gospel of new life (along the lines of Edward Carpenter), and recognizably Benthamite liberalism, in a mode that folds liberal rationalism into a series of secularized socialist utopias. What's being represented here, more than the confused humanitarianism of a single character, is the confusion of beliefs and values contained by late Victorian liberalism in general. When Stephen professes a weary disinterest in signing, MacCann accuses him of reactionary aestheticism.

—The affair doesn't interest me in the least, said Stephen wearily. You know that well. Why do you make a scene about it?
—Good! said MacCann, smacking his lips. You are a reactionary then?
—Do you think to impress me, Stephen asked, when you flourish your wooden sword?
—Metaphors! said MacCann bluntly. Come to facts.

Stephen blushed and turned aside. MacCann stood his ground and said with hostile humour:

—Minor poets, I suppose, are above such trivial questions as the question of universal peace.[25]

Stephen's refusal to sign the petition is aligned with his other refusals, the negations of anti-liberal modernist self-definition through rejection of Victorian religious and political culture. But MacCann leaves Stephen blushing in a way that the parallel confrontations with the nationalist Davin, the religious dean of studies, and the hermetic Cranly do not.

One primary reading of politics in this scene contrasts the explicit, propagandistic emancipatory politics of MacCann (a figure modeled on Joyce's university friend Skeffington, a radical new-life socialist and feminist) to the more profound artistic emancipation that Stephen's (and Joyce's) art hopes to effect. Thus Dominic Manganiello writes, "For Joyce ... the emancipation made possible through literature transcended those notions of freedom embraced by nationalists and socialists. ... The transformation of institutions does not depend on force, lobbying for peace, or pleading for social justice, but can only follow upon this unsuspected process of changing basic attitudes and prejudices."[26] This summary inherits Percy Shelley's notion of poets as "the unacknowledged legislators of the world" and positions Joyce's authorial politics as the "transcendence" of mere political claims on freedom through the greater freedom afforded by art.[27] At a further level of abstraction, Joyce's *nego* can be taken to stand for the negative capacity of an autonomous modernist art to "point to a practice from which they abstain: the creation of a just life," as Adorno puts it.[28] The *non serviam* of Joyce's "toughminded art" thus stands in for our received notion of modernism's relationship to liberal politics in general, and MacCann's late Victorian utopian politics in particular.

More interesting than this conventional reading of Joyce's refusal of the political horizon of his time, however, is the way in which the constitutive boundaries of modernist politics—between autonomy and commitment, bourgeois progressivism and avant-garde reaction, engagement and impartiality, material fact and ideological illusion—are continually traduced by the texts that supposedly exemplify those boundaries. Recall the blush on Stephen's face, like the scarlet brush during his pandying, the visible sign of a disavowed reality ("Metaphors! ... Come to facts"). A blush is a peculiar cultural–material conjunction, a response of blood that registers a recognition, an uncomfortable affinity between outer world and inner life. The blush moves across the boundary between nature and culture in response to MacCann's call to "facts," however illusory we (and perhaps Stephen) know those facts to be. We register the blush within language, of course, both the more general *langue* and as an element of

Portrait's own particular language, but we may read (and experience) the blush as a resistance of our materials to the metaphors we use to contain them—including the systematic chain of metaphors that sustain Stephen's artistic self-creation in this final chapter of *Portrait*.

Both the hybridity of this particular response—the way the blush engages cultural and material co-actors to create its response—and the specific political materials responded to matter (and are matter) here. Stephen Dedalus blushes to recall his metaphoric relationship to material life, and blushes in particular at the invocation of a utopian world political scene. We recall the emotion of a much younger Stephen: "It pained him that he did not know well what politics meant and that he did not know where the universe ended."[29] Both are real questions—what is the Collective which we are called to assemble, Latour would ask—and both questions return in the later scenes of disciplinary violence.

After the confrontation with liberal-ethical ideology, Stephen's long walk at the conclusion of Portrait stages an encounter with Donovan, a final representative of imperial disciplinary power. After the encounters with his counterparts MacCann and Davin, and in the midst of Stephen's exposition of his aesthetic theory to Cranly and Lynch, "a fat young man, wearing a silk neckcloth, saluted them and stopped":

> —Did you hear the result of the exams? [Donovan] asked. Griffin was plucked. Halpin and O'Flynn are through the home civil. Moonan got fifth place in the Indian. O'Shaughnessy got fourteenth. The Irish fellows in Clark's gave them a feed last night. They all ate curry.

> His pallid bloated face expressed benevolent malice and, as he had advanced through his tidings of success, his small fat-encircled eyes vanished out of sight and his weak wheezing voice out of hearing.[30]

After exchanging a few unpleasantries, Stephen and his mates see Donovan off to a dinner of pancakes, and Stephen resumes his exposition of neo-Thomist aesthetics. Donovan, in this brief interlude from aesthetics, stands in for what Stephen earlier anticipated as the "worldly voices" urging him to raise his father's fallen state, and clearly also for the contact of British imperial order on both the habitus and life-trajectories of Stephen's young peers. His necktie (silk), education ("constitutional history"), aesthetic tastes (second-hand Goethe and Lessing), leisure pursuits (botanical walks), and culinary tastes (pancakes and curry) all mark him as a member of the internationalized Anglo-British civil servant caste, and his disposition and bodily dissipation figure that caste as "excrementitious," in the words of Lynch.³¹ Donovan intervenes within Stephen's lecture as a kind of abject disavowal of the habits and tastes encouraged by imperial order. Pierre Bourdieu would describe Donovan as a typical representative of the politically and culturally dominant bourgeoisie, and would position Stephen as an antagonistic member of the dominated-dominant caste, the caste of Flaubert, Mallarmé, and *l'art pour l'art*.³² The dominant allegory of the encounter, in the view of critical sociology, would certainly be the process of class differentiation by which the artist at once claims familiarity with the institutional thresholds of late Victorian imperial power and at the same moment abjects them through the "excrementitious" figure of Donovan.

This analysis of the liberal imperialist protagonist in relation to the modernist protagonist, as the confrontation of two antagonistic and yet intertwined positions or possibilities within the dominant and dominated-dominant class fractions, certainly clarifies some elements of Donovan's specific characterization. What Bourdieu's form of sociological critique tends to elide, however, is exactly the material substrates of this small scene of class antagonism (in a different sense that the "material and social reality" which his account takes as its ground): the silk neckcloth that Donovan wears, which arises out of specific networks of imperial trade (not merely internal class distinction); and his relationship to the natural world as part of a "walking club," which Donovan treats as a field of disinterested contemplation (rather than sustenance: "bring us a few turnips and onions the next time you go out ... to make a stew," Stephen asks him).³³ Donovan's abstract interest in the natural world is the corollary of his comfortable place outside it, firmly in the realm of a pancake and curry-eating global administrative caste.

Then there is the civil service and imperial exams which sort Stephen's classmates into their fates. The civil service exams were a major institution of colonial rule as well as bureaucratic domination. Just the exam posting itself is left in the frame: compare Sally Rooney's recent exploration of scholarships at Trinity in *Normal People*, which registers the full force of an institutional process at which Joyce here only hints.³⁴ We learn of Donovan, in response to an absent question from Stephen, that he will matriculate in "constitutional history," with a solid future as a member of the political-governmental elite. Out of these cultural and material networks of educational discipline, which evade mere categorization as the "sartorial," "natural," and "educational-bureaucratic," Joyce shapes Stephen's specific material antagonism to the disciplinary nets of nation, class, and empire.

Class antagonisms and class-fractional positions are intrinsic to the material networks that subtend the scene, of course, but are created out of a swarm of intersecting actors and agents whose work brings class, empire, and nature into view. Rather than reading material markers as the mere correlates of class distinction—as Bourdieu's distinctive statistical tables and lists in *Distinction* tend to do—we should read the elements of Donovan's distinctive overmaterialized, gluttonous, excremental body as actors in their own accounts, with intriguing stories to tell about what Wyndham Lewis calls "the art of being ruled."[35] Latour's revision of critical sociology should allow literary scholars to take up the thinking of Bourdieu and the classical sociologists on the rationalization of governance and its intersections with class position, but with a reversal of focal position. Rather than examining how the concrete is subsumed into the system and the agent placed within the institution, as elements of the "ideological determination" of the aesthetic or the "cultural field of production" within which modernist texts much be understood, we should read governmental institutions, forms of discipline, and their material correlates as co-actors within modernist texts, actors with their own movement, scope, and attachments.

Foucault's treatment of governmentality might seem to point the way here, defined as an "ensemble formed by the institutions, procedures, analyses and reflections, the calculations and tactics that allow the exercise of [a] specific albeit complex form of power."[36] Yet the Foucaultian notion of the governmental *dispositif* slides into place all too easily, from the Latourian point of view. Governmentality comes pre-packaged with procedures, analyses, tactics, discourses, and a political economy ready to deploy. Is the scene of governance really to be found in the writings of the German ordoliberals, as Foucault will argue in his work on biopolitics, or is it rather to be found in the posting of imperial exams, the striking of the clock tower, Donovan's silk ties, his bourgeois tastes, and his "field club" walking tours? The scene of government is far more micropolitical and more pervasive, on the Latourian reading, than the history of Western macroeconomics might suggest; the sites of discipline are filled not with racks and whips but with "useless old papers and empty earthenware ink bottles," old statistical charts and rulebooks, walking sticks and exams. Out of these small scenes we might begin to reassemble the collective life of the disciplinary state in the way that literature asks us to attend to it: slowly, contingently, one office closet and one blush at a time.

Notes

1. Rita Felski, *The Limits of Critique* (Chicago: University of Chicago 2015), 18–19.
2. See Paul Saint-Amour's summary of recent work in "Weak Theory, Weak Modernism," *Modernism/Modernity* 25, no. 3 (2018): 437–59.
3. Franz Kafka, *The Trial*, 1925, trans. Willa and Edwin Muir (New York: Schocken Books, 1995), 83.
4. Ibid., 86.
5. Ibid.
6. Ibid., 87.
7. James Joyce. *Ulysses* 9. 1049, Gabler edition (New York: Vintage, 1981).
8. Theodor Adorno, *Prisms*, trans. Samuel and Shierry Weber (Cambridge: MIT Press edition, 1981 [1967]), 245.
9. Kafka, *The Trial*, 83.
10. "A Kafka-machine is thus constituted by contents and expressions that have been formalized to diverse degrees by unformed materials that enter into it and leave by passing through all possible states." Gilles Deleuze and Félix Guattari, *Kafka: Towards a Minor Literature*, trans. Dana Polan (Minneapolis: University of Minnesota Press, 1986), 7. Bruno Latour, Marina Brilman, and Alain Pottage. *The Making of Law: An Ethnography of the Conseil D'état* (Cambridge: Polity, 2015).
11. Kafka, *The Trial*, 83.
12. Cornelia Vismann, *Files: Law and Media Technology*, trans. Geoffrey Winthrop-Young (Stanford: Stanford University Press, 2008).
13. See the introductory essays in *Franz Kafka: The Office Writings*, ed. Stanley Corngold, Jack Greenberg and Benno Wagner, trans. Eric Patton with Ruth Hein (Princeton: Princeton University Press, 2009).
14. Letter to Felice Bauer, cited in Corngold et al., x.
15. James Joyce, *A Portrait of the Artist as a Young Man*, ed. Seamus Deane (New York: Penguin, 1992), 51–2.
16. Sarah Cole, *At the Violet Hour* (Oxford: Oxford University Press, 2012), 9.
17. Kafka, *The Trial*, 86.
18. Joyce, *A Portrait of the Artist as a Young Man*, 43.
19. Ibid.
20. See Nancy Armstrong, *How Novels Think: The Limits of Individualism from 1719–1900* (New York: Columbia University Press, 2005), and Franco Moretti, *The Way of the World: The Bildungsroman in European Culture* (London: Verso, 1987).
21. Joyce, *A Portrait of the Artist as a Young Man*, 220.
22. Ibid., 136.
23. Ibid., 149.

24 Ibid., 151.
25 Ibid., 152.
26 Dominic Manganiello, *Joyce's Politics* (London: Routledge and Kegan Paul, 1980), 38–9.
27 Percy Shelley, *A Defense of Poetry*, ed. Albert Cook (Boston: Ginn, 1890), 46.
28 "Commitment," in *Aesthetics and Politics*, Theodor Adorno, et al. (London: Verso, 1977), 194.
29 Joyce, *A Portrait of the Artist as a Young Man*, 11.
30 Ibid., 228.
31 Ibid., 163.
32 See Pierre Bourdieu's reading of Flaubert in *The Rules of Art: Genesis and Structure of the Literary Field*, trans. Susan Emanuel (Stanford: Stanford University Press, 1996).
33 Joyce, *A Portrait of the Artist as a Young Man*, 228.
34 Sally Rooney, *Normal People* (London: Faber and Faber, 2018).
35 See Pierre Bourdieu, *Distinction: A Social Critique of the Judgement of Taste*, trans. Richard Nice (Cambridge: Harvard University Press, 1987 [1979]). Wyndham Lewis, *The Art of Being Ruled* (London: Chatto and Windus 1926).
36 Michel Foucault, *Security, Territory, Population: Lectures at the Collège de France, 1977–1978*, ed. Micheal Senellart, trans. Graham Burchell (New York: Palgrave Macmillan, 2009 [2004]), 108.

Bibliography

Adorno, Theodor W. *Aesthetics and Politics*, Theodor W. Adorno, et al., London: Verso, 1977.

Adorno, Theodor W. *Prisms*. 1967. Translated by Samuel and Shierry Weber. Cambridge: MIT Press, 1981.

Armstrong, Nancy. *How Novels Think: The Limits of Individualism from 1719–1900*. New York: Columbia University Press, 2005.

Bourdieu, Pierre. *Distinction: A Social Critique of the Judgement of Taste*. Translated by Richard Nice. Cambridge: Harvard University Press, 1987 [1979].

Bourdieu, Pierre. *The Rules of Art: Genesis and Structure of the Literary Field*. Translated by Susan Emanuel. Stanford: Stanford University Press, 1996.

Cole, Sarah. *At the Violet Hour*. Oxford: Oxford University Press, 2012.

Deleuze, Gilles, and Félix Guattari. *Kafka: Towards a Minor Literature*. Translated by Dana Polan. Minneapolis: University of Minnesota Press, 1986.

Felski, Rita. *The Limits of Critique*. Chicago: University of Chicago Press, 2015.

Foucault, Michel. *Security, Territory, Population: Lectures at the Collège de France, 1977–1978*. Edited by Micheal Senellart. Translated by Graham Burchell. New York: Palgrave Macmillan, 2009.

Joyce, James. *A Portrait of the Artist as a Young Man*. 1916. Edited by Seamus Deane. New York: Penguin Books, 1992.

Joyce, James. *Ulysses* 9. 1049, Gabler edition. New York: Vintage, 1981.

Kafka, Franz. *Franz Kafka: The Office Writings*. Edited by Stanley Corngold, Jack Greenberg, and Benno Wagner. Translated by Eric Patton with Ruth Hein. Princeton: Princeton University Press, 2009.

Kafka, Franz. *The Trial*. 1925. Translated by Willa and Edwin Muir. New York: Schocken Books, 1995.

Lewis, Wyndham. *The Art of Being Ruled*. London: Chatto and Windus, 1926.

Manganiello, Dominic. *Joyce's Politics*. London: Routledge and Kegan Paul, 1980.

Moretti, Franco. *The Way of the World: The Bildungsroman in European Culture*. London: Verso, 1987.

Rooney, Sally. *Normal People*. London: Faber and Faber, 2018.

Vismann, Cornelia. *Files: Law and Media Technology*. Translated by Geoffrey Winthrop-Young. Stanford: Stanford University Press, 2008.

6

Michelet's Nonmodernity

Maxime Goergen

One should never waste an occasion, my friend, to reiterate that Michelet is the very genius of history. First because it is the truth; and also because it annoys so many people; and it is such a torture for our good friends the moderns.[1]

"It is urgent, it is properly vital for philosophy that we use the 19th century as the new Middle Ages at last," pleaded Michel Serres in conclusion to a study on Michelet's *The Sorceress*.[2] This suggestion was scrupulously heeded by Latour, for whom the legacy of the post-Revolutionary period acts as a philosophical and political matrix. In a similar way to Serres, Latour sees the nineteenth century as a crucible of contradictions: a rational and modern century, it resolutely partitions practices, disciplines, and agents into binary oppositions, but in so doing it also causes hybrids and quasi-objects to proliferate. While it may think of itself as the heyday of modernity, it is in fact the golden era of the nonmodern.

This interpretation is implicit in *The Pasteurisation of France* (1988) and fully developed in *We Have Never Been Modern* (1991). When the latter was published, the nineteenth century had become an object of intense scrutiny for Latour. As the first section of this study will show, the French intellectual climate of the 1980s lent itself favorably to a critical reassessment of the post-1789 period; the concept of nonmodernity is a distinct product of this Zeitgeist. The first goal of these pages is to analyze how Latour's ideas contribute to a change in the perception of the cultural and ideological legacy of the nineteenth century, and to show how, in bypassing the modern/antimodern binary in which it was circumscribed, the concept of nonmodernity restores the nineteenth century to its complexity. The second and third sections of this study will illustrate the crucial role played by literature in the reappraisal of the nineteenth century as nonmodern and define literature as the very place of origin of nonmodern sensibility. Finally, nonmodernity can also help us make sense of specific works and authors that had become unreadable or out of fashion under the restrictive paradigm of modernity. Latour's critical toolbox, which is clearly inspired by semiotics and narrative theories,[3] has the potential to rejuvenate our historical approach of nineteenth-century literary "classics." This is what the final section will illustrate. Jules Michelet will be used as one of the most prominent representatives of the nonmodern strand that runs through nineteenth-century French literature. His works exemplify the ambivalence of a century which, while apparently upholding the constitutional principles of modernity, was also actively undermining them. Hopefully these pages will be in keeping with Serres's suggestion: re-reading Michelet with Latour can help us recover networks of meanings and agents that had been discarded, and read the French nineteenth century anew, as both unfamiliar and yet surprisingly relevant for early twenty-first-century readers.

I

In *We Have Never Been Modern*, the post-1789 period is represented as coterminous with the golden age of modernism, conceived both as a temporal rupture between past and present and as an epistemological rift between the natural and the social. It coincides with the peak era of stabilization of the modernist fallacy, a "Second Enlightenment" during which the critical discourse of social sciences further widens the great schisms initiated by Descartes and Kant, whether it be between nature and culture, the human and the nonhuman, or science and politics. *We Have Never Been Modern*, which by Latour's own admission was written on the smouldering ashes of naturalism and socialism, therefore clearly articulates a critique of the political, scientific, and intellectual heritage commonly associated with "the nineteenth century." It denounces and unmasks the triumph of the parallel project of scientific domination and political emancipation, whose delusional nature was brutally revealed in 1989, a year dubbed by Latour the "year of miracles." Crucially, 1989 seems to be the final nail in the coffin of a waning nineteenth century, whose illusions were finally dispelled with the fall of the Berlin wall.

For Latour, two watershed moments illustrate the illusions inherent in the modernist construction of history: 1789 and 1989, the year of the French Revolution and the commemoration of its bicentenary, two events which coincide with the beginning and the end of the modernist narrative. In the eyes of a modern, the French Revolution is a *tabula rasa*, the mythical point of inception of a new world to come. This is an interpretation that has been dominant for the better part of the twentieth century, under the influence of Marxist historiography. In *We Have Never Been Modern*, Latour joins ranks with thinkers of various ideological backgrounds who, in the favorable intellectual climate of the 1970s and 1980s, will challenge these erstwhile commonplace assumptions about the Revolution and the "modern" century that it spawned. Latour self-admittedly aims to do for modernity what François Furet did for the French Revolution in *Interpreting the Revolution* (1978), namely, to emancipate the events and the objects it created from the ulterior discourses that organized their coherence. The years 1789 and 1989 therefore function for Latour as two historical markers around which the very notion of history can be revised. Ultimately, he relies on the deconstruction of the historicized concept of Revolution—with 1789 and 1989 as its external margins—to write a nonmodern history of modernity, in other words a history in which the liminal value of these dates ceases to be functional.

As Latour was writing *We Have Never Been Modern*, French intellectual history was at a crucial point of juncture. Marxism, as a hegemonic intellectual and political school of thought, was steadily losing ground as the last vestiges of the regimes it inspired crumbled in eastern Europe. The Revolution had ceased to be a promised land rising on the historic horizon: it had been confined to the mute strangeness of the past. Against this backdrop, the concept of nonmodernity is highly representative of what François Dosse recently called the "1989 moment," during which the critical bequest of Marxism is re-evaluated. What is also at stake in this intellectual moment, beyond Marxism itself, is a revision of the ulterior reading of the nineteenth century that was underpinned by the hermeneutic totalitarianism of Marxist discourse. Latour's nonmodernity is a paradigm that emerges in the midst of a flurry of publications by French historians, intellectuals, and essayists, which are testament to a newfound interest in a century whose meaning has suddenly ceased to be predicated on a political eschatology. A few representative examples will illustrate this revival. In the wake of Furet's revisionist reading of the Revolution, claiming that *la Révolution française est terminée* (the French revolution is over), the publication of Pierre Nora's *Lieux de mémoire* (*Rethinking France*) relegates the nineteenth century's ideological legacy into the past: for Nora, it has ceased to be ingrained in living national *memory*, and should be now treated with the distance and dispassionateness owed to earlier periods of *history*. Over the same period of time, the Orsay museum opens its doors to the public (1986), making the nineteenth century a state-funded object of musealization and commemoration in its own right, in a gesture that further stresses its uncanny remoteness. Meanwhile, Philippe Muray denounces the collusion of socialism and illuminism in a ferocious pamphlet, *Le 19e siècle à travers les âges* (*The 19th Century through the Ages*) (1984). The 1980s and early 1990s are a long procession of farewells to the preceding century. Be they nostalgic or revengeful, they always feature the same line of arguments: the nineteenth century is to blame for a historical promise it didn't keep (socialism), while the alliance of technical mastery of nature and social progress it heralded (naturalism) also proved to be a fallacy.

Latour's concept of nonmodernity evidently feeds into this moment of French thought. The idea that we have never been modern is rooted in the belief that revolutions in fact never really happened, and indeed *cannot* ever happen: there never was an unbridgeable rift between a "before" and an "after," but only ulterior intellectual and political interpretations that constructed and imposed a discontinuous narrative of history.

A welcome side effect of this theoretical reassessment in philosophy, politics, and literary studies is that it also paved the way for the rediscovery of figures that had been rejected by modernity, or until then confined to obsolescence. These figures, through Latour's lens, can now be interpreted as the main protagonists of a nonmodern narrative of the nineteenth century. In political philosophy for instance, the 1970s and 1980s were hailed as a "return to Tocqueville," inaugurated by liberal philosopher Raymond Aron. This philosophical comeback gained momentum, once again, thanks to Furet's book, which commends Tocqueville's moderation and nonteleological perception of history. Tocqueville's intellectual patronage is one that Latour also readily acknowledges when he states that "modernity still awaits its Tocqueville."[4] By virtue of his emphasis on permanence and continuity in history (or, as Latour would put it, extension and acceleration of practices by a greater number of agents) rather than on rupture and purity, Tocqueville is the building block on which a heterodox (i.e., non-Marxist) reassessment of the historical legacy of the nineteenth century can be built. Other figures re-emerge in his wake, among which those writers and thinkers who, after having been idolized by the French Third Republic and made into national prophets of progress and democracy, had subsequently been shunned by advocates of political or aesthetic modernity. The most remarkable of these towering literary figures are Hugo and Michelet, to whom I will turn in the final section of this text. The loose corpus of ideas these writers adhered to was aptly named "humanitarianism" by historian of ideas Paul Bénichou, who highlighted their attempts at determining a new secular faith for post-Revolutionary France, based on a blend of political and moral optimism, a belief in the pacifying and progressive impact of education and technology, a trust in the inevitability of democracy, and the celebration of the people as the historic agent behind this drive toward progress. Victor Hugo, the most universally recognized of these figures, is also the one who most remarkably returned to the limelight in the mid-1980s. In 1985, the French government celebrates the centenary of the writer's death with a series of events aimed at reminding younger generations of his importance in the construction of French Republican identity. The backdrop of these celebrations is distinctly one of ideological disarray that chimes in with Latour's critique of revolutionary eschatology: at this point François Mitterrand's socialist administration had long given up its early ambition of breaking away from capitalism and of *"changer la vie"* (changing life), and steadily initiated a conversion to market economy. As the lyrical illusions of May 1981 subsided, the left looked for alternative narratives that would allow it to abandon its radical legacy, which was still ripe with the promise of a new revolution to come. The French socialist party tried to reinvent itself as a progressive force whose main task was now to curb the excesses of a liberal democratic order whose foundations it no longer wished to challenge. At this stage in the dissolution of the ideological corpus of the left, pre-Marxist humanitarian figures could provide a welcome fallback narrative. This is precisely what Philippe Muray pinpoints in his 1984 controversial study. According to Muray, the reason why returning to references such as Tocqueville or Hugo proves so effective is that, however different they might be on other counts, they provide an alternative plot to the Manichaeism of revolutionary teleology. They do so, essentially, by reintroducing two elements that Marxism rejected: first, the idea of Providence (the crossed-out God, in Latour's words); second, and crucially for the scope of this chapter, they challenge the process of purification that led to the division between human and nonhuman subjects. Here again, Tocqueville and Hugo foreshadow a distinctly nonmodern take on the century. A chapter in Tocqueville's *Democracy in America* emphasizes, for instance, an environmental agency in the felicity conditions of American democracy: "There are a thousand circumstances independent of the will of men that make it easy to have the democratic republic in the United States,"[5] Tocqueville writes, among which is nature itself: "In the United States, it is not only legislation that is democratic; nature itself works for the people."[6] As Pierre Charbonnier notes, Tocqueville here is hinting that there might be "ecological conditions to freedom and equality."[7] As to Hugo, his providentialist ontology refuses to separate humans, animals, and objects: "In this century," he claims, "I am the first who has spoken not only of the soul of animals, but of the soul of things":[8] human and nonhuman agencies are coterminous and underpinned by a hidden principle of unity. Muray points out that what defines "19th-centuryness" is precisely the idea that all forms of life stem from the same vital unity. Politically, this bolsters an optimistic vision of the "people" or the "masses," represented as being instinctively closer to this common vitalist matrix than other classes, such as, say, bourgeois intellectuals. This has a distinct appeal for the 1980s, especially for the left, as it looks for new "historic agents" to represent, and new ways to articulate its own mission, now that it has abandoned its ambition to make a clean break with the past. An emphasis on unity and connection is what Jean Baudrillard signposts as the characteristic ideological sidestep of the left as he publishes the ominous *La Gauche divine* (*The Divine Left*) in 1985: socialism has become a pure celebration of interaction and social links. It extols the virtues of the "circularity of exchanges,"[9] putting forth vitalism and mediation as foundations of the body politic, at the expense of "the violent myth of the social"[10] embodied by Revolutionary tradition. It has, in a word, forfeited modernity in favor of nonmodernity.

There is evidence, then, to suggest that toward 1989, the "year of miracles," France operated a return to heretofore neglected aspects and figures of the nineteenth century, in order to counteract the ideological void left by the simultaneous collapse of two pillars of modernity: confidence in the domination of nature on the one hand, faith in the emancipation of humanity on the other hand. The rise of the nonmodern marks a period of ideological reshuffle for the left.

It makes sense, as a result, to include Latour's philosophical stance into what Bernard Hours defined as "the thought of the bicentenary":[11] Latour's denunciation of the pitfalls of modernity chimes in perfectly with contemporary reassessments of the mission, purview, and agents of the French left. But within this broad movement, Latour's approach is unique. Its originality lies in the resolutely anachronistic bias of his critical apparatus. In refusing to take the premise that history is made of clearly defined "befores" and "afters" for granted, Latour fundamentally differs from the many iterations of postmodern or antimodern discourses that have determined the oppositional boundaries of the French intellectual field for the last forty years. In contrast, Latour insists that the idea that "time passes" is itself a byproduct of the modern Constitution: "The connections among beings alone make time. It was the systematic connection of entities in a coherent whole that constituted the flow of modern time."[12] History, and the process of division it implies, is hence always potentially guilty of a typically modernist sin. It theoretically splinters past and future, which are rendered incommensurable by the denial of their common mediations—when in fact any given point of history is filled with resurgences: "the past remains, and even returns."[13]

It is obvious that what Latour is denouncing here is a vision of history and progress that is typically attached to the very Constitution of the nineteenth century as a stable ideological point of reference, and that I have outlined above. However, as Jean-Baptiste Fressoz argues, "modernity has never been unequivocal in its mechanistic view of the universe and in its project to attain technological mastery of the world [...] nineteenth-century technological modernization did not occur in a fog of unconsciousness or a modernist frenzy."[14] If, as Latour shows in the wake of François Furet, the French Revolution was not revolutionary as its events unfolded, then we should also entertain the possibility that the nineteenth century, as a whole, was already aware of its own nonmodernity even as it unfolded the thread of the modern narrative; we can think afresh our relation to the nineteenth century by considering it as the cradle of nonmodernity. This is one of the many avenues of research opened by *We Have Never Been Modern*: is it not precisely over the course of this undisputed century of triumphant modernity, as the exclusions underpinning the modern Constitution were at their most inflexible, that the most fascinating hybrids were likely to be spawned?

II

The hypothesis of this section is that these hybrids found a welcoming environment in literary and artistic production. As the nineteenth century tries to define "modernity" in literature and the arts, it is in fact already tiptoeing toward a definition of the nonmodern. Literary modernity is defined not as a process of purification and rupture, but as its exact opposite, namely a trigger for the production of hybrids and for the representation of mediations. This justifies why we should turn to it now to look for an alternative to the all-too implacable logic of modernity as a rift.

It is perhaps inevitable to refer to Baudelaire, as he provides both the most comprehensive and most influential definition of "modernity" available in France at a time when the word modernity was still a neologism. "By modernity," Baudelaire writes, "I mean the ephemeral, the fugitive, the contingent, the half of art whose other half is the eternal and the immutable."[15] Baudelaire's "modern" is a far cry from the polarizing mainstream interpretation of modernity that is condemned in *We Have Never Been Modern*. As a matter of fact, it is essentially not incompatible with Latour's nonmodern, to the extent that both notions can be seen as cognates. This is true in particular with respect to their perception of time and of the teleological construction of history. H.-R. Jauss rightly points out that Baudelaire's conception of modernity "no longer even understands itself as epochally opposed to some determinate past [...]."[16] In this definition, Jauss adds, "the great historical antithesis between the old and the new, between ancient and modern taste, gradually loses its currency."[17] Baudelaire sees modernity as nothing else than an experience of entanglement and heterogeneity.

As a result, the aesthetic experience of modernity is in effect one of blurred boundaries. It challenges the radical rupture between past and present, between "them" and "us," that Latour sees as the act of faith of the modern mindset. Indeed, in line with Baudelaire's definition, the modern literary canon develops an ambivalent and critical reaction to the experience of the acceleration of technical and social times, as well as to the process of political rationalization. As Antoine Compagnon has shown, this points to a fundamental ambivalence at the heart of the modern project: masterpieces of modern literature developed into a haven of antimodern political feeling: "Historically, modernism, or true modernism, worthy of this name, has always been antimodern, that is ambivalent, self-reflective, and experienced modernity as an uprooting."[18] At least within the specific province of literary experience, then, the seemingly irreconcilable notions of the modern and the antimodern overlap and contaminate each other.

As far as I know, Latour doesn't explicitly refer to this Baudelairian etymology, nor does he pay particular attention to literary incarnations of the concept of modernity. This is despite their evident proximity to some aspects of the nonmodernity he advocates. For what is true of the French Revolution does apply to the literary experience of modernity as well: one should differentiate the "modalities of historical action" from the "process."[19] "Modern" writers used the concept of modernity to understand what they were going through and to give it meaning, but this does not mean that, in practice, their writing was modern, no more than—in Furet and Latour's eyes—the French Revolution was revolutionary.

III

Before I turn to Jules Michelet's works as a prime example of nonmodern practice, it is useful to illustrate how nonmodernity can be used to challenge certain undisputed premises of literary history. The great shift of modernity in literature can be summarized in very broad sweeps as affecting first and foremost the status of imitation. Before modernity, models prevail; the order of mimesis is one of conformity with tradition and with an essentialized reality that it is the mission of the literary text to illustrate and reconfigure. After modernity, though, the text becomes its own standard of evaluation, liberated from the shackles of aesthetic norms; its relation to reality becomes increasingly conscious of its mediated nature; the type of connections that can be drawn between reality and its textual representation becomes contingent on highly subjective, and potentially infinite, variations. With Latour, it is the two main tenets of literary modernity, namely its self-reflexive nature and its autonomy from nonliterary discourses, that are questioned. They correspond to a twofold and complementary process of purification (in the affirmation that there is a separate type of discourse called "literature" which is incommensurable with others) and mediation (literature claiming to be a unique and privileged channel for the expression of the whole of human experience): this is the very same process as the one defining the modern paradox as a whole.

To an extent, then, Latour's nonmodern does justice to the way modern literature defined itself in the nineteenth century: not as a clean break or a new dawn, but as an unresolved encounter of darkness and light, populated with uncertain creatures. It places the notions of hybridity and mediation at its center. In doing so, it also radically decenters the focus of literary history. If nonmodernity is a valuable category to understand literary history, then it can potentially, and considerably, alter the composition of our traditional nineteenth-century literary Pantheon—*exit* Flaubert, say, and enter Michelet.

Another exciting promise carried by the concept of nonmodernity in literary studies is that it prompts us to scrutinize the way writers negotiated their own aesthetic practices and to refuse to take their (or anyone else's) ulterior discursive rationalizations for granted. It does so, however, in a way that notably differs from the French tradition in the field of the sociology of literature. This discipline, in the wake of Bourdieu's *The Rules of Art*, has developed a methodology that aims to account for the positions occupied by writers within the cultural, social, and economic spheres of their time, using concepts of habitus and capital. Specialists of sociopoetics, such as Alain Viala or Jérôme Meizoz, made effective use of the notion of "posture auctoriale" ("auctorial posture," or "author's image") to describe the way writers negotiated their identity within the literary field. What this school of criticism takes for granted, however, is that auctorial postures are necessarily predicated on the existence of an autonomous literary field that singlehandedly steers a writer's social and artistic trajectory. As William Paulson pointed out,[20] the very existence of this divide between literary and nonliterary discourses is something that the concept of nonmodernity challenges: this divide can be seen as a prime example of purification, akin to the one that artificially separates nature and society. A nonmodernist literary history would hence challenge the misplaced sociological polarities of the nineteenth-century French literary field—between "art for art's sake" on the one hand and "bourgeois art" on the other—and focus instead on the "Middle Kingdom," especially on those productions that have been expelled from the realm of institutionalized literature. It would consider literature as moving "via spirals and eddies, forever reviving dead forms in new guise"[21]—genres, tropes, *topoi*, and types would then have to be understood in their entanglement and recurrences rather than in the brutal breakups that set them apart. It would also strive to bridge the age-old gap between authorial intentionality on the one hand and reader's freedom of interpretation on the other hand, by conferring agency to other elements within and outside of the text, as Latour himself suggests, citing the writer who perhaps best embodies the demiurgic ambitions of the French nineteenth century: "Balzac is indeed the author of his novels, but he often writes, and one is tempted to believe him, that he has been 'carried away' by his characters, who have forced him to put them down on paper."[22]

I have already mentioned that the concept of nonmodernity was implicit in Baudelaire's definition of modernity, and that the apparent rift between moderns and antimoderns had, in fact, always spawned literary hybrids. The argument could be made—it is implicit in Compagnon—that "literature," rather than being the name given in the nineteenth century to the institution of an autonomous field of cultural production with its own set of values and rules of inclusion and exclusion, is in fact the very embodiment of the "Middle Kingdom," the place where the combined work of purification and mediation is at its most visible, finds its most welcoming environment, and reveals its profound solidarity. For in spite of all attempts at defining its essence, literature remains indeed an experience of hybridity, a discourse that can only be defined by what it does to other discourses, and by the extent to which it alters subjectivities. "As for texts, why deny them the grandeur of forming the social bond that holds us together?"[23] asks Latour: literature can be envisaged as a network of bonds, material, subjective, and textual at one and the same time, making it the paragon of quasi-objects.

Someday, perhaps, teachers and scholars will refer to "nonmodern literature" with the same aplomb and self-confidence that they have when talking about romanticism or realism. The reality of nineteenth-century writing practices cannot be fully explained away by the ulterior justifications provided by the modern/antimodern divide. Latour prompts us to take a new approach to the construction of the literary canon—via a rereading of the Baudelairian construction of "modernity"—and to turn our attention to works that slipped through the cracks, works that had been nonmodern all along, and therefore remained somewhat invisible or unreadable.

IV

Latour's concepts invite us to consider the text as a quasi-object, as a bond, as the utopian milieu where different agents, things, beings, and events find a space of negotiation and mediation. In so doing, they help us constitute the paradigm of a nonmodern literary history, which does justice to the nineteenth century's own complex relation to modernity. Assuredly, Jules Michelet, a historian and a moralist, a professor at the Collège de France and the author of a monumental and passionately subjective history of the French Revolution, would figure prominently in any textbook on nonmodern writing. Michelet sits uncomfortably between genres and disciplines: besides his historical writings, he was also the author of natural histories such as *The Insect* (1858) or *The Sea* (1861), or of moral treatises such as *The People* (1846). He was also a prolific diarist. What makes him an exemplary case study is that his intellectual career is also an evolution from modernity to nonmodernity. He was originally very much the shining example of a modern in Latour's sense—a thinker who believed in the unbridgeable differences between humans and nonhumans—so much so, in fact, that it is in Michelet's works that some of the most prescient definitions of what Latour will describe as the constitutional conditions of modernity can be found. Let us now follow the trail of Michelet's conversion to nonmodernity.

In the very first paragraph of his *Introduction to World History* (1831), Michelet posits an absolute separation between nature and man as the foundation of his vision of human agency: "With the world, a war began that will end with the world, and not before: the war of man against nature, of spirit against matter, of liberty against fatality. History is nothing but the story of this endless struggle."[24] This separation, more brutally expressed by Michelet than by any other thinker of his time, spells out what Latour defines as the first conditions of the modern Constitution, namely the absolute separation of nature and society. In Michelet's early texts, this separation is coextensive with a rejection of the Christian dogma of Grace, to which he substitutes the revolutionary ideal of Justice. As Bénichou notes, "In fact, invoking Justice against Grace is wanting God's justice to be our own: God, in Michelet's eyes, can only love us according to Law, Reason and Justice, that is according to the idea Man has of God."[25] In rejecting Grace, Michelet candidly exposes one of the guarantees of Latour's modern Constitution, the "crossed-out God": the divine is simultaneously transcendent (Grace is rejected from the realm of human actions) and immanent (in the form of Justice, which is defined by humans). The principles of Christianity and those of the Revolution were as incompatible to the early Michelet as those of nature and human progress.

And yet, as Mitzman points out, Michelet's ideas change over the course of the 1840s and 1850s: "From a basic belief in the linear progress of freedom through conflict with and liberation from the natural world, he came to accept a cyclical view of nature and spiritual existence built on the principle of harmony."[26] The watershed moment for this change is June 1848 and the disillusions brought about by the demise of the Second Republic and the December 2 coup by Louis-Napoléon Bonaparte. This troubled historical context is exacerbated by personal circumstances, as Michelet is dismissed from the Collège de France on March 12, 1851. Michelet's view of history had thus far been predicated on the idea of the French Revolution as a clean break, revealing new universal principles to France and to the world: "Did France exist before that time? It might be denied."[27] The Revolution functions theoretically as an absolute origin: "Grand, strange, surprising scene! To see a whole people emerging, at once, from nonentity to existence [...]."[28] But what June 1848 challenges for Michelet is the confidence in a linear perfectibility of societies that was implicit in this vision of Revolution as ground zero. Michelet's appraisal of history changes accordingly. Rather than being represented as a clean break, performed at an identifiable moment in time by a defined set of rational agents, the Revolution becomes a spiritual principle, one whose incarnation is limited neither to human agency, nor to a distinct chronology. So much so that historical discourse is no longer sufficient to explain it away: it is now treated, as Gossman points out, as an "ever-renewed promise of redemption,"[29] in which all of creation—man, nature and things—equally partakes.

The year 1848 is to Michelet what Latour showed 1989 to be for his generation: a "year of miracles" in which the contradictions of modernity are crudely exposed, and the shortcomings of dominant ideologies brutally unmasked. Now that the Revolution as a historical process had proved to be reversible, its true nature is to be found elsewhere: in other *agents*, in other *temporalities*. Michelet's latter intellectual production is increasingly keen to find a space of representation for agents that had had little or no voice in historical discourse so far, whether these agents are human (the people, the sorceress) or, more interestingly perhaps, nonhuman (the sea, the bird, the mountain, the insect). In doing so, Michelet does not seek to impose his own human rationality on them, but rather embraces the idea that history is a form of alchemy that involves the participation of a multiplicity of subjects and objects, as well as the coexistence of historical time and natural cycles of recursivity and renewals. Michelet's premonition, which leads to a fundamental reappraisal of his ideology in the 1840s and 1850s, is as follows: while human and nonhuman agencies, or indeed human and nonhuman temporalities cannot be conflated, they are in fact underpinned by a profound unity, that it is the mission of the writer to reveal.[30] In Michelet, as Barthes noted, there is "no barrier of essence between the orders of nature: the mineral is the plant, the animal contains the human dream."[31] Michelet's work becomes a meditation on the relation between nature and culture,[32] supported by two principles that anticipate Latour's nonmodern paradigm: irreducibility on the one hand, and translatability on the other. Nothing in Michelet's world can claim to be the universal equivalent of anything else; yet, everything is equally correlated and worthy of representation. In *The Insect*, for instance, Michelet addresses nonhuman agents as equal partners: "If thou toilest and lovest, O Insect, whatever may be thy aspect, I cannot separate myself from thee. We are truly somewhat akin. For what am I myself, but a worker?"[33] Michelet's world is one without stitchings, where the smallest elements of inert nature are bestowed with the same intensity of agency and subjectivity, down to the tiniest ant: "However humble the insect may seem in appearance [...] it exists independently; it moves, goes, comes, advances or returns [...] it suffices for itself; it foresees, provides, defends, and boldly confronts the most unexpected chances. In this, then, do we not discern, as it were, a first glimpse of personality?"[34]

No discourse then, be it the discourse of the historian as opposed to the discourse of "the people," and no isolated agent, be it the "great man" as the subject of history as opposed to the insect, the mountain, or the bird, can be said to encapsulate and express the meaning of others. Yet everything may become the object of a translation—humans and nonhumans can become allies to each other. As Latour puts it, "An actor expands while it can convince others that it includes, protects, redeems, or understands them."[35]

Expansion and understanding are precisely the missions assigned to writing by Michelet. Writing triggers a process of empowerment of other agents, during which the writer's autonomous rationality gets profoundly altered by mediations. In *The People*, Michelet represents himself as a spokesperson for the different classes that make up the social fabric of France, for, he claims, "I unite them all in my own person":[36] his word becomes the very nexus of mediation where different beings, who have no other space or voice, find their natural habitat. Beings and things are porous in Michelet's ontology, which also means that, conversely, the writer's own subjectivity can merge with nonhuman agencies, as in this famous example in *The Mountain* [1866], in which Michelet recounts the experience of taking mud baths at Acqui:

> The only image that I could then cherish was that of Mother Earth—Terra Mater. I felt her very plainly, caressing and pitying and warming her wounded child. Without? Ay, and internally also. She interpenetrated my frame with her vivifying principles, entered into and blended with me, insinuated into my being her very soul. The identification between us grew complete. I could no longer distinguish myself from her.[37]

As this example shows, Michelet advocates a fundamental ontological equality between human and nonhuman subjects, hereby anticipating Latour. Unsurprisingly for the graphomaniac that he was, however, Michelet endows the practice of writing, and books as objects, with a privileged status within this flat metaphysics. Michelet clearly insists on the capacity of the written word to have the same ontological status as other human and nonhuman subjects. Texts are to be understood as having their own agency. But also, because everything can eventually be translated into a textual form, Michelet hints that a book might indeed be the most welcoming space of all, one in which all temporalities can be deployed, and all voices are represented—while epiphanies like that of the Aqui mud baths are rare in the extratextual world. Texts, therefore, are the ultimate mediators, the most effective environment for networks to reveal themselves, and for the limitations of modernity's oppositional structure—human vs. nonhumans, subject vs. object, science vs. politics, etc.—to be exposed. For Michelet, the most meaningless duality of them all is no doubt the separation of the self and the world. We have to take Michelet seriously when he writes, in the *Preface to the History of France* (1869): "My life is in this book, it has been transformed into it. This book has been my life's only outcome":[38] for the extraordinary power of the text is that it suspends, however briefly, the antagonism of the self and the world. In the written word, Michelet seeks the ideal unity he can no longer find in history, the elusive balance between his own subjectivity and its dissolution within a collective of other actants. This moment of equilibrium defines both what a writer should be for Michelet—the momentary spokesperson of a variety of different and potentially conflicting agents—and what he also ends up seeing as the real incarnation of the Revolutionary spirit, namely a moment of unity and harmonious polyphony that can be both eternally preserved by texts and yet forever reactualized in the act of reading. As Gossman suggests, "is it not, in fact, by transforming [the Revolution] into literature that Michelet hopes to suspend the fragile epiphanic moment and make it eternal, indefinitely re-presentable and renewable?"[39]

Michelet's writing established a continuum between human and nonhuman, facts and subjectivity, autobiography and collective narratives, science and fiction. These are seamlessly entangled in his works. In Latour's word, Michelet's books can be read as *factishes*: he writes them as much as he is written by them, with "the robust certainty that allows practice to pass into action without the practitioner ever believing in the difference between construction and reality, immanence and transcendence"[40]—to the extent that it threatens the very integrity of both himself as a writer and his book as a historical or scientific artifact. Michelet's originality and exemplarity is that the very essence of his work is to display and dramatize these negotiations rather than to hide them. The writer himself is torn between a sense of failure—the impossibility to purify, the feeling that an excess of language and meaning is constantly created—and the acknowledgment, more and more consenting and enthusiastic as Michelet gets older, that other agents do have a right to be represented, and that at the root of history and human experience lies the mysterious unity postulated by translatability. Michelet increasingly conceived of his role as writer and as a historian as that of the delegate of a parliament of things.

Three short conclusions can be drawn from this reading of Michelet and the notes that precede it. First, if Michelet is indeed a nonmodern, it is no doubt because he was also, at first, a disillusioned modern, shaken by the possibility of history going backwards or of the Revolution being erased. Nonmodernity is present, in other guises, in "progressive" writers such as Hugo or Zola, who shared Michelet's fears. There is a nonmodernist vein that runs through the French nineteenth century and that is still largely unexplored. Second, while Michelet did not primarily consider his production as literary, what he does is precisely to define a characteristic of nonmodern literature: by granting all agents the same ontological status, nonmodernity unveils the essentially narrative nature of all disciplines: ultimately, distinctions between the literary and the scientific, the factual and the fictional, are secondary. As suggested before, a great number of texts which sit halfway between disciplines—this is, of course, Michelet's case, but one can think of the works of Fourier or Pierre Leroux, among others—could be reassessed in this light. Third, as Roland Barthes hinted in an article aptly called "Michelet's Modernity,"[41] what made writers like Michelet "unreadable" before the "year of miracles" is precisely what makes them relevant and young again today: their interest for symbolic mediations, their concern for the problems of delegation of authority and voice—who is entitled to speak, and on whose behalf? What channels of communication/translation can be used? How can nonhuman agency be represented? These questions seem more pressing in the early twenty-first century, as we are negotiating ways of defining a democratic and natural contract that can accommodate both humans and nonhumans in the face of political and ecological disaster. Nonmoderns, such as Michelet, offer a fictional model of life in common.

Notes

1 Charles Péguy, *Clio. Dialogue de l'histoire et de l'âme païenne* (Paris: Gallimard, 1932), 45. My translation.
2 Michel Serres, *Hermès I: la communication* (Paris: Minuit, 1948), 226. My translation.
3 See Bruno Latour, *Reassembling the Social: An Introduction to Actor-Network-Theory* (Oxford: Oxford University Press, 2005), 54–6.
4 Bruno Latour, *We Have Never Been Modern*, trans. Catherine Porter (Cambridge: Harvard University Press, 1992), 40.
5 Alexis de Tocqueville, *Democracy in America*, ed. Eduardo Nolla, trans. James T. Schleifer vol. 1 (Minneapolis: Liberty Funds, 2010), 453.

6   Ibid., 456.
7   Pierre Charbonnier, "Les Aventures écologiques du libéralisme," *AOC,* April 24, 2018, https://aoc.media/analyse/2018/04/25/aventures-ecologiques-liberalisme/#_ftnref1 (accessed June 20, 2019).
8   My translation. Cited in *Victor Hugo on Things that Matter*, ed. Marva A. Barnett (New Haven: Yale University Press), 214.
9   Jean Baudrillard, *The Divine Left. A Chronicle of the Years 1977–1984*, trans. David L. Sweet (Cambridge: MIT Press, 2014), 130.
10 Ibid., 89.
11 Bernard Hours, "Compte-rendu de *Nous n'avons jamais été modernes*," *L'Homme et la sociét* 109 (1993): 133.
12 Latour, *We Have Never Been Modern*, 77.
13 Ibid., 69.
14 Jean-Baptiste Fressoz. "The Lessons of Disaster: A Historical Perspective of Postmodern Optimism," *Books and Ideas*, https://booksandideas.net/The-Lessons-of-Disasters.html (accessed June 24, 2019).
15 Charles Baudelaire, *The Painter of Modern Life and Other Essays*, trans. Jonathan Mayne (London: Phaidon Press, 1995 [1863]), 13.
16 Hans Robert Jauss, "Modernity and Literary Tradition," *Critical Inquiry* 31 (2005): 359.
17 Ibid.
18 Antoine Compagnon, *Les Antimodernes. De Joseph de Maistre à Roland Barthes* (Paris: Gallimard, 2005), 12. My translation.
19 Bruno Latour, *Cogitamus. Six lettres sur les humanités scientifiques* (Paris: La Découverte, 2010), 60–1.
20 William Paulson, "Nous n'avons jamais été dix-neuviémistes, ou l'avenir d'un avant-dernier siècle," *Nineteenth-Century French Studies* 24 (1996): 34–9.
21 Graham Harman, *Bruno Latour: Reassembling the Political* (London: Pluto, 2014), 165.
22 Bruno Latour, *An Inquiry into Modes of Existence. An Anthropology of the Moderns*, trans. Catherine Porter (Cambridge: Harvard University Press, 2013), 158.
23 Latour, *We Have Never Been Modern*, 90.
24 Jules Michelet, *Introduction to World History* (1831), in *On History*, trans. Flora Kimmich, ed. Lionel Gossman and Edward K. Kaplan (Cambridge: Openbooks, 2013), 25.
25 Paul Bénichou, *Le Temps des prophètes. Doctrines de l'âge romantique* (Paris: Gallimard, 1977), 541.
26 Arthur Mitzman, "Michelet and Social Romanticism: Religion, Revolution, Nature," *Journal of the History of Ideas* 57 (1996): 668.

27 Jules Michelet, *History of the French Revolution*, vol. 1, trans. C. Cocks (London: Bohn, 1847), 201.
28 Ibid., 74.
29 Lionel Gossman, "Michelet's Gospel of Revolution," in *Between History and Literature* (Harvard: Harvard University Press, 1990), 218.
30 On this point, see Paule Petitier, "Un Discours sur la mort; Michelet et le modèle de L'Insecte," *Romantisme* 64 (1989): 101–12.
31 Roland Barthes, *Michelet*, trans. Richard Howard (Berkeley: University of California Press, 1987), 33.
32 As Robert Mandrou points out, this is the object of *The People* (1846), which reflects on the influence of natural and material conditions on the way social groups come to life. See Robert Mandrou, "Pourquoi relire *Le Peuple*," *L'Arc* 52 (1973): 50–3.
33 Jules Michelet, *The Insect*, trans. W.H. Davenport Adams (1858; London: Nelson and Sons, 1875), 22.
34 Ibid., 89–90.
35 Bruno Latour, *The Pasteurization of France*, trans. A. Sheridan and J. Law (Cambridge: Harvard University Press, 1988), 173.
36 Jules Michelet, *The People*, trans. G.H. Smith (New York: Appleton, 1846), 25.
37 Jules Michelet, *The Mountain*, trans. W.H. Davenport Adams (London: Nelson and Sons, 1872), 111.
38 Jules Michelet, *Preface to the History of France* (1869), in *On History*, 143.
39 Gossman, "Michelet's Gospel of Revolution," 222.
40 Bruno Latour, *On the Modern Cult of the Factish Gods*, trans. Heather McLean and Cathy Porter (Durham: Duke University Press, 2010), 22.
41 Roland Barthes, "Michelet's Modernity," in *The Rustle of Language*, trans. Richard Howard (Berkeley: University of California Press, 1989), 208–11.

Bibliography

Barthes, Roland. *Michelet*. Translated by Richard Howard. Berkeley: University of California Press, 1987.
Barthes, Roland. "Michelet Today." In *The Rustle of Language*. Translated by Richard Howard. 195–207. Berkeley: University of California Press, 1989.
Barthes, Roland. "Michelet's Modernity." In *The Rustle of Language*. Translated by Richard Howard. 208–11. Berkeley: University of California Press, 1989.
Baudelaire, Charles. *The Painter of Modern Life and Other Essays*. Translated and edited by Jonathan Mayne. 1863. London: Phaidon Press, 1995.

Baudrillard, Jean. *The Divine Left. A Chronicle of the Years 1977–1984*. Translated by David L. Sweet. Cambridge: MIT Press, 2014.

Bénichou, Paul. *Le Temps des prophètes. Doctrines de l'âge romantique*. Paris: Gallimard, 1977.

Bowman, Frank. "Michelet et les métamorphoses du Christ." *Revue d'Histoire Littéraire de la France* 5 (1974): 824–51.

Bourdieu, Pierre. *The Rules of Art. Genesis and Structure of the Literary Field*. Translated by Susan Emanuel. Stanford: Stanford University Press, 1995.

Charbonnier, Pierre. "Les Aventures écologiques du libéralisme," AOC. https://aoc.media/analyse/2018/04/25/aventures-ecologiques-liberalisme/#_ftnref1 (accessed June 24, 2019).

Compagnon, Antoine. *Les Antimodernes. De Joseph de Maistre à Roland Barthes*. Paris: Gallimard, 2005.

Dosse, François. *L'Avenir en miettes, 1968–1989*. Vol. 2 of *La Saga des intellectuels français, 1944–1989*. Paris: Gallimard, 2018.

Fressoz, Jean-Baptiste. "The Lessons of Disaster: A Historical Perspective of Postmodern Optimism," *Books and Ideas*. https://booksandideas.net/The-Lessons-of-Disasters.html (accessed June 24, 2019).

Furet, François. *Interpreting the French Revolution*. 1978. Translated by Elborg Forster. Cambridge: Cambridge University Press, 1981.

Gossman, Lionel. "Michelet's Gospel of Revolution." In *Between History and Literature*. 201–24. Cambridge: Harvard University Press, 1990.

Harman, Graham. *Bruno Latour: Reassembling the Political*. London: Pluto, 2014.

Heinich, Nathalie. "Une Sociologie très catholique? A propos de Bruno Latour." *Esprit* 5 (2007): 14–26.

Hours, Bernard. "Compte-rendu de *Nous n'avons jamais été modernes*." *L'Homme et la société* 109 (1993): 132–4.

Hugo, Victor. *Victor Hugo on Things That Matter. A Reader*. Edited by Marva A. Barnett. New Haven: Yale University Press, 2009.

Jauss, Hans Robert. "Modernity and Literary Tradition." *Critical Inquiry* 31 (2005): 329–64.

Latour, Bruno. *Cogitamus. Six lettres sur les humanités scientifiques*. Paris: La Découverte, 2010.

Latour, Bruno. *An Inquiry into Modes of Existence: An Anthropology of the Moderns*. Translated by Catherine Porter. Cambridge: Harvard University Press, 2013.

Latour, Bruno. *On the Modern Cult of Factish Gods*. Translated by Heather McLean and Catherine Porter. Durham: Duke University Press, 2010.

Latour, Bruno. *The Pasteurization of France*. Translated by A. Sheridan and J. Law. Cambridge: Harvard University Press, 1988.

Latour, Bruno. *Reassembling the Social. An Introduction to Actor-Network-Theory*. Oxford: Oxford University Press, 2005.

Latour, Bruno. *We Have Never Been Modern*. Translated by Catherine Porter. Cambridge: Harvard University Press, 1992.

Mandrou, Robert. "Pourquoi relire *Le Peuple*." *L'Arc* 52 (1973): 50–3.

Michelet, Jules. *History of the French Revolution*. Translated by Charles Cocks. Edited by Gordon Wright. Chicago: University of Chicago Press, 1967.

Michelet, Jules. *On History. Introduction to World History* (1831); *Opening Address at the Faculty of Letters*, January 9, 1834; Preface to *History of France* (1869). Edited by Lionel Gossman. Translated by Flora Kimmich, Lionel Gossman, and Edward K. Kaplan. Cambridge: OpenBook, 2013.

Michelet, Jules. *The Insect*. Translated by W.H. Davenport Adams. London: Nelson, 1875.

Michelet, Jules. *The Mountain*. Translated by W.H. Davenport Adams. London: Nelson, 1872.

Michelet, Jules. *The People*. Translated by G.H. Smith. New York: Appleton, 1846.

Mitzman, Arthur. "Michelet and Social Romanticism: Religion, Revolution, Nature." *Journal of the History of Ideas* 57 (1996): 659–82.

Muray, Philippe. *Le 19e siècle à travers les âges*. Paris: Denoël, 1984.

Nora, Pierre and David P. Jordan (eds.). *Rethinking France*. 1984–1992. 4 vols. Translation directed by David P. Jordan. Chicago: Chicago University Press, 2001–2010.

Paulson, William. "Nous n'avons jamais été dix-neuviémistes, ou l'avenir d'un avant-dernier siècle." *Nineteenth-Century French Studies* 24 (1995–1996): 34–9.

Petitier, Paule. "Un Discours sur la mort; Michelet et le modèle de *L'Insecte*." *Romantisme*, 64 (1989): 101–12.

Péguy, Charles. *Clio. Dialogue de l'histoire et de l'âme païenne*. Paris: Gallimard, 1932.

Serres, Michel. *Hermès I: la Communication*. Paris: Minuit, 1968.

Tocqueville, Alexis de. *Democracy in America*. Edited by Eduardo Nollo. Translated by James T. Schleifer. Minneapolis: Liberty Funds, 2010.

Part Three

Latour's Contributions to the Field of Contemporary Animal Studies

7

Landing in Animal Territories

Vinciane Despret

*"En un sens, ce que nous faisons tous
c'est de la pédologie philosophique comparée!
Nous comparons des types de sol, de profils, d'horizons qui sont très différents."*
Bruno Latour, "Redécouvrir la terre," dialogue avec
Baptiste Morizot et Pierre Charbonnier[1]

Furry Sociologists

To say that baboons ghost-wrote the research of Bruno Latour's *Reassembling the Social: An Introduction to Actor-Network Theory* would be overstating things somewhat.[2] Yet I cannot help thinking that their role was not insignificant. Indeed, what became the book's major theme develops intuitions advanced, almost twenty years earlier, in an article which called baboons to witness. That same article attempted to think with these baboons and to learn from them what a proper sociology would look like: a sociology capable of taking into account the many deeds that members of a society perform to make this society what it is. The article, "Redefining the Social Link: from Baboons to Humans," was co-written with primatologist Shirley Strum and published in 1987. It constitutes, if my genealogical hypothesis is correct, a kind of empirical test—involving baboons—of the hypothesis developed in the 2005 text *Reassembling the Social*. Before getting to this particular article, let us recall that the book's major concerns are linked to the attempt to define sociology's very identity, thanks to the use of the actor network theory (ANT)—now used explicitly. ANT, which formally defines this identity (as problematic as this appellation may otherwise be[3]), "is not an alternative theory *within* sociology" but "an alternative to the sociology of the social."[4] It is also less a theory and more of a grasp, a method, or "a technique to detect how the connections between heterogeneous entities, human and non-humans, compose a given situation, customarily called 'social.'"[5] A sociology defined in this manner—and such definition undoubtedly remains faithful to the etymology and original intuition of the term clearly discernible in the root (*socius*)—will not be a "science of the social," but "the tracing of associations."[6] Latour insists: if one is to understand the nature of society, one must not think of a social matrix in which actors would insert themselves or a social context that sociologists would have to explicate. One must instead follow step by step the continuous creation of associations, of links that become social.

In their 1987 article, Strum and Latour begin by differentiating two ways of doing sociology associated with two rival definitions of the social: on the one hand, the ostensive definition adopted by traditional sociology, and on the other, the definition which has been called "performative" and is being taken up by both authors. In the case of the first, ostensive definition, we can remember that: "[s]ocial actors [...] are *in* the society [...] to the extent that they are active, their activity is restricted because they are only part of a larger society";[7] in the case of the second performative definition, "*[i]n practice*, actors [...] define, for themselves and for others, what society is, both its whole and its parts."[8] In other terms, "society is constructed through the many efforts to define it [...]. This shifts the emphasis from looking for the social link in the *relations between* actors to focusing on *how* actors achieve this link in their search for what society is."[9]

Their broadly sketched primatological history of the baboons[10] shows that studies about baboons relied for a long time on the first definition of the social, the ostensive one. Primatologists adopted this definition all the more readily in that it suited their practical and theoretical habits: indeed, the search for specific invariants has long guided their observations, according to the idea that there must be "one" social model for the entire species. Baboons, in other terms, were supposed to "fit" the social mold forged by evolution. With the proliferation of research at the end of the 1960s, however, a disquieting variety has begun to appear within baboon societies. It became quite difficult to find *one* societal model valid for all social groups. How was one to make sense of all these different organizations of the social? According to the same ostensive social paradigm, scientists suggested either that research was still too rudimentary—all the while continuing to bet on its eventual coherence in the long run—or that ecological conditions made society diverge from the norm, or yet again that researchers' subjectivities or methodological differences might be responsible for these divergences.

But a new research trend—one that is deeply transforming what we thought animals in general and baboons in particular were capable of—suggests that another variability factor be taken into account. When ethologists start to question their own problematic habit of asking animals questions that "give" them no "chance," they also begin to credit them with progressively more sophisticated skills and social awareness—such as negotiating, testing, assessing, and manipulating.[11] Thus, if the theory of dominance (which claimed to uncover the universal organization of baboon societies) can indeed provide some kind of explanation, it is still unable to explain how baboons decide who is dominant. And if, as is entirely possible, it is an artifact, where does it originate? With the baboons or with their observers? In short, as the authors conclude: "If baboons are constantly testing, trying to see who is allied with whom, who is leading whom, which strategies can further their goals, as recent evidence suggests, then both baboons and scientists are asking the same questions. And to the extent that baboons are constantly negotiating, the social link is transformed into a process of acquiring knowledge about 'what the society is.'"[12] In other terms, "baboons are not *entering into a stable structure* but rather negotiating what that structure will be [...]."[13]

The variety of organizational modes, then, is not the simple product of external variations—whether they be research conditions, ecological contexts, or the differences of the observers. It is more easily explained as that which clearly appears when one asks societies a performative question: baboons do not enter into a society nor do they join a hierarchy or a system of alliances that is already formed and waiting for them. Instead, they explore, which means that they experiment and inquire about what their societies may be. And, in order to do that, they never cease to test "the availability and solidity of alliances without knowing for certain, in advance, which relationships will hold and which will break."[14] This last assertion leads Latour and Strum to propose another contrast, this time between baboon and human societies: the former are complex societies, the latter appear to be complicated ones. The performative definition of the social raises the following questions: How does one do it? What are the practical means actors have to enforce their version of society? When one attempts to answer these questions, however, one of the singularities of baboon society readily appears: they have very few ways of *simplifying*.

Complicated societies have at their disposal symbols and material resources which stabilize some factors, keep them constant, and authorize actors to *take for granted* certain facts, elements, and characteristics; but baboons must ceaselessly renew the inquiries and negotiations that allow them to reach their objectives. Indeed, if, in their social lives, some individual qualities such as age, family ties, or sex appear stable, most of the characteristics that allow them to predict the behavior of others remain subject to constant renegotiations within their relations. Baboons, then, experience a complex society, which means that the solutions they implement to construct or repair the social are never stable and must always be put to work once more. Or, to say it differently, they can only negotiate with the help of their bodies, their social competencies, and the strategies they are able to invent: "Baboons have only 'soft tools' and can only build 'soft' societies. They have nothing more to convince and enlist others in their definitions than their bodies, their intelligence and a history of interactions built up over time. This is a *complex* task and only socially 'smart' and skillful individuals may hope to be successful in baboon society."[15]

Zoo Politikon

Given that baboons, as social actors, "'perform' society to some degree [and] are active participants from the beginning, probing and investigating, negotiating and renegotiating, where would we comfortably place the beginning of political behaviour?"[16] If political relationships are those that consist in negotiating and controlling the behavior of others in order to impose a version of what society should be, it goes without saying that baboons are political beings and that their social ties have to be seen as their means of negotiating and controlling the society they wish for. This is equally true for countless animal societies.

In the past several years, several attempts have been made to break with the "exceptionalist" thesis of the human as sole political animal.[17] I leave aside, here, the abundant research which only recognizes animals as political through the status they may be given within human institutions—whether as citizen or through the attribution of rights.[18] I prefer to adopt another perspective, such as that which Baptiste Morizot has magistrally developed (2016). In his long inquiry about the figure of the diplomat—a figure which helps negotiate new relations with animals and in particular wolves, Morizot suggests that we not "impose upon them the conceptual structures of human politics and join them [instead] in their own political animal interactions."[19] He explains that the conceptual apparatus of modern political philosophy relies on a rigid alternative between contractual relations and trials of strength. One may either be endowed with logos as well as the ability to enter into a contract, or be deprived of it and condemned to exercise or succumb to relations of strength. "A relationship based on rights [*rapport de droit*] is only possible with beings that are able to follow and recognize conventions, rules formulated by speech; that is to say human beings. Every one and everything else depend on trials of strength [...]."[20] The author adds that it is in this dichotomy that the ontological error regarding the animal takes root. The wolf's absence of speech, for example, does not situate it outside the sphere of conventions, rules, and laws. "For if wolves do not enter into contracts, they nonetheless have behaviors that are political, that is to say symbolic: geopolitical behaviors that establish borders, hierarchies, *conventional* behaviors which are intra- and inter-specific."[21]

Thus, wolves' feeding practices are highly ritualized, and access to the product of the hunt follows a precise and complex etiquette, where the dominants (often the parents of the pack) do not necessarily have to assert priority; in a similar vein, but indicative of an even better symbolic ability, marking behaviors via urine, fecal matters, and glandular secretions are signals through which wolves communicate with other packs as well as other species. They mark their territories' boundaries. Morizot explains that, with these markings, a wolf from the same pack can recognize that he is home but a wolf from another pack will see a limit that cannot be transgressed without risk. Along each border delimiting the outside limit of the territory, one can notice another borderline, following the other's inner border and forming in this way a true cartography of territorial distribution, a "geopolitical map, whose signaling system is built upon scents" and whose analogy with human maps is striking.[22] These borders are not rigid; a series of conventions which remain obscure to us organize, once again, the exchanges: a pack venturing upon a foreign territory discontinues its marking; some dispersing[23] wolves do not react to borders as do packs, and likewise, packs behave differently in response to the intention of transient wolves. Other animals, such as badgers and martens, will also leave markings often in close proximity to those of the wolves, as if to initiate a dialog through the intermediary of these markings. These marks, continues Morizot, do indeed belong to the symbolic order since, according to the definition given by anthropologist Roberta Hamayon, their scope is external to them and allows them to evoke something "other" than themselves.[24] They are indeed conventions, "a shared knowledge which, if agreed upon, has a normative effect on behaviors, akin to limitation, incitation or inhibition, and which does not require any physical trial of strength or conflict to be established."[25]

According to this view, borders that are thus materially defined have a geopolitical relevance: they institute, writes Morizot, "complex territorial entities that rely on conventional limits and demand a symbolic activity from animals. Animals do indeed take part in political relations because their decisions about these borders and their spatial structuring, have effects of different scales upon their collective interactions [...]."[26] If we come back to the proposition formulated by Strum and Latour and further extend the hypothesis of a complex dimension of animal political societies, it becomes clear that wolves use their bodies to negotiate their relations with others on the question of the occupation and appropriation of space. The same is true also, when pondering what is the behavior most suitable to the crossing of a previously "settled" space. Where fences oppose a physical barrier to anyone's passage, droppings and marks exert control over others, and the conventional dimension of the control grants it a relatively stable status in terms of its signification—something that might be interpreted as a form of decomplexification of the fabrication of the social. This stability, however, is seriously limited since the conventions established by the marks may be stable (albeit relatively) but the material marks themselves have little stability and need to be maintained to keep their effectiveness—after a few days, these marks evaporate or lose their evocative power, which explains why wolves are always attentive to their freshening.

I would like, next, to combine these two propositions, that of Strum and Latour according to which animals, as political actors, perform their societies by negotiating relations that *give them form*, and that of Morizot who envisions territories as proofs of wolves' membership in the sphere of political beings. The latter theory, that of Morizot, suggests a similar relationship with forms, a double relationship even: the territory is a *form of the social* (a form inscribed in space and geographically distinguishable) and the behaviors it brings forth attest to the animals' capacity to create as well as obey conventions, that is to say *to respect forms*. If Strum and Latour's hypothesis interests me so much, it is because it is a powerful proposition and as I believe or, at least wager, a very fecund one. Because it widens the scope of what is at stakes in the political behavior of animals—not only as a pursuit of local interest but also as that which gives form to the social—it forces us to broaden our attention. One can understand, for example, an animal's defense of its territory as a response to the need of insuring the exclusivity of its resources (although it is not always the case), to gather for itself the conditions that allow it to reproduce, to regulate the rythms of the couples, etc. If, however, one adopts Morizot's thesis according to which "to create a territory" involves geopolitical behaviors, and if one puts to the test Strum and Latour's hypothesis concerning the stakes of the political behaviors, these territorial functions can be read differently. The way animals actively inhabit these territories would appear to be a way that they give form to their societies. This translation opens the inquiry up to other kinds of questions: how can a way of inhabiting a space manufacture sociality? And what kind of sociality is manufactured with it?

To Deterritorialize

If I choose to study the question of animal territories, it is because I would like to answer the proposition made by Latour in *Down to Earth: Politics in the New Climatic Regime*, which states that we need to investigate.[27] To "investigate" here means to describe "dwelling places" (a name Latour proposes to give territories in order to free them from the connotations given to them by the administrative grid of the State), "to add conflicts of interpretation regarding what a given actor is, wants, desires or can do, to conflicts about what other actors are, want, desire or can do."[28] "To define a dwelling place, for a terrestrial, is to list what it needs for its subsistence, and, consequently, what it is *ready to defend*, with its own life if need be. This holds as true for a wolf as for a bacterium [...] What must be documented are the properties of a terrestrial—in all the senses of the word property—by which it is possessed and on which it depends."[29]

To begin this inquiry, I have chosen to focus on birds. This choice is not fortuitous and is not due to any personal preference—except, of course, that birds, namely israeli babblers, were the heroes of my first field study and that Latour and his work were instrumental in making me understand how much they could teach me.[30] I could also have invoked them again in the context of what I just elaborated since these babblers—whom I learned to know by following Israelian ethologist Amotz Zahavi into the Neguev desert—continually invent the most sophisticated strategies to negotiate a society which authorizes competition for a rank in the hierarchy all the while reducing its potential effects. To say it quickly, babblers negotiate constantly, through altruistic acts (rather than open conflicts and trials of strength), the possibility of augmenting their prestige, a prestige that can modify their status in the hierarchy (this status is itself due to the rank of the parents and the birth order). Babblers, in other terms, ceaselessly reinvent the art of compromise.

Birds became the obvious choice because they were, historically, the first to make the territorial question visible and intriguing. The first zoologists who took an interest in that question at the end of the nineteenth century were, as their first descriptions show, visibly impressed and surprised by the pugnacity of the territorial behavior.[31] The first theories put forward motifs that came to be debated in the first decades of the twentieth century: intolerance, male jealousy, and the guarantee of exclusive access to a feeding space. Thus, in a book published in 1868, a German ornithologist, Bernard Altum, states that the distances observed between territories account for their necessity: they are needed to insure food for the young. All species of birds that have a specialized diet will limit their movements to small spaces. They should not settle near other couples because of the danger of famine. They consequently need a territory with a specific size, dependent upon the space's productivity. According to Altum, the function of bird songs is to allow birds to mutually perceive each other and to establish their territories' borders. The author observes that conflicts often begin with songs and that songs continue to be heard during the fights. In 1903, Charles Moffat proposes a theory suggesting that the territory itself is the object of the conflict. The function of the song, as Moffat conceives it, is to advertise the presence, in a particular site, of an unvanquished male, who claims the site as his and announces that he will not allow any male to enter without starting a fight. Why, however, use such an elaborate song where a few notes would suffice? According to Moffat, an elaborate song is an advantage. Given that only winners sing (vanquished birds being reduced to silence), the victorious bird perfects his song. The talentuous singer, therefore, demonstrates his long experience with success and his ability to protect his territory.[32] With this hypothesis, Moffat takes position against the theory of sexual selection (which stated that the function of the song was to attract females). In the same vein, the author states that the birds' brilliant plumage probably evolved, not to seduce a companion but as *war paint* (a kind of warning coloration).[33] "Without, then, wishing to push arguments on this subject too far, I say these bright colors [...] are means by which cock birds impress certain lessons on one another, and if they do not help a bird to *win* his plot of ground, they, at any rate, render his subsequent possession of it less liable to disturbance."[34] In support of this hypothesis, he claims that he has never seen conflicts where birds did not exhibit their most remarkable feathers during the fight. He also asks whether or not the presence of such colored birds obviously perched above a bush "does [...] remind us of a bright little flag, put up—as it were—to mark that such and such area is under such and such dominion?"[35] Furthermore, still according to Moffat—and this is a theory also found in Lorenz (as a convention this time)—the function of a territory is to regulate demographic growth: parcels that distribute a given space end up being integrally distributed between the birds, with the effect of preventing the unchecked growth of the bird population.

Most ornithologists give credit to the Englishman Eliot Howard for the scientific concept of territory. He mentions the theory of territory in *The British Warbler* in 1907 and again in 1920 in *Territory of Bird Life*. It is from this moment on that the question of territory generates enormous interest among the ornithologists. Howard, unaware of the works of Altum and Moffat, will nonetheless come to share some of their intuitions. At a certain moment, males living in a group during winter become intolerant of others; they isolate themselves progressively and confine their movements within a defined space. According to Eliot, a territory serves to meet the need for food and to regulate population. For species living in a colony with unlimited food supply, such as sea birds, the role of the territory is to control the population due to the fact that nesting sites are scarce. Interestingly for Howard the need to regulate the population can be dissociated from the need to secure a zone of sufficient alimentation. Birds can therefore follow different motives when establishing a territory. For example, maintaining exclusive access to resources, which had been accepted as an evident function of territory, does not seem to constitute a universal motive. Thus willow-wrens, which J. M. Dewar observed in 1915, occupy territories with borders that are often quite flexible. Each territory contains a nesting area surrounded by a larger feeding zone that seems to constitute a "common property" where all the birds of the area come to feed undisturbed.[36] Similarly, and there are other examples, David Lack noted in 1933 that the species most pugnacious toward territorial issues do not seem to maintain strict territorial boundaries when feeding their youngsters:[37] if it were a question of resources, however, they would be much more aggressive. With certain birds, females feed outside the territory; this leads Lack (and many others) to suggest that the function of a territory may be to help couples to form by isolating the male. Moreover, certain members of a species can be territorial at certain moments and choose to live in colonies at other times, and they seem to do so without being dictated by a reproductive agenda. David Lack concludes that there is no sufficient proof to affirm that territory constitutes the overarching rule that governs the life of birds. In fact, they suggest that territory seems to be nothing more than a male preoccupation: its real signification may be to "provide the male with a more or less prominent isolated headquarters where he can sing or otherwise display." Except that barely a year later, Tinbergen reports that for the Northern Phalarope, it is the female that claims and defends the territory and attempts to attract a male by sending out mating calls. Still a year later, in 1936, Barbara Blanchard recounts that while tracking the Nuthal White-crowned Sparrows, she realized that what appeared to be a fierce territorial conflict between males was in fact carried out by females.[38]

In two chapters of his book *Evolution of Habits in Birds* (1933), the ornithologist Edmund Selous asks: "Are birds really landed proprietors?" He gives an answer: "Before either a man or a bird can privately appropriate even the narrowest space of land, meaning to resist any other attempts at occupancy thereof because of its own prior right of possession, there must be a conception in the mind of each of what such right personal possession with consequent effect is." He asserts that we are in a position to think that birds "do not appropriate sources of food for themselves," reminding us not to forget that "many of us are familiar with despotic behaviors of individuals *at feeding shelves*."[39]

Territorial Exuberance

I have, so far, considered only a handful of the many scientific findings that were coming out at a remarkably pace during the 1930s and the following decade. But these few cases already show, quite early in the territory debate, what will become the main characteristic of the notion of territory itself: the fact that there are no, or very little, controversies. There is certainly no lack of contradictory data, but these contradictions do not seem to be due to errors of observations (which was the case with baboons when the observations of primatologists went counter to what was expected), nor do they invalidate other studies or allow a particular theory to definitively exclude a competing hypothesis.[40] Researchers became quickly aware of the vast diversity in the ways birds organize themselves. There are no real theoretical controversies, except to contest the power of a hypothesis to provide generalization. There is neither a single rule nor evidence that a territory constitutes a social mold because such rule or evidence does not exist. For these birds, there can be an identical solution to a wide variety of issues, and a single problem can generate multiple solutions. Robert Hinde foregrounds this in his introduction to the special issue of the journal *Ibis* devoted to territories: "The diversity of nature can never be fitted into a system of pigeon-holes."[41] He adds further that "categories are intended only as an aid to discussion"; they are all the more debatable that they can be put to use in many different ways by the same species either simultaneously or in succession; and in other species the usage will vary according to age, sex, habitat, or population density.

It almost feels as if birds were successful in imposing their own questions on the researchers, even warning them against drawing hasty conclusion (Edmund Selous has given a fine example of such impact when he questions the possible effects of feeding on our knowledge of birds).[42] I can't really explain why birds succeeded in such a short time span what will take baboons a few decades to achieve. Could it be that their burden of accounting for the origins of humans exerted such constraints on the sociology that was to study them?[43] It is possible. We also need to take into account the fact that ornithologists, confronted from the start with a diversity of species, have, from early on, cultivated a comparative approach which enabled them to be attentive to the plurality of organizations.[44] But it is also possible that something is happening around territorial behavior: a behavior which, as I have noted, puzzles researchers. Birds often manifest such vitality and power of determination; they spend so much energy and seem in fact so "possessed" by what they are defending that it is not impossible to think that researchers themselves have been compelled by this behavior and have thought: here is something crucial that needs to be accounted for.

Beyond diversity, however, common traits emerge especially in the accounts of those who have observed birds "making" their territory. Most often, during the territorial period (just before the start of spring, but there are many counter-examples because some have winter territories, others occupy them all year, etc.), birds distance themselves progressively from the group and begin to survey a place. They fly over the space in all directions starting from what is progressively being designated as the center (often an overhang, a hill, or a tree branch), passing by repeatedly as if coloring a surface with invisible ink, going from the center to the periphery that is gradually emerging. The boundary becomes a place brimming with activity since it generally lies alongside a neighbor's space that may also spread out. It is probable that these "surveys" accomplish at least two things: on the one hand, the bird makes itself "at home" by forming a deep intimacy with a place it has thus "appropriated" along with its particularities; the space becomes "familiar" and "to inhabit," in this sense, amounts to transforming and making a place one's "own." On the other hand, the way in which birds survey a space to make it their "own" lends support to Jakob von Uexküll's idea that a territory can be the extension of one's own body. Hence all these bodily markings, songs, traces: all these extensions of the body in space that allow it to become itself, and that Michel Serres considered a bit hastily as marks of dirtiness and pollution—it seems to me that Serres's error stems most likely from ascribing to animals a modern and uncritical conception of property, turning birds into little bourgeois landlords concerned with exclusivity.[45]

These practices resemble clearly practices of *appropriation* for two main reasons: they involve the process of making a place one's own and turning it into an extension of one's body. This depends, however, upon keeping the term property and its cognates free from the limits the moderns have imposed upon them. Margaret Morse Nice's observations of the Song Sparrows she followed from March 1928 to February 1938 in Columbus, Ohio, help clarify this. Some of these birds migrate during winter, whereas others remain in the same place and occupy it permanently. Yet their attitude changes entirely depending on the season. The same inhabited space can be a territory at certain times and not at others. The space, I would say, is of variable affectivity. The bird is not the same at all, depending on the time of the year we observe them, and the change is remarkable. Thus, if we can say that the bird makes the space its "own," we can also say the same thing perhaps about the effect the territory has on the bird: the bird has become territorial as an effect of the territory. It is the space that conquers, or appropriates, might we say, the bird. In other words, from our perspective, the space Nice's Song Sparrows inhabit in winter and the one they occupy in summer remain (geographically) the same, whereas from the birds' perspective they cease to be the same at a moment in spring or summer because *the birds themselves are no longer the same*: to qualify the birds at this moment as being territorial is to designate not an essence but a way of being: a way of inhabiting that transforms being or, more precisely, *metamorphoses the assemblages of being and space in time*.

Territory belongs therefore to the regime of appropriation, which is not to say, as I indicated above, that it is an object of appropriation. I use "appropriation" in the sense Souriau gave to the term. As David Lapoujade writes, "To possess does not consists in appropriating a thing or a being. Appropriation involves not property but what is proper. The verb of appropriation should not be used in the reflexive form but in the active form: to possess is not to take ownership of but to render appropriate for …, that is, to cause to exist properly."[46] Or, to further clarify, we could say of being that it makes its existence appropriate to new dimensions.[47] We find a similar idea in a fascinating book that explores within French law itself the possibility of breaking away from the conception of property as sovereign power over things and to think of things instead as environments one may inhabit. The author, Sarah Vanuxem, a jurist, explains that "in the Chleu's mountainous Douars, to appropriate a place consists in conforming it to oneself and in conforming oneself to it; to appropriate a land amounts to attributing it to oneself as well as to making oneself appropriate for it."[48] We can say, again, in reading observations that puzzled researchers, that if the bird *possesses*, it is equally *possessed*: the territory *takes hold* of it. The bird is territorialized: the territory compels it to sing, to survey (as if its existence as a territory depended in this surveying, which is indeed the case), to roam along the borders, and give itself over/lend itself to conflicts. The most enigmatic, and the most intriguing, feature of the conflicts now emerges: according to the majority of researchers, these are conflicts whose outcome is always predictable. The vast majority of conflicts have the same result: the intruder withdraws. But before coming to this enigma, I would like to mention another thing that will be useful not for entirely solving the enigma but for offering some further speculations.

To Territorialize by the Middle

As I mentioned, a theory, long supported by scientists (and popularized by Konrad Lorenz), attributes to territory the function of regulating population density by limiting the possible number of reproductive couples. This theory has received numerous critiques (that it is mostly applicable to humans, for example). The most interesting of these critiques was formulated by the ecologists of the Chicago School working under the direction of Warder Clyde Allee. At the end of the second decade of the twentieth century, they started to focus on "ecological assemblages" and worked within the perspective of an ecology they define as "the science of communities."[49] This has given a highly interesting orientation to their research. Regarding the hypothesis of regulation, they underscore the fact that the effects of overpopulation have been exclusively studied. Overpopulation does present a problem for the animals and is disabling (reducing fertility, delaying the hatching of eggs, reducing food, accumulating waste and excrements, deteriorating the chemical makeup of the environment, spreading diseases and parasites), but the deleterious effects of underpopulation should not be ignored. Under a certain threshold, the effects of the group disappear and, in some species, animals no longer reproduce under certain circumstances. For certain highly visible species, underpopulation has only a benign effect on reproduction; but for others, such as the Muskrat, who live spread out in space, it affects females greatly. Since their period of sexual receptivity is very short, their chance of meeting a male in underpopulated areas would be quite reduced. Territories might thus play a role in what I call *composition* (the expression is the author's): reassembling and separating.

This compositional characteristic of territories could very well prove essential. It might be even more clearly relevant to questions of political organization.[50] By reminding us that territories do more than just separate and that they also reassemble in an *organized manner*, the above-mentioned scientists make perceptible a dimension of territories that is evident but neglected: the fact that they are always *adjacent*. There are no territories without neighbors. There are no territories without exteriority, that is, without another territory. An animal is territorial always in relation with others; a territorial organization, in other words, is a *composition of neighbors*. From this perspective, one could suggest that territories are *forms in space* (and in time), that is, a shaping of form in relation to other forms. Thus, with territories space changes property: it becomes a form that engenders other forms—a milieu, in fact. Birds create forms that compose; that is, elements that give form to society. Each territory is the manifestation of the political invention of a form that composes relations with other forms in a regime of *affinities* in the etymological sense of the word (*ad finitum* or the limit).

Let us presently return to conflicts, whose spectacular dimension has gradually given way to other observations and to another hypothesis. It is because they are spectacular that they impressed researchers; and perhaps it is their whole point: they partake of spectacle. They are postures of threat: songs, parades, agitated gestures, puffing of feathers. Observers discover in fact that territorial conflicts, so often described as fierce, generally make very few victims. This is not all: one should note that their outcome is always highly predictable which, as I mentioned, is a paradox given what is at stake. This predictability owes to a very simple reason: the defensive vigor of the occupier is always superior to the aggression of the intruder. In a 1939 study of dominance in canaries, Shoemaker reports that a bird that is a subordinate in a neutral terrain becomes dominant in its territory. In 1940, Kirkman experiments with moving closer the nests of laughing seagulls that are normally spread 45 cm apart and finds that the pugnacity changes camp depending on whether the same seagull is the current occupant of the nest or the intruder. Aggressive and self-assured when the rapprochement takes place on its own terrain, the bird becomes timid and tentative when it takes the role of the intruder. In his book on aggression, Lorenz notices an invariance in territorial conflicts: the individual bird fights with much more vigor when the fight takes place on its own territory. Moreover, the bird's combatting strength does not stay constantly elevated throughout the space to be defended: it always increases according to how near one gets to a certain territorial center where the conflict occurs, and it decreases as much in the intruder. It is as if there were a gradient of forces at the start of the center, and each bird's affect were correlated to this center.

In the majority of situations involving territorial conflicts, the power to win is always, or almost always, given to the defender so long as it finds itself in the situation of defending the borders of its territory whether it be by force, mimicry, or voice. Howard has already mentioned this in his work, writing "that overmuch importance is attached to the conflicts, that in large number of instances they are mere 'bickerings' and lead to nothing, and that they are now only 'formal,' which means, I suppose, that they are vestigial-fragments of warfare that determined the survival of the species in bygone ages."[51] For Howard, what determines the form and the outcome of conflicts is "the position which a bird occupies whilst fighting is in progress, so its pugnacious nature gains or loses susceptibility."[52] And it is the gain or loss relative to the position that leads Howard to affirm that the conflict is "controlled."[53]

Evidently, we are entitled to ask why these conflicts occur if their outcome is so predictable. They might be chiefly predictable, perhaps, for the observers who accumulate an incredible quantity of experimentations; the experiences of thousands of birds patiently gathered from hundreds and thousands of hours of observations. Birds have no reason to share our outlook—although they most likely learn the forseeable outcome of conflicts through cumulative experience. But perhaps this is also the power of territories which "take," "capture," "possess" those they transform into territorial beings: there may be something in these stories that has to do with "it's stronger than me." Territory, as should now be clear, emerges truly as a device of convention for mobilizing affect—the fact that affects are modified by the birds' position relative to the territory alone should attest to that.

As a conventional device, territory is the object of experimentation by and on conventions: a tentative process of trial and error of borders drawn, negotiations, provocations, challenges, learning, trajectories of experiences creating the forms whereby birds define what will henceforth be their territorialized society: conventions are negotiated, then stabilized. The fact that after a while things very often calm down and conflicts become rarer supports this hypothesis. Birds can move onto other things. This suggests that territory, as a creation of neighborhood, could be, as Baptiste Morizot proposes, a *conventional device for pacification*.[54] This hypothesis could be supported, in certain cases, by what scientists have called the "dear enemy effect"—I say "could be" because we also observe in highly competitive species the inverse effect, known as the "nasty neighbor effect." A number of observations show indeed that the reactions of certain birds are much less aggressive if the intruder is a close neighbor than if it is a less familiar animal occupying a distant territory.[55] Furthermore, this effect is often dynamic because it takes hold gradually (without it being explicable as the effect of habituation) and is modified when circumstances change. More recently, this effect has been observed in interspecific relations.[56]

Moreover, we observe that in a number of cases the intruders of the same species are tolerated as long as they feed but are chased away if they start to parade around or sing. Morizot thinks that wolves also support the hypothesis of pacifying convention: when they pass a border, they cease to mark. According to this conception, the territory would be a spatial configuration that requires proper use: from this border on, certain things are not done—this is what I have called the respect for forms. It is a device-site (dispositif-lieu) that in a way protects against troubles stemming from life in community. Warder Clyde Allee reminded us that territory is not only a space of protection but also a space of rupture with the regime of activity. He contends that continuous activity in a community would lead to excessive demand resulting in exhaustion or death. In protected places, there can be periods of recuperation and relative inaction, when an animal responds no longer, or not very rapidly, to stimuli. In the life of animals, a quantity of "dramatic incidents occur, and there is a strong tendency to record and overemphasize these. Animals, under many conditions, and plants as well, may merely persist […] The quiet retirement of animals capable of extreme activity is often a fundamental part of living."[57]

We could mention many other versions of what could constitute a territory for a bird. As we advance in our research, other territories with other forms, other motifs, and other conventions will appear. Territories could also be sites of creation (*matter for expression*, think of songs), sites that modulate love, sites of life, sites of habit; or still, simply, sites one loves.[58] With these researchers I learned no longer to content myself with saying other "hypotheses," other "perspectives," but other *territories*, other ways of inhabiting and thus of making the world. This is where I believe I follow most faithfully what Latour has taught me and never ceases to teach me: to endeavor to lead this type of inquiry that has so deeply modified anthropology, and of which he recently said that when it is addressed to animals, it entails most of all "learning from other species that there are other ways of existing."[59]

(Translated by Elisabeth Arnould-Bloomfied and Claire Chi-ah Lyu)

Notes

1. "In a sense, what we do is comparative philosophical pedology! We compare types of soils, profiles and horizons that are quite different" [editors' translation]. Bruno Latour, "Redécouvrir la terre," dialogue avec Baptiste Morizot et Pierre Charbonnier, *Tracés: Revue de Sciences humaines* 33 (2017): 229. Online Journal. URL: http://journals.openedition.org/traces/7071; DOI: 10.4000/traces. 7071 (accessed July 31, 2018).
2. "Furry sociologists" is the lovely expression used by Bruno Latour in his post-face to the French translation of Shirley Strum's *Almost Human*, in order to designate baboons since one has stopped asking them the same old questions of hierarchy and dominance. See Bruno Latour, Postface to the French translation of Shirley Strum, *Presqu'humain: Voyage chez les Babouins* (Paris: Eshel, 1990), 337.
3. "A name that is so awkward, so confusing, so meaningless that it deserves to be kept." Bruno Latour, *Reassembling the Social: An Introduction to Actor-Network Theory* (Oxford: Oxford University Press, 2005), 9.
4. Gérard De Vries, *Bruno Latour: Une introduction*, trans. Fleur Courtois-L'Heureux (Paris: La Découverte, 2018), 112.
5. Ibid., 113.
6. Latour, *Reassembling the Social*, 5.
7. Shirley Strum and Bruno Latour, "Redefining the Social Link. From Baboons to Humans," *Social Science Information* 26, no. 4 (1987): 784.
8. Ibid., 785.
9. Ibid. Original emphasis.
10. I speak specifically of the "the primatological history of the baboons" to underline the fact that this history is only one aspect of the baboons' history. These particular episodes have contributed to the knowledge we have of them and has undoubtedly affected their lives and histories—if only because researchers intervene sometimes actively in the course of their lives, accompanying their peregrinations, modifying their relations within the group, with local populations, and more generally with

all those that become interested in the project. One must also add that researchers figure also quite often in the baboons' very designs, as witnessed by Hans Kummer or Thelma Rowell who remarks that they let observers approach when realizing that their presence protects them from predators and enemies. See Hans Kummer, *Vies de singes. Moeurs et structures sociales des babouins hamadryas* (Paris: Odile Jacob, 1993), 109–10. Rowell's interview was carried out as part of a pre-documentary research. Vinciane Despret and Didier Demorcy, "Non Sheepish Sheep," Documentary produced for the exhibition "Making Things Public. Atmospheres of Democracy." dir. Bruno Latour and Peter Weibel. ZKM of Karlsruhe, Spring 2005.

11 See Bruno Latour on Thelma Rowell's sheep: "A Well-articulated Primatology. Reflections of a Fellow Traveler," in *Primate Encounters: Models of Science, Gender and Society*, ed. Linda Fedigan and Shirley Strum (Chicago: University of Chicago Press, 1986), 367, 8.
12 Strum and Latour, "Redefining the Social Link," 788.
13 Ibid. Original emphasis.
14 Ibid., 796.
15 Ibid., 795.
16 Ibid., 797.
17 See, for example, one of the best known of these attempts: that of Frans de Waal and his "political chimpanzee."
18 See Pierre Charbonnier's very interesting article on this subject: "Prendre les animaux au sérieux: de l'animal politique à la politique des animaux," *Tracés: Revue de Sciences humaines*. Online Journal. URL: http://journals.openedition.org/traces/6273; DOI: 10.4000/traces. 6273 (accessed September 5, 2018).
19 Baptiste Morizot, *Les Diplomates: Cohabiter avec les loups sur une autre carte du vivant* (Marseilles: WildProject, 2016), 107 [editors' translation].
20 Ibid., 108.
21 Ibid., 109. Original emphasis. It is possible to broaden the definition of "contract" and to give legitimacy to the wolves' political ability to make contracts with each other and with humans if we follow Latour's second chapter of *Facing Gaia* (a chapter inspired by Michel Serres): "The natural contract is not a deal between two parties, humanity and nature [...], but rather a series of transactions in which one can see how, all along and in sciences themselves, the various types of entities mobilized by geohistory have exchanged the various traits that define their agency." *Facing Gaia: Eight Lectures on the New Climatic Regime,* trans. Catherine Porter (Cambridge: Polity, 2017), 64. Latour evokes the term "morphism" to name these exchanges, a word we will find again linked to politics (and the politics of territories) later in this chapter (politics being understood here as what gives and receives form).
22 Morizot, *Les Diplomates,* 111.

23　"Dispersing" is an ethological term that signifies roaming. [translators' note]
24　Morizot, *Les Diplomates,* 115.
25　Ibid., 5.
26　Ibid., 116.
27　Bruno Latour, *Down to Earth: Politics in the New Climatic Regime*, trans. Catherine Porter (Cambridge: Polity, 2018).
28　Ibid., 87.
29　Ibid., 95. Original emphasis.
30　See Vinciane Despret, *Naissance d'une théorie éthologique: La danse du cratérope écaillé* (Paris: Les Empêcheurs de penser en rond, 1996); and *What Would Animals Say If We Asked the Right Questions?* trans. Brett Buchanan (Minneapolis: University of Minnesota Press, 2016).
31　The term territory appears for the first time in the seventeenth century for European nightingales. It can be found in John Ray's book (1627–1705) *Ornithology of Francis Willughby.* In it, he explains that, as soon as it arrives, the nightingale lays hold of a site which it considers as its property and on which it tolerates no conspecific rival, except for its female—Ray quotes Giovanni Pietro Olina, the author of an ornithological treatise published in Rome in 1622, *L'Uccelliera.* If the term territory appears only in the seventeenth century, the idea that eagles defend a space in order to protect their food exclusivity or that, in some places, one finds only a couple of crows where food is scarce, is mentioned in *l'Historia Animalium* of Aristotle. For a history of these theories and scholarship from the seventeenth century until the first half of the twentieth century, I turned to the works of Margaret Nice ("The Role of Territory in Bird Life," *The American Midland Naturalist* 26, no. 3 [1941]: 441–87) and David Lack ("Early References to Territory in Bird Life," *Condor* 46 [1944]: 108–11).
32　Morizot recalls that the Old Viking law spells out a very different version of Roman law regarding the right to property: "You really possess only what you can protect." *Sur la piste animale* (Arles: Actes Sud, 2018), 49.
33　Charles Moffat, "The Spring Rivalry of Birds," *The Irish Naturalist* 12 (1903): 165.
34　Ibid., 166.
35　Ibid., 165.
36　J. M. Dewar, "The Relation of the Oyster-Catcher to Its Natural Environment," *Zoologist* 19 (1915): 281–91, 340–6.
37　David Lack, "Territoriality Reviewed," *British Birds* 27 (1933): 179–99.
38　Nice, 452.
39　Cited by Nice, 450.
40　See Strum and Latour, "Redefining the social Link."
41　Robert Hinde, "The Biological Significance of the Territory of Birds," *Ibis* 98 (1956): 342.

42 This echoes the later findings in primatology: the suspicion that the theory of domination is linked to the habit of using food to approach them or precisely to make dominance visible. See Thelma Rowell, "The Concept of Social Dominance," *Behavioral Biology* 11 (1974): 131–54.

43 See Bruno Latour and Shirley Strum, "Human Social Origins: Please Tell Us Another Story," *Journal of Social and Biological Structures* 9 (1986): 169–87.

44 I thank Baptiste Morizot, a generous and attentive reader, who drew my attention to this aspect.

45 Michel Serres, *Le Mal propre: Polluer pour s'approprier?* (Paris: Le Pommier, 2012). In this context it would have no doubt been more judicious to look for a model in Roman law since "roman legal matter evades entirely the Cartesian category of the *res extensa*": *dominium*, as property, refers to *dominus*, the master of the house, and constitutes an extension of his person. See Sarah Vanuxem, *La Propriété de la terre* (Marseilles: Wild Project, 2018), 60.

46 [Translators' note: We have translated "*s'approprier*" as "to take ownership of," "*approprier à*" as "to render appropriate for," and "*faire exister en propre*" as "cause to properly exist"].

47 Davis Lapoujade, *Les Existences moindres* (Paris: Minuit, 2017) 60–1.

48 Vanuxem, 13. [Translators' note: A "Douar" is a village or camp and the term "Chleus" designates what is proper to the Berber populations of western Marocco, their language, culture, and territories.]

49 Warder C. Allee, Alfred E. Emerson, Orlando Park, Thomas Park, and Karl P. Schmidt, *Principles of Animal Ecology* (Philadelphia: Saunders, 1949), vii, 3.

50 Bruno Latour, "La Société comme possession: La 'preuve par l'orchestre,'" in *Philosophie des possessions*, ed. Didier Debaise (Dijon: Les Presses du Réel, 2011), 9–34.

51 Eliot Howard, *Territory in Bird Life* (London: Collins, 1948), 112.

52 Ibid.

53 Ibid., 80.

54 Morizot, *Sur la piste animale*, 71.

55 Elodie Briefer, Fanny Rybak, and Thierry Aubin, "When to Be a Dear Enemy: Flexible Acoustic Relationships of Neighbouring Skylarks, *Alauda arvensis*," *Animal Behaviour* 76, no. 4 (2008): 1319–25.

56 Allison E. Johnson, Christina Masco, and Stephen Pruett-Jones, "Song Recognition and Heterospecific Associations between 2 Fairy-Wren Species (Maluridae)," *Behavioral Ecology* 29, no. 4 (2018): 821–32.

57 Allee et al., 6.

58 Nice, 448; Allee et al., 8.

59 Bruno Latour, "Qui a la parole ? Anti- ou multi-espèce?" Review, published in *Le Monde,* march 1, 2018 of *La Révolution antispéciste,* ed. Ynes Bonnardel, Thomas Lepeltier, and Pierre Sigler (Paris: PUF, 2018).

Bibliography

Allee, Warder C., Alfred E. Emerson, Orlando Park, Thomas Park, and Karl P. Schmidt. *Principles of Animal Ecology.* Philadelphia: Saunders, 1949.

Briefer, Elodie, Fanny Rybak, and Thierry Aubin. "When to Be a Dear Enemy: Flexible Acoustic Relationships of Neighbouring Skylarks, *Alauda arvensis.*" *Animal Behaviour* 76, no. 4 (2008): 1319–25.

Charbonnier, Pierre. "Prendre les animaux au sérieux: de l'animal politique à la politique des animaux." *Tracés: Revue de Sciences humaines.* Online Journal. URL: http://journals.openedition.org/traces/6273; DOI: 10.4000/traces. 6273 (accessed September 5, 2018).

Charbonnier, Pierre, Bruno Latour and Baptiste Morizot. "Redécouvrir la terre" dialogue avec Baptiste Morizot et Pierre Charbonnier. *Tracés: Revue de Sciences humaines* 33 (2017). URL: http://journals.openedition.org/traces/7071; DOI: 10.4000/traces. 7071 (accessed September 5, 2018).

Despret, Vinciane. *Naissance d'une théorie éthologique. La danse du cratérope écaillé.* Paris: Les Empêcheurs de penser en rond, 1996.

Despret, Vinciane. *What Would Animals Say If We Asked the Right Questions?* Translated by Brett Buchanan. Minneapolis: University of Minnesota Press, 2016.

Despret, Vinciane, and Didier Demorcy. "Non Sheepish Sheep." Documentary produced for the exhibition "Making Things Public. Atmospheres of Democracy." Directed by Bruno Latour and Peter Weibel: ZKM of Karlsruhe, 2005.

De Vries, Gerard. *Bruno Latour: Une introduction.* Translated by Fleur Courtois-L'Heureux. Paris: La Découverte, 2018.

Dewar, J. M. "The Relation of the Oyster-Catcher to Its Natural Environment." *Zoologist* 19 (1915): 281–91, 340–46.

Hinde, Robert, "The Biological Significance of the Territory of Birds." *Ibis* 98 (1956): 340–69.

Howard, Eliot. *Territory in Bird Life.* London: Collins, 1948.

Johnson, Allison E., Christina Masco, and Stephen Pruett-Jones. "Song Recognition and Heterospecific Associations between 2 Fairy-Wren Species (Maluridae)." *Behavioral Ecology* 29, no. 4 (2018): 821–32.

Kummer, Hans. *Vies de singes. Moeurs et structures sociales des babouins hamadryas.* Paris: Odile Jacob, 1993.

Lack, David. "Early References to Territory in Bird Life." *Condor* 46 (1944): 108–11.

Lack, David. "Territoriality Reviewed." *British Birds* 27 (1933): 179–99.
Lapoujade, David. *Les Existences moindres*. Paris: Editions de Minuit, 2017.
Latour, Bruno. *Down to Earth: Politics in the New Climatic Regime*. Translated by Catherine Porter. Cambridge: Polity Press, 2018.
Latour, Bruno. *Facing Gaia: Eight Lectures on the New Climatic Regime*. Translated by Catherine Porter. Cambridge: Polity Press, 2017.
Latour, Bruno. Postface to the French translation of Shirley Strum. *Presqu'humain: Voyage chez les Babouins*. Paris: Eshel, 1990.
Latour, Bruno. "Qui a la parole? Anti- ou multi-espèce?" *Le Monde*, March 1, 2018. Review of edited collection: Yves Bonnardel, Thomas Lepeltier, and Pierre Sigler, eds. *La Révolution antispéciste*. Paris: PUF, 2018.
Latour, Bruno. *Reassembling the Social: An Introduction to Actor-Network Theory*. Oxford: Oxford University Press, 2005.
Latour, Bruno. "Redécouvrir la terre," dialogue avec Baptiste Morizot et Pierre Charbonnier. *Tracés: Revue de Sciences humaines* 33 (2017): 229. Online Journal. http://journals.openedition.org/traces/7071; DOI: 10.4000/traces. 7071 (accessed July 31, 2018).
Latour, Bruno. "La Société comme possession: La 'preuve par l'orchestre.'" In *Philosophie des possessions*. Edited by Didier Debaise. 9–34. Dijon: Les Presses du Réel, 2011.
Latour, Bruno. "A Well-Articulated Primatology. Reflections of a Fellow Traveler." In *Primate Encounters: Models of Science, Gender and Society*. Edited by Linda Fedigan and Shirley Strum. 358–82. Chicago: University of Chicago Press, 1986.
Latour, Bruno, and Shirley Strum. "Human Social Origins: Please Tell Us Another Story." *Journal of Social and Biological Structures* 9 (1986): 169–87.
Latour, Bruno, Baptiste Morizot and Pierre Charbonnier. "Redécouvrir la terre." *Tracés: Revue de Sciences humaines* 33 (2017). URL: http://journals.openedition.org/traces/7071; DOI: 10.4000/traces. 7071 (accessed 5 September 2018).
Moffat, Charles. "The Spring Rivalry of Birds." *The Irish Naturalist* 12 (1903): 152–66.
Morizot, Baptiste. *Les Diplomates: Cohabiter avec les loups sur une autre carte du vivant*. Marseilles: WildProject, 2016.
Morizot, Baptiste. *Sur la piste animale*. Arles: Actes Sud, 2018.
Nice, Margaret. "The Role of Territory in Bird Life." *The American Midland Naturalist* 26, no. 3 (1941): 441–87.
Rowell, Thelma. "The Concept of Social Dominance." *Behavioral Biology* 11 (1974): 131–54.
Serres, Michel. *Le Mal propre: Polluer pour s'approprier?* Paris: Le Pommier, 2012.
Strum, Shirley. *Presqu'humain: Voyage chez les Babouins*. Paris: Eshel, 1990.
Strum, Shirley, and Bruno Latour. "Redefining the Social Link. From Baboons to Humans." *Social Science Information* 26, no. 4 (1987): 783–802.
Vanuxem, Sarah. *La Propriété de la terre*. Marseilles: Wild Project, 2018.

8

Composing with the "Animal Side"

Elisabeth Arnould-Bloomfield

This work comes out of a concern that my research on animals was both removed from their lives and skirting the vast domain of animal science and practical knowledges. The recent tradition of philosophical and anthropological critique I was working from was certainly not foreign to these concerns. Several of the most important philosophers of the last twenty years have staged encounters with real animals and called upon us to replace our philosophical abstractions with less instrumental creatures. Derrida, as you well know, casts his cat as the star of his critical performance in *The Animal Therefore That I Am*.[1] J. C. Bailly follows a deer into the conceptual thickets of *The Animal Side*. These animals and the new attention they commend have become something of a litmus tests for all who want to think about animals today. They keep reminding us that, regardless of discourse, philosophical tradition, or critical voice, speaking about animals cannot be done in absentia. It requires seeing and being attentive to those we meet.

Although this recent appeal to flesh and blood animals remains compelling to me, I have also found it disappointing. Instead of fostering animal knowledge and connecting with its practices—both scientific and mundane—this new "animal realism" has remained largely skeptical and intransitive. Bound to a post-Kantian critical outlook which insulates nature from thought, it has made quick work of the reality it unearthed. Derrida's lively cat, for example, is soon reframed within issues of reference and linguistic inscription and written off as ultimately unknowable. Likewise, in Bailly's essay, and despite a detour through the science of ethology, animals are wrested away from general knowledge—scientific or otherwise. They stay on "their sides" of the world, real but radically other.

Although this postmodern approach has its usefulness, it is also problematic. Skepticism may indeed be helpful when pointing at the arrogance of anthropocentrism or the ethical limitations of our "rights" tradition, but it also hinders our relationship with animals. Its emphasis on the "radical otherness of nature" encourages both respect for its sublimity and incuriosity for the mundane. It furthers our traditional disregard for ordinary skills and practices (husbandry, training, domestic relations) and participates as well in philosophy's disdain for positivistic "animal science." This separation with "external" knowledge is, of course, problematic and, in the long run, untenable. It cuts itself off from most recent important discoveries about animal lives and behaviors. And it perpetuates, however unwittingly, the purifying dualism of neo-Kantian philosophies which keeps nature out of bounds and apart from culture. Postmodern animals are relegated on the side of a reality without clear translation. They do not participate in our knowledge any more than we are implicated in their nature.

It is easy to see how this approach, which grants animals the dubious benefit of an unthinkable nature, is at once a critical boon and a liability. It may help Derrida or Bailly with their critique of anthropocentrism but it also furthers the illusion of human exception by keeping us alone on the side of culture and denying animals a role in the construction of knowledge. Recent thinkers, ethologists, and philosophers of science have underscored the limits of these postmodernist and skeptical philosophies and shown that, in contrast with these formulations that keep apart pure mind and world, a hybrid approach that focuses on natural–cultural relations and beings is central to a rethinking of both animals and humans. Bruno Latour, in particular, advocates a "middle-knowledge" that studies "the way things are tied with our collectives and subjects" instead of focusing on "animals in themselves."[2] This relational approach frees the multiplicities of contacts and translations previously immobilized by the epistemological reticence of the postmoderns. It furthers many of their posthumanist goals but also calls for the inventions of experimental practices and the speculations of science. For Latour and many of his fellow relational thinkers, animal "reality" is not ours to decide, nor does it oppose itself to the limits of our thinking. It exists within propositions and practices that actively create the conditions for its understanding. And it is, most importantly perhaps, contingent upon what animals have to say.[3]

In what follows, I propose to read the French writer and philosopher Jean-Christophe Bailly's recent essay on animals in light of Latour's nonmodern approach to knowledge and epistemology. Bailly's essay is a particularly good candidate for such revisioning because it is torn between a deep longing for intimacy with animals and an equally sturdy belief in the abyssal nature of human–animal difference. Unlike other contemporary philosophers who remain more clearly focused on a deconstructive reappraisal of humanist discourse, Bailly follows animals into the deepest recesses of their worlds. His pursuit, like Derrida's critical tracking, begins with the kind of representational "epoche" that comes with today's questioning of anthropocentrism. He takes us inside the worlds and behaviors of animals and even uses an early (Uexküllian) version of ethology to buttress his intuitions about animal awareness. For all its insights, however, Bailly's knowledge remains provisional and vacillating. He may sidle up ("*côtoyer*") to the animal world but struggles to connect with it. And it is the etiology of this disconnect that I would like to study here in contrast with Bruno Latour's relational approach. Retracing the steps Bailly follows to get closer to the fullness of nature's meaning—his revisiting of the Rilkian open and subsequent recourse to a Merleau-Pontian brand of ethology—I will show that the remote connections these steps establish can be tightened and fleshed out.

I

The tension between Bailly's desire for closeness and skeptical caution is apparent at the very outset of the essay in the encounter between the author and a deer on a dark country road. As I mentioned earlier, chance encounters such as this play an important critical role in animal philosophy. They act as a kind of epistemological shifter that interrupts discourse and makes way for the apprehension of a pure phenomenal presence. In the case of this particular encounter, the author's sudden contact with the bounding deer brings what Jane Bennett describes as a transfer "from knowledge to acute sensory activity."[4] And this transfer is in turn so impactful that it creates the feeling of a perfect, synaesthetic, apprehension that fuses contact and vision in a singular "eye touching." "It was," writes Bailly, "as if, with my eyes, in that instant, for the duration of that instant, I had touched some part of the animal world, Touched, yes, touched with my eyes, despite the impossibility."[5] As Bailly dutifully notes here, "touching with one's eyes" is literally impossible—no empirical or theoretical pursuit can appropriate the truth of its object. I will come back later to this skeptical assessment. For now, I would like to note that this improbable synaesthesia is nonetheless a good paradigm for

Bailly's animal knowledge because it programs an approach that needs to be both striving for perceptual immediacy and preserving its neutrality of vision. Bailly is looking for a knowledge that would offer this perfect combination of percept and vision, intimacy and distance; and if he turns to the science of ethology, or rather its Uexküllian iteration, it is because ethology appears to offer both empirical immediacy and theoretical distance and neutrality.

Ethology is, however, the second of two methodological steps in Bailly's progressive account of animal awareness. Before coming to his more pointed investigation of the creatures behind the gaze, Bailly makes a first incursion into their modalities of being—and seeing—through a reading of the Rilkian "open."[6] The notion is a well-rehearsed one. It is a favorite and often polemical tool of philosophers from Heidegger to Agamben. And if Bailly chooses to engage with it anew, it is because it helps him redefine, against Heidegger's critical read—and also against Rilke's effusive one—the inchoate expanse of animal vision. What the Rilkian notion allows, first and foremost, is a way to address the question of animal awareness without comparing it to human mental processes. The "open" eludes classical questions of animal intelligence or degree of consciousness because it names a perceptual expanse: a place where "no formative intention has yet to penetrate."[7] This formlessness is the very reason why Heidegger finds it profoundly lacking in meaning and calls it "poor in world."[8] But it is also, and conversely, the source of the power Rilke and Bailly grant it. For the latter thinkers, the open designates a dimension of the world which precedes understanding and the mobilization of language. It opens a space of "signifiance […] a possible open, still indeterminate meaning" which "substitutes a sort of dispersal […] to the percussive impact of difference that is produced by discourse."[9] Bailly calls this formless apprehension of the world "pensivity"—the equivalent of human contemplation—and it is clear that this pensive approach, however different it may be in each and every species, is what allows all animals their "share of the visible."[10]

All of this is well known. What is newer, and perhaps more interesting, is Bailly's pointed focus on the sharing of the open between men and animals. Rilke himself has touched upon this idea of a common sensual sharing among and between creatures. But Bailly's take on this community of the visible—and on its epistemological potential—is much soberer than Rilke's romantic view. What the latter perceives as a perceptual medium that allows living beings to apprehend the world in common, the former sees as a bare dimension of general awareness. Bailly does believe, like his predecessor, that all life draws "from a sort of phreatic layer of the perceptible, a kind of remote, undivided, uncertain reservoir."[11] But he also sees the sharing of this reserve as strictly *distributive* and not *transitive*: it is what all species apprehend perceptually but do not interpret and communicate identically. And the suggestion that we all share the open is, for Bailly, quite a minimalist affair. It simply means that all living creatures are aware of sharing a phenomenal world and that "their perceptual experience, without implying reflexive consciousness, gives meaning to the possibility of an exploratory activity."[12] What is at stakes then, in this assertion that we share the world of percepts, is both minor yet momentous in its impact on our understanding of the animal world. It is minor because the idea that animals are present to a world they see and hear is certainly not new. But it is also significant because the shifts in meaning that come with this focus on sensory awareness have both ethical and epistemological consequences. To say, indeed, that making sense is not exclusive to man's reflexive (Cartesian) consciousness but is a component of the sensual experience of all creatures is a true game changer. First, because establishing that the world is "seen by other creatures" puts an end to the credo of "human exclusivity," and suggests—as does Bailly himself—that we should give them a say in a new zoopolitics of nature. Second, because betting on these different yet equal animal experiences implies that we should change, quite radically, our approach to animal knowledge. This break with an anthropocentrist tradition is precisely what Bailly has in mind when he critiques Rilke's bet on the universal familiarity of the open. For Bailly, any suggestion that interspecies differences can be bridged is not only hopelessly angelic but also part of a scheme that trivializes the very notion of perceptual animal awareness. If all animals—including humans—have a unique sensual perspective, no one perspective can reflect and understand all others. To believe otherwise is to have already stepped out of the open's democratic "sharing of the visible" and opted for the old exceptionalist take on human experience and knowledge. We are all familiar with this view—that of Heidegger—according to which the open (and animals) can only be meaningful in reference to human thinking. Such reference, as Bailly well knows, can only bring us back to old dualist dogmas and bring us down the wrong epistemological path. It leads us to either anthropomorphize animal awareness or disqualify its interiority as unknowable. Either way, it is the belief that we are "more equal"[13] in perception and awareness than other animals, which allows us to think that we can divine their minds from the recesses of our own psyche. And it is because such dogmatic anthropomorphism contradicts most clearly the empirical lessons of the open that Bailly turns to a different kind of experience and knowledge.

It is not by chance, then, that Bailly chooses to end his sections on the open with a second and more problematic version of his initial deer encounter. This rewriting, which he borrows from a pre-romantic novel (*Anton Reiser*), offers a thoroughly intransitive meeting scene: one in which communication and understanding remain suspended.[14] The meeting takes place at the knackers where Anton Reiser, the eponymous hero of the novel, comes to see and feel the elusive difference between men and cattle. A quote from the novel shows him

> often (standing) for hours observing a calf's head, eyes, mouth and nose, and just as with strangers, he leaned as close as possible toward it, often in the foolish delusion that it might perhaps be possible to gradually think himself into the being of such an animal. His greatest desire is to know the difference between himself and the beast, and occasionally he became so absorbed in observing it that he truly believed he has sensed for a moment the nature of the creature's existence.[15]

Bailly's reading of this scene links Anton Reiser's strange and inconclusive embrace with the animal to the hero's existential instability. Anton Reiser is lost in the world, gripped by anguish and unsure of the limit that separates man and cattle. This shaky foundation does not allow him to "frame his encounter," let alone enter the calf's mind through experiment or empathy. His only option, says Bailly, is to let "border vacillate" and "wander with the calf in a space without limits," which he describes as a "reservoir of existence."[16] And this vacillation at the limit of knowledge creates, writes Bailly, "a threshold effect" that speaks to the possibility of relation but only within the division of difference.[17]

Bailly's reading of Anton Reiser's encounter appears to emphasize the emptiness of a liminal space where experience yields very little. But this skeptical moment is also open to a more pragmatic interpretation in which this threshold is a perfect paradigm for the kind of limited perceptual encounter Bailly has attempted to describe. The contemplation of the calf's head, in particular, offers a useful illustration of the vision Bailly is after because it describes an instance of opacity and myopia in an essay otherwise full of far-seeing gazes. Until now, vision in Bailly's text has had a mostly expansive role: parsing out the visible, unlocking its "*signifiance*," reflecting animal pensivity. It is, here, short-circuited: jammed against the fragmented pieces of the calf's head and obscured by their materiality. Instead of a meaningful exchange between the observer and the calf's *visage*, Morris's text shows a gaze that pores over and touches, again and again, the material and opaque limit of the animal's head. Anton Reiser literally "*touches with his eyes*,"[18] the physical threshold of the calf's body. He does so over and over because his vision fails to give him access to the being of the calf, but also because this failure is the very condition for the success of a different kind of experience: one that opens to the material singularity of the other.

II

Bailly's treatment of Anton Reiser's encounter is an obvious echo of the first peculiar visual touch associated with the initial encounter. Here again, the eyes "touch" tentatively what their gaze hopes to theorize and grasp. But the scope and meaning of this grasping is narrowed down. To "touch with one's eyes," according to Anton Reiser's experience, is to experience the paradoxical intimacy of an outside gaze. Such contemplation does not interpret or penetrate. Instead it lets itself be informed by another's form and style. And its intimacy comes from being passively, but thoroughly, opened to the singularity of what it sees. The approach it prescribes, then, is the same as that of ethology. It is an empirical method observing from outside the appearances and worlds of animals. And if Bailly turns to this science, or rather its early Uexküllian rehearsal, it is because its "observable melding of subjective experience and world" is uniquely able to rectify overly romantic interpretations of Rilke's open and give it its true, external meaning.[19]

At the time Bailly writes the *Animal Side*, ethology is a familiar science. Uexküll is, by then, an almost obligatory reference in contemporary philosophical texts, from Agamben to Deleuze.[20] And Bailly turns to ethology for the same reasons many animal thinkers do: because it corrects both mechanical views of nature and post-romantic anthropocentric views on animal interiority. His recourse to ethology is therefore not particularly new nor does it claim to be. It is nonetheless useful in that it allows him to transform the more obsolete (interior) part of the Rilkian open into a modern, objective, and zoocentric animal science. What Bailly sees in Uexküll's theory is a knowledge that acknowledges the perspective of individual animals while disentangling it from human subjectivity. He also sees a method which reconstructs these points of views from outside and without any of the projections of human psychology or cognitive science. Uexküll's approach and methods are, indeed, based on two fundamental principles: (1) that animals do not live in the seemingly global world of human percepts and meanings and (2) that they only perceive things that have meaning for them and construe their meaning in acting. In the world of an animal, in other terms, objects take the meaning of the action they are involved with. (The famous Uexküllian tick, for example, perceives only three things: the smell of the butyric acid, the heat of the mammal's body, and the warm liquid of the mammal, because these affects are what makes it feel the mammal, drop on its body and drink its blood.) This meaningful synergy between sensory organs, milieu, and affects is what Uexküll has called an "umwelt." Bailly also describes it as "the skein that every animal forms for itself by winding itself into the world according to its means" (Bailly, 49).[21] This conception of an animal umwelt as a visible interplay of creature and world allows Bailly to give a thoroughly unromantic, external rather than internal, reading of the open. The umwelt is a behavioral map ("skein") drawn by the scientist "who makes an inventory of what makes an animal act and react [and who may then] infer what the animals perceive and what the perceived things mean for them."[22] Ethology makes it possible, in other words, to observe and describe rather than speculate on animal subjectivity. Because it defines this subjectivity as an ethos—a constellation of behavior—rather than an interiority—the inner essence of a mind—it offers an altogether different idea of animal consciousness, as far removed from Cartesian reflexivity as it is from eighteenth-century romantic interiority. And because it gives us insight into each animal's singular solution to the problem of its existence, it brings us in close proximity with an animal's manner of being.

But what is exactly Bailly's understanding of Uexküll's ethology in *The Animal Side*? What are the power and limitations of its outside vision? And what exactly does it allow us to see? These questions are important for a couple of reasons. First, ethology is neither a unified science nor a homogenous philosophy. As a science, it runs the gamut from the behaviorisms of its early scientific formalizations to today's self-searching practices. As an ontology, it is equally split between such interpretations as Heidegger's that see umwelts as captive systems and the more generous and relational readings of Merleau-Ponty and Deleuze.[23] It is therefore important to show where Bailly's own onto-ethology fits. Second, if it is relatively easy to understand Bailly's attraction to ethology's visual epistemology, it is difficult to pin down exactly the kind of knowledge it affords him. There seems to be a kind of rift in Bailly's ethology. On the one hand, he proposes a version of umwelt theory that shows animal worlds to be immediately manifest. On the other, the natural side is presented as disconnected and not readable in its entirety. It appears to be made of fragments, partial images such as: "the stippled feathers of a peregrine falcon,/the pink and green of the body and wings of an elephant hawkmoth,/the infinite tracking shots of great swarms of birds,/the way ducks and Swans have of putting their head under their wings."[24] These ethological fragments abound in the last part of the essay. They conjugate a kind of Adamic dictionary: man's imperfect pastiche of what Bailly calls, after Plotinus, the "poem of nature."[25] But why is Bailly's vision so split and what are the gnoseological consequences of this rift on his onto-ethology?

Bailly's ethological vision remains divided because it continues to be faithful to the dualism of post-Kantian phenomenology and its implicit "bifurcation of nature." Whitehead has called "bifurcation of nature" the separation of the world into secondary qualities—which belong to the perceiving subject—and primary qualities—which belong to physical nature.[26] The red of the sunset, for example, is a product of our minds, while the molecules and electric waves are elements of nature. Bailly's ethology, based on observing animal's sensual appearances likewise keeps separate the subjective and the objective: animals' styles and their noumenal reality. It ignores in particular, as has been made clear earlier, any scientific speculation and limits itself to the deciphering of phenomenal appearances. Its apprehension of animals seems therefore limited to their visible forms and it is difficult to see, indeed, how the grasp of Bailly's experiential ethologist could bridge the gap that separates him from "real nature" to articulate anything like a "primary knowledge."

Bailly, who is undoubtedly aware of these epistemological difficulties, has devised an apparent solution to this dilemma: to shift all knowledge on the side of nature and to reduce the role of human subjects to that of contemplators of an auto-poietic and auto-noetic nature. This solution which eliminates man's role in the knowledge process and makes nature the creator and interpreter of its own grammar is an interesting one—and a favorite of phenomenologists such as Merleau-Ponty. It suggests that the gap between human experience and the realities of nature can be mended if one renounces man's external knowledge—whether subjective or rational—to make him mere contemplator of nature's meaningful spectacle. The knowledge gap exists, indeed, only if man adds his own perspective to nature's spectacle, but it is eliminated in a scheme where nature is creator of its own laws (of the noumenal world) and interpreter of the forms (phenomenal reality) which it decodes for us. Bailly's solution, then, is to replace the human "book of nature" with the "poem of nature." The human book allows an opaque nature to become imperfectly readable through experience or scientific calculations. The "poem of nature," on the other hand, requires no translations. It thinks and writes itself in its beings.[27]

This agential shift from humans to animals is already, as we remember, at the core of Uexküll's ethology. The main move of his behavorial biology was indeed to step away from mechanical science toward an observation of meaningful animal umwelts. The German scientist was also beholden to a religious ontology that saw in nature a plan or musical composition harmonizing the semiotic bubbles of the umwelts. And Bailly shares these two principles of Uexküll's onto-ethology. What remains different, however, between Uexküll's and Bailly's ethology is the degree to which humans (scientists and philosophers) participate in the elaboration of the picture. Although Uexküll's observational method gives animals their dues in the construction of meaning (animals make the signs we read), it also draws from other biological practices to determine the sensory apparatus of the animals he observes—dissecting the eye of the fly for example. Uexküll scientists, therefore, still do half of the work, whereas for Bailly, nature does all the work. Humans merely contemplate it.

Bailly draws both from Merleau-Ponty and Plotinus to work out this displacement of knowledge onto nature. These two approaches are for him complementary. Merleau-Ponty's own reading of Uexküll offers him an individual perspective showing each animal to be its very own creator of meaning.[28] Plotinus's nature's philosophy extends this auto-poietic and auto-noetic power to the entirety of nature. For Merleau-Ponty, thus, animals are not simply determined by an immutable link between perception and environment. Their behavior is adaptive and plastic. It is an interpretive response which elaborates itself according to their needs and wants. Contrary to Heidegger, who sees the umwelt as a closed behavioral loop and deprives animal responses of both freedom and meaning, Merleau-Ponty believes it to be creative and meaningful. For Merleau-Ponty, animal behavior is indeed creative because it is a relation: a co-elaboration with a changing environment and not a mechanical construct. As such, it is not a conditioned or instinctual response and cannot be accounted for through the simple causality of traditional science. Merleau-Ponty prefers to think of behaviors as "styles": forms enacting their own meaning. The behavior of an animal, he writes, is never "the manifestation of a finality, but rather of an existential value of manifestation, of presentation."[29] It is "a melody that sings itself […] at once a song proffered and a song heard within the self."[30]

This shift from instinct to style (and from human meaning to animal performance) is the crux of Bailly's ethology. It is also the most important feature of an ontology which he borrows from Plotinus's philosophy of nature. Plotinus, like Merleau-Ponty, believes that life does not need the complement of thought. It *is* thought. As he writes in his *Enneads* (30th treatise), nature (*phusis*) "contains in itself a silent contemplation […] every [one of its] li[ves] is a form of thought."[31] In this philosophy, which conflates the world's productions (*poien*) with its thinking (*theorein*), nature's deployment is also a hermeneutic performance. Like Ion's *hermeneia* in Plato's text, its truth is not external.[32] It does not refer to outside schemes: it is its own production, its own "poem." And it is easy to see the appeal of this vision of nature for Bailly and his ethology. The link it establishes between beings and thought echoes what Bailly explored earlier in the text as the "pensivity" of animals—their participation to a "logos" that is not ours but the incorporated *nous* of the sensible world. If, indeed, as Bailly explains in "Le Moindre souffle" ("The Slightest Breath"), nature is no longer assimilated to the thought we have but to the thought it is; it no longer is the passive recipient of our intellection but "that by which the perceptible thinks itself into intelligibility."[33] Such thinking deeply transforms traditional scientific and philosophical approaches by not only equating intellection and process, but also giving nature meaning and agency. In this reenchanted vision of a meaningful world, nature is no longer the passive object of human thought. It becomes the "effectuation of its own cogito," folding being and thought into each other as the "logos of the sensible world."[34] And what Bailly's re-materialized Cogito appears to offer here is a solution to the problem of knowledge: it seems to solve the dilemma of bifurcated thinking by moving all semiosis onto the nature pole.

What remains open, however, within this new *cosmo-cogito*, is the question of what to do with human knowledge. How do you "know" a poem? How do you evaluate its performance without measuring or translating it? The answer Bailly suggests is not really an epistemological one. It is more of an aesthetic solution that keeps knowledge within nature and only allows for human contemplation. Nature's auto-poiesis needs no other translation than that of its phenomena. These phenomenal appearances are, on Bailly's account, its thoughts, and merely need to be reflected in the very kind of light mirroring ("touching") gaze that has been Bailly's graal since the onset of the text. Contemplation, for Bailly, is the only modality needed to grasp the semiotic dance of nature's animal forms. Yet, what remains obviously unsettled in this phenomenal and contemplative scheme is the question of translation: How do you find out how nature works, not just how it looks? How can ethology—or any science for that matter—be simply contemplative? And is Bailly's phenomenal contemplation a real solution to the modern "bifurcation of knowledge"? Can it ever mend the gap between the phenomenal and noumenal worlds? Or does it simply deepen the gap between perception and knowledge?

Bailly's depiction of his contemplative encounter with a bat in the *Animal Side* illustrates the need for these questions. The meeting is set up, as expected, so as to reflect the now familiar agential shift from human to animal. The bat, Bailly writes, "puts together a sort of three dimensional map in which every irregularity (a wall, a reed, a wire, a flying insect), identified by the return of a sound wave the creature sends out, becomes a point or a series of points that the small winged mammal integrates and interprets at full speed."[35] Bailly's choice of the map trope is brilliant but problematic. It is a good demonstration of how the bat's behavior (its haphazard flight) creates its own material-semiotic diagram, a diagram readily read by men. But it also provides a very simplified version of what a map is for the bat as well as for us. The bat's map Bailly draws, here, is strictly *analog*. It is an exact physical replica of its movements. This implies that the bat's map is literal through and through. To say it with a well-worn phrase, the implication here is that *the bat's map is the territory*. But like any map, the bat's is only partially analog and implies some degree of *digital* encoding. The analog or mimetic element of spatial movement is only the transposition of an entirely different and inaccessible code: echolocation. And not only is this perceptual system invisible to us, it is also perfectly opaque, without the help of the human mind, its speculations and, in this particular case, its biological science.

My point, here, which I make with Whitehead's and Latour's help, is that bat's maps are not readily readable. It is certainly possible to become better acquainted with them and to decipher what they mean, but it requires more than contemplation. And Bailly's empiricism is not enough because his contemplation continues to involve only the sensual and perceptual operations of the human mind in the knowledge of nature. His solution privileges what Whitehad calls "knowledge (only) in the mode of presentational immediacy," such as contemplation.[36] And it continues to foster the modern division of knowledge between perception and reason, subject and object, appearances and reality because it is incapable of imagining, a more radical empiricism, one that would also include "perception in the mode of causal efficacy."[37] This other, non-sensuous form of intuition, which concerns the apprehension of causal relationships, time and space, process etc., is needed to ensure that the experimenter be present in the world in the same manner as his experiment—or, to say it differently, that he be assured of the commensurability between nature's expressiveness and his own intuitions on the relatedness of things. Indeed, if Bailly's ethologist wishes to know animals beyond a mere play of shadows, he needs to stop limiting himself to his strict sensualism, get back to the thinking he has set aside and recognize that it is made of the same stuff as the world and its process. This would allow him, for example, to give a more accurate picture of ethology and show that his animal contemplations are nothing if not co-created with other, more formal, knowledges. Without this co-construction, the bat's map would be strictly unreadable and the bat itself would appear to us as a fuzzy object flying erratically.[38] I do not mean to be crass in pointing out this small inconsistency in Bailly's vision. This vision is compelling and is truly borne by a desire to connect and communicate with animal styles and manners of being. But Bailly's genuine longing for connection with a meaningful world does not follow through to its radically empiricist conclusion—one that states that human concepts and natural things are immanent. It is hijacked by a modern epistemology that keeps our minds separate from intelligent nature.

In spite of its attempt to give animals more say in our knowledge, Bailly's contemplative empiricism fails to offer a convincing alternative to more traditional epistemologies. This failure is not entirely his alone. It is that of a modern epistemology which insists upon separating human and animal sides, experience and science. Such dualism condemns knowledge to shuttle itself from the subjective pole to the objective and back again. But it is incapable structurally to conceive of a hybrid way of knowing. It cannot *compose*—in all senses of the word—with the animal side.

III

So how do we know nature or animals without getting hung up on one or the other pole of the modern dualism? Latour offers an answer: we start "in the middle." In a 2004 article entitled "How to Talk About the Body: The Normative Dimensions of Science Studies," he gives an example of this "middle" or relational knowledge that directly challenges Bailly's distant contemplation and centers on the co-constitution (or articulation) of a body and a "thing." Taking as an example the training of a perfumer's nose, Latour proposes to show how the perfumer's body—not his subject or mind—is both affected and "effectuated [...] by other entities, human or non-human."[39] He starts with the device that plays a major role in the training of a "nose"[40] within the perfume industry—

the "odour kit"—and shows how its graduated register of pure fragrances is designed to train the nose to distinguish progressively finer contrasts. His further description of the training includes an instructor, a week-long protocol of odor discriminations, as well as quantity of mediations hidden in the background—such as the creation and bottling of the odor kit, the teaching of skills, and the behind-the-scene participation of the chemical industry. What this list of mediations emphasizes, of course, is the artificiality of a process of "effectuation" that co-constructs both nose and odors through training. It shows that, contrary to common beliefs about the inner workings of knowledge, mediations and their processes are primary. They are not instruments for use by a subject in order to represent, more or less accurately, the object "out there" any more than the objects exist in the world independently of the subject. As Latour himself writes: no nose preexists its "learning to be affected by hitherto unregistrable differences."[41] Symmetrically, no object or "world of complex odoriferous contrasts exists prior to its remapping with the odor kit."[42] What comes about with this process of learning, then, is not a mirror-like mediation between primary qualities of a world and the immediate faculties of a body. It is a material articulation that "allows, because of the artificiality of the instrument, the differences of the world to be loaded into what appeared at first as an arbitrary set of constrasts and onto an affected nose."[43]

How does this compositionist[44] scheme affect Bailly's own? How do we re-entangle together knowledge and things to recompose his split vision of nature? One way of starting to scramble Bailly's modern approach might be to take his own hint and portray him walking deeper into the woods, getting truly "affected" by a creature and touching it. This scenario would undoubtedly alter his perspective, reverse the problematic fiction of "touching with one's eyes," and propose a better mediated and embodied *seeing with one's touch*. Yet this tableau is also misleading and does not allow for an effective Latourian remapping of Bailly's epistemological landscape. Such remapping requires indeed that we let go of the still modern belief that a pure and embodied mediations might be better than artificial ones. Touch, unless it is already set—as in Haraway's *When Species Meet*[45]—in a hybrid, natural–cultural, context, remains too strictly material and does not provide an alternative model to Bailly's purifying vision. It still gives legitimacy to an "organic" model of knowledge in which perception is the key to nature. And what is needed to alter Bailly's split map is not another immediate access to the purity of nature's embodied thought, but a radical scrambling of his dualist topography. If Bailly wishes to escape his modern dilemma—and avoid both the naturalism and skepticism that are unavoidably linked to his modern stance—his best bet is the nonmodern solution Latour shares with the pragmatic tradition of James and Whitehead: radical empiricism or immanentism. This approach is uniquely situated to "settle" the interminable dilemma of modernity—or its debates about the respective merits of nature and culture—because it does not recognize the transcendence of the human mind or the separation between nature and culture. Latour's immanentism stipulates that everything—subjects and objects, spirits and things—is on the same plane of immanence and is equally relational and "factish." And this "democracy of actants" has profound and dynamizing consequences on Bailly's bipolar approach. If everything is natural–cultural, and if knowledge is a composition of mediations in which all "actants" (things and ideas) are equally involved in hybrid collectives, nothing—no subject or object—is ever unknowable or completely known. An animal that enters into propositions such as the classic "ethograms" of ethology is not a *natural* being whose behavior is readily visible and can then be represented by a neutral science. It has already been articulated and transformed by this ethogram in the same exact way that scents were mobilized and transformed by the odor kit. It is no longer simply "natural" but neither is it purely constructed. It is rather coextensive—as is the ethologist's grasp—with the proposition that mediates and articulates its differences. According to this Latourian construct, getting close to animals is always a matter of knowing more rather than less. It requires multiplying connections and translations. Any ethologist worth his/her salt relies, for example, not only on fieldwork and observational data, but on multiple concepts and translations, other disciplines (biology, sociology, history), and numerous steps that include "alliances (fund-raising), autonomisation of the field (peer-review), public appeal of a discipline."[46] These steps are essential, not only because they "vascularize" ethological knowledge, but because they, alone, can make the facts they create, "real." Facts need to travel along complex chains and networks of information to become referential.[47] Bailly's bat—if I can belabor this example one last time—is a perfect case in point. The author used the trope of the "tri-dimensional map" to highlight the visibility of its umwelt while hiding the artificiality of the echolocating construct. Yet Bailly's attempt to hide the technical mediations behind the bat's umwelt is an excellent demonstration of the crucial reality-building role Latour gives articulations. Seen solely through the contemplator's gaze and deprived of the specificity of her biosonar apparatus—and its poetic translation—the bat, says Latour, is invisible because "direct perception of form requires being experienced in the relevant field of thought."[48] To make it visible, it has to be fleshed out through the building of propositions, their contexts, and the debates they engage in. The bat is, therefore, like the perfumes of Latour's example, "articulated" by the science of ultrasonic echolocation as the contemplative ethologist is himself redone in this complicated knowledge. And it is perhaps no small irony that Bailly's unique example of "pure" contemplative knowledge turns out to also be the best illustration of Latour's principle of articulation. It shows us that animals and their scholars can only understand and meet each other in the middle of hybrid mediation networks, not in the purifications and polarizations of modern epistemology.

I will briefly conclude with two remarks. First, it is important to note that there are, today, in the animal studies field, a number of theoreticians who have left behind modern paradigms and have adopted the empiricist and hybrid approach of Latour. Animal practitioners, philosophers, ethologists, and historians—such as Vicky Hearne, Donna Haraway, Thelma Rowell, Eric Baratay, Vinciane Despret, Philippe Morizot, and others—are making animals visible within "associations of beings that take complicated forms" and cannot be "include[d] in an inhuman and a-historical nature."[49] They work squarely in the middle of Bailly's human and animal sides, crossing practices that have long been kept apart, and producing fascinating hybridized objects such as interspecies histories (Baratay, Haraway), speculative ethologies (Rowell, Despret, Morizot), the linguistic of animal trainings (Hearne). Their works are changing the way we think about animals far more significantly and quickly than anyone could expect, given the resistance of modern science and postmodern philosophy. They are also—and this is my second point—helping us think the complexity of our current biopolitical crisis far beyond what is proposed by traditional eco-philosophy. As Latour has shown in *Politics of Nature*, modern ecology has entertained a similarly purifying and isolationist view of nature as Bailly's, and has therefore been quite unable to deal effectively with the entanglements of the current climate crisis as well as other urgent biopolitical issues. My hope is that Latour's thinking—and the exuberant practice of the scholars who work in his vicinity—can help recompose Bailly's divided "sides" and foster a much-needed natural–cultural politics.

Notes

1. Jacques Derrida, *The Animal That Therefore I Am*, ed. Marie-Louise Mallet, trans. David Wills. (New York: Fordham University Press, 2008), 1–52.
2. Bruno Latour, *We Have Never Been Modern*, trans. Catherine Porter (Cambridge: Harvard University Press, 1999), 4.
3. See, for example, Vinciane Despret, *What Would Animal Say If We Asked the Right Questions?*, trans. Brett Buchanan (Minneapolis: University of Minnesota Press, 2012).
4. Jane Bennett describes such a "phenomenology of enchantment" in *The Enchantment of Modern Life: Attachments, Crossings, and Ethics* (Princeton: Princeton University Press, 2001), 5.
5. Jean-Christophe Bailly, *The Animal Side*, trans. Catherine Porter (New York: Fordham University Press, 2011), 2.
6. Bailly offers in the first half of his text a reading of the notion of the "open" Rilke presents in the 8th Elegy of the *Duino Elegies*.
7. Bailly, *The Animal Side*, 19.
8. Ibid., 18.
9. Ibid., 14. The word "signifiance" is not readily translatable. The translator notes that "The term […] refers to the semiotic modalities and processes of making and conveying meaning."
10. Ibid., 15.
11. Ibid., 22.
12. Isabelle Stengers, *Thinking with Whitehead: A Free and Wild Creation of Concepts*, trans. Michael Chase (Cambridge: Harvard University Press, 2011), 32.
13. This is, of course, an allusion to Orwell's *Animal Farm*.
14. The novel, *Anton Reiser*, was written by a pre-romantic German author, Karl-Philip Morris. It is not currently available in English or French.
15. Bailly, *Animal Side*, 24.
16. Ibid., 24–5.
17. Ibid., 25.
18. Ibid., 2. My emphasis.
19. Ibid., 13.
20. Jakob von Uexküll, "A Stroll through the Worlds of Animals and Men: A Picture Book of Invisible Worlds," in *Instinctive Behavior: The Development of a Modern Concept*, ed. and trans. Claire H. Schiller (New York: International Universities Press, 1957).
21. Ibid., 49.
22. Vinciane Despret, "From Secret Agents to Interagency," *History and Theory* 52, no. 4 (2013): 31.

23 See Gilles Deleuze and Félix Guattari, *A Thousand Plateaus: Capitalism and Schizophrenia*, trans. Brian Massumi (Minneapolis: University of Minnesota Press, 1987) and Maurice Merleau-Ponty, *Nature: Course Notes from the College de France*, ed. Dominique Séglard, trans. Robert Vallier (Evanston: Northwestern University Press, 2003).
24 Bailly, *The Animal Side*, 58.
25 Ibid., 56.
26 Alfred North Whitehead, "Theories of the Bifurcation of Nature," Chapter 2 in *The Concept of Nature* (Cambridge: Cambridge University Press, 1920), 26–48.
27 Bailly borrows this trope of "nature's poem" from Plotinus, *Enneads*, Third treatise.
28 See Maurice Merleau-Ponty, *Nature: Course Notes from the College de France*.
29 Merleau-Ponty, quoted in Bailly, *The Animal Side*, 49. For both Merleau-Ponty and Bailly, it is the image of the bird in flight that best conveys the power of animal behavior to constitute the unity of its own movement.
30 Bailly, *The Animal Side*, 49.
31 Ibid., 56.
32 Plato, *Ion*, trans. R. E. Allen (New Haven: Yale University Press, 1998).
33 Bailly, "Le Moindre souffle," *Le Parti-pris des animaux*, 66. My translation.
34 Ibid., 66–67.
35 Ibid., 51.
36 Alfred North Whitehead, *Process and Reality: An Essay in Cosmology* (New York: Free Press, 1978 [1929]), 168–70.
37 Ibid.
38 Latour, "A Texbook Case Revisited: Knowledge as a Mode of Existence," in *The Handbook of Science and Technologies Studies*, ed. Edward Hackett, Olga Amsterdamska, Michael Lynch, and Judy Wacjman (Cambridge: MIT Press, 2007), 12.
39 Latour, "How to Talk About the Body: The Normative Dimension Of Science Studies." *Body and Society* 10, no. 2–3, 207.
40 This is, of course, the term used by the perfume industry to designate a specialist skilled in the identification of complex odors.
41 Latour, "How to Talk About the Body," 208.
42 Ibid.
43 Ibid., 210. If this paradigm seems a bit foreign, it should not be. The embodied "middle" knowledge it offers is of the same contingent, situated and entangled cloth than the one theorized by feminists such as Butler, Haraway, or Barad. Latour describes a knowledge where everything happens "in the middle" —"au milieu," which, if we pay attention to the double significance of the French expression, means both the middle ("without grounding definitions or an ideal horizon")

and the surrounding habitat ("without being able to disentangle something from its particular surrounding"). "Au milieu," then, defines a knowledge that rests on purely "contingent foundations" and one that is strictly worldly and "on the ground." It is a process of worldy co-emergence, which is always ongoing. It is therefore a highly historical and situated knowledge where such dualities as nature and culture, human and animals are valid and understandable only in a process of specific relation and difference.

44 I borrow the term from Bruno Latour, "An Attempt at a Compositionist Manifesto," *New Literary History* 41 (2010): 471–90.
45 Donna Haraway, *When Species Meet* (Minneapolis: University of Minnesota Press, 2008), 3.
46 Latour, "A Well-Articulated Primatology: Reflections of a Fellow Traveller," in *Primate Encounters: Models of Science, Gender, and Society*, ed. Shirley C. Strum and Linda Marie Fedigan (Chicago: University of Chicago Press, 2000), 6.
47 Ibid.
48 Ludwig Fleck, quoted by Latour, "A Textbook Case Revisited: Knowledge as a Mode of Existence," 12.
49 Bruno Latour, *Politics of Nature*, trans. Catherine Porter (Cambridge: Harvard University Press, 2004), 21. The exact citation is as follows: "Political ecology does not speak about nature and has never sought to do so. It has to do with associations of beings that take complicated forms, rules, apparatuses, consumers, institutions, mores, calves, pigs, broods—and that it is completely superfluous to try to include in an inhuman and a-historical nature."

Bibliography

Bailly, Jean-Christophe. *The Animal Side*. Translated by Catherine Porter. New York: Fordham University Press, 2011.
Bailly, Jean-Christophe. *Le Parti-pris des animaux*. Paris: Christian Bourgois, 2013.
Bennett, Jane. *The Enchantment of Modern Life: Attachments, Crossings, and Ethics*. Princeton: Princeton University Press, 2001.
Buchanan, Brett. *Onto-Ethologies: The Animal Environments of Uexküll, Heidegger, Merleau-Ponty and Deleuze*. Albany: SUNY Press, 2008.
Deleuze, Gilles, and Felix Guattari. *A Thousand Plateaus: Capitalism and Schizophrenia*. Translated by Brian Massumi. Minneapolis: University of Minnesota Press, 1987.
Derrida, Jacques. *The Animal That Therefore I Am*. Edited by Marie-Louise Mallet. Translated by David Wills. New York: Fordham University Press, 2008.
Despret, Vinciane. "From Secret Agents to Interagency." *History and Theory* 52, no. 4 (2013): 29–44.

Despret, Vinciane. *What Would Animals Say If We Asked the Right Questions?*. Translated by Brett Buchanan. Minneapolis: University of Minnesota Press, 2012.

Haraway, Donna. *When Species Meet*. Minneapolis: University of Minnesota Press, 2008.

Latour, Bruno. "An Attempt at a 'Compositionist Manifesto.'" *New Literary History* 41 (2010): 471–90.

Latour, Bruno. "How to Talk About the Body? The Normative Dimension of Science Studies." *Body and Society* 10, no. 2–3 (2004): 205–29.

Latour, Bruno. *Politics of Nature*. Translated by Catherine Porter. Cambridge: Harvard University Press, 2004.

Latour, Bruno. "Primate Encounters: For a Well-Articulated Primatology." In *Primate Encounters: Models of Science, Gender, and Society*. Edited by Shirley C. Strum and Linda Marie Fedigan. 358–81. Chicago: University of Chicago Press, 2000.

Latour, Bruno. "A Textbook Case Revisited: Knowledge as a Mode of Existence." In *The Handbook of Science and Technology Studies*. Edited by E. Hackett, O. Amsterdamska, M. Lynch, and J. Wacjman. 83–112. Cambridge: MIT Press, 2007.

Latour, Bruno. *We Have Never Been Modern*. Translated by Catherine Porter. Cambridge: Harvard University Press, 1999.

Merleau-Ponty, Maurice. *Nature: Course Notes from the College de France*. Edited by Dominique Séglard. Translated by Robert Vallier. Evanston: Northwestern University Press, 2003.

Stengers, Isabelle. *Thinking with Whitehead: A Free and Wild Creation of Concepts*. Translated by Michael Chase. Cambridge: Harvard University Press, 2011.

Uexküll, Jakob von. "A Stroll through the Worlds of Animals and Men: A Picture Book of Invisible Worlds." In *Instinctive Behavior: The Development of a Modern Concept*. Edited and translated by Claire H. Schiller. 5–80. New York: International Universities Press, 1957.

Whitehead, Alfred North. *Process and Reality: An Essay in Cosmology*. New York: Free Press, 1978 [1929].

Part Four

Issues of Practical Concern Related to Latour's Thinking

9

Latour's Interpretation of Donald Trump

Graham Harman

For the present collection on nonmodern practices in the humanities, I can think of few topics as relevant as Bruno Latour's recent thinking on climate change. If by "nonmodern" we mean an end to the usual artificial separation between thought and world, then Latour's critique of modernism by way of nature/culture hybrids stands with Karen Barad's own concept of entanglement as one of the most widely utilized approaches in the humanities today.[1] For Latour, to "modernize" means the pointless attempt to purify nature and culture from each other: treating the former as inert and mechanical or characterized by clockwork precision, and the latter as amounting to nothing but the free projection of arbitrary cultural values untethered to anything in the nonhuman sphere. Once the theoretical weakness of this sort of modernism is demonstrated, the imperative becomes to "ecologize" rather than to modernize. By ecologizing, Latour means paying attention to the increased intertwining of human and nonhuman elements, with James Lovelock's Gaia theory providing an outstanding example. In Lovelock's theory, the climate is no longer treated as a neutral background for human activity, but as something that results in large part from the vital activity of humans and all other life forms.[2] Most recently, Latour has zeroed in on the new chief political enemy of Gaia: the American President Donald J. Trump. This chapter will consider Latour's interpretation of this powerful climate ignoramus.

Trump is not just a fool, but an unusually dangerous one. While this view is by no means original, and is even fairly widespread among those forced to live through his embarrassing and often frightening tenure as president of the United States, only a relative handful of philosophers have ventured their diagnoses of the man in print, one of them being Latour. More importantly, Latour does not just lambast Trump in the expected manner of a public intellectual responding to the crisis of the hour, but manages to place the Trump phenomenon at the center of his most recent thinking. This makes it possible that Latour's assessment will outlive the direct historical relevance of Trump himself. In any case, his take on the forty-fifth president is more unsettling than Slavoj Žižek's apparently provocative pro-Trump stance: the latter being too immediately digestible due to its intellectually familiar Leninist trope that liberals are a greater barrier to the future than the Right.[3]

This chapter will be concerned with Latour's two main writings on Trump currently available in English. The first is a brief article from *The Los Angeles Review of Books*, dating from shortly after Trump's election.[4] The second is the book-length essay *Down to Earth*, composed in the wake of additional reflection, and containing a more systematic treatment of the historical significance of Trumpism.[5] We should now take them in order.

Political and Metaphysical Realism

First, a word is needed about the title of Latour's post-election editorial: "Two Bubbles of Unrealism." The word "realism" remains unpopular in intellectual life even though its purported double, "materialism," is exploding in popularity: everywhere we read about new materialisms, vital materialisms, feminist materialisms, but much less about different variants of realism, despite the wide familiarity of the Speculative Realist movement.[6] I will turn to materialism shortly, but let's speak briefly about realism, in order to set the table for a discussion of Latour's Los Angeles piece. Although realism comes in numerous guises, two in particular are important for our discussion.

We can speak first of political realism, which is normally associated with those strategic political thinkers who favor the hardball calculus of national interest over moralizing sermons on social justice and international law. Political realism is considered "realist" because it prides itself on not wasting its time on empty dreams of utopia, but instead faces up to the way the world "really is" rather than how it ought to be. As such, political realism is normally associated with what we call the political Right, ranging from sobering political philosophers such as Niccolò Machiavelli, Thomas Hobbes, Carl Schmitt, and Eric Voegelin to cunning statesmen like Cardinal Richelieu or Henry Kissinger. Although such figures are generally reviled by progressive activists and liberal citizens, it is hard to deny a certain grain of truth in their vision of human affairs. Latour expressed awareness of this at the London School of Economics, when he stated that it is "a common thing in political philosophy, that reactionary thinkers are more interesting than the progressive ones ... in that you learn more about politics from people like Machiavelli and Schmitt than from Rousseau."[7] More generally, Latour in early career coupled his remorseless ontology of actors entering networks and engaging in power struggles with an eye-opening fondness for the politics of Machiavelli and Hobbes.[8] Thus, we could speak of the early Latour as a political realist in this sense of the term, although he has always been more or less a mainstream liberal (in the American rather than European sense) in most of his explicit political positions. Latour's youthful deference to power politics only began to shift with *We Have Never Been Modern*, in which he suddenly took issue with Steven Shapin and Simon Schaffer's defense of Hobbesian power plays over Robert Boyle's notion of a scientific truth that lies beyond all social considerations.[9] From that point forward, Latour showed some degree of commitment to something in politics beyond the mere struggle for victor. Less than a decade later, he grants a key political function to both scientists and moralists simultaneously: detecting realities currently unrecognized by the body politic.[10] Namely, scientists are supposed to identify previously unknown entities in nature, while the job of moralists is to discover who remains voiceless or oppressed under our current political settlement. The latter is an especial surprise, given the early Latour's open contempt for moralists, defined as those who are content to be "right" without taking the trouble to gain "might."

To summarize, the meaning of "political realism" had changed completely for Latour by the year 2000. If in his early career it referred to a candid assessment of the actual forces in play in a situation—as in Machiavelli's modern tradition—it had come to mean an awareness of relevant factors *beyond* the current situation, whether scientific or moral in character. Now, a progressive critic might lazily assume that the young Latour was somehow cynical, but that with growing wisdom he came to realize that there is an actual political-moral truth that must govern all political decisions. But Latour's suspicions about Rousseau, as expressed in his London statement, indicate that he does not think morality can govern politics any better than science can. Note as well that his recent philosophy treats morality [MOR], politics [POL], and science [REF] as three completely separate modes of existence that must never be confused.[11] It is easy to see how politics differs from the other two modes if we consider their respective relations to power plays. Morality, in almost mystical fashion, thinks itself able to grasp *directly* a truth that transcends all concrete facts; it is this feature that makes political moralists either stirring and selfless orators or self-righteous finger-waggers, depending on the occasion. As for science, although it is more aware than moralism of its own fallibility, it also thinks it can grasp *directly* some truths about nature that transcend the supposed corrupt compromise of sleazy professional politicians. It is interesting that Latour prefers politics to both science and morality, though we must remember that it is no longer the winner-take-all of power politics, which he left behind in rejecting Shapin and Schaffer's celebration of Hobbes. Instead, it is a politics that contains an element of the unknown, and indeed of the unknowable.

With this point we reach the most recent incarnation of Latour's political realism, inspired in part by the work of his one-time student Noortje Marres.[12] To be specific, Latour zeroed in on the early-twentieth-century debate between the American thinkers Walter Lippman and John Dewey.[13] In response to Lippmann's bleak diagnosis that American democracy is plagued with an ignorant populace and will therefore need to give way to technocracy, Dewey responded that the public is not a preexistent whole, but comes into being through specific issues, and thereby assembles limited and ever-changing publics. Given Latour's career-long interest in inanimate things, it is unsurprising that his appropriation of Dewey would leave a place for nonhuman stakeholders in the political sphere, as the pages of *Down to Earth* will remind us.[14] The more surprising result, perhaps, was that Latour's Dewey is focused on consensus while nonetheless leaving room for what is left *outside* the current political settlement.[15] Whereas Hobbesians celebrate the immanence of all political things, the Latour of the early twenty-first century maintains his recently discovered interest in that which transcends the current polis, and which perhaps will always slip from its grasp.

We turn now to a second form of realism, the *metaphysical* kind, which—at a minimum—entails the thesis that there is something real outside the human mind. In Latour's case, however, the human mind was never at the center in the first place, at least not in the hard-core manner of most post-Cartesian philosophy, and that means we need to tweak this definition a bit. Accordingly, let's say that metaphysical realism is the thesis that there is something real not just outside the mind, but outside *any* actor, which for Latour includes nonhumans no less than human beings. As we consider this new definition, it looks as if Latour has never quite been a metaphysical realist: after all, he tends to define reality as the sum total of actors performing actions on each other, much as in the relational metaphysics of Alfred North Whitehead.[16] Hence, there seems to be no room for any sort of "outside" in Latourian actor-network theory. As we read in one of the most candid passages of *Pandora's Hope*, an entity is nothing more than whatever it "modifies, transforms, perturbs, or creates," and holds nothing in reserve beyond this—no hidden substantial core.[17]

Although I have tried to show briefly that Latour's mature political philosophy comes to focus on an unknowable political object, he makes the same move even more boldly in his neglected critique of materialism, "Can We Get Our Materialism Back, Please?"[18] In this short but brilliant article, Latour rejects materialism precisely because it replaces our perpetual *uncertainty* about what matter really is with a ready-made philosophical or scientific theory that purports to exhaust matter's essential features. Whereas philosophical realism usually means that there is a world outside the mind and that we can know it—as long as we follow the proper rational procedures—Latour's theory turns out to be that there is a world outside the mind, but we can never really know it. This is much the same lesson he drew from Marres's reading of Dewey and it is far removed from the utter Hobbesian immanence of both politics and knowledge that was the young Latour's trademark.

To summarize, what realism has come to mean for Latour over time is threefold: (a) there is something residually existent outside the current state of affairs in the world, (b) we can never know it, but (3) there is still a specifically political way of facing up to it. Only now are we prepared to understand what Latour means when he portrays Trump as an anti-realist or escapist. Unfortunately, the same will turn out to hold for Trump's enemies as well, so that we are all threatened by our own respective bubbles of anti-realism.

The View from 2016

Written just days after Trump's stunning election victory, "Two Bubbles of Unrealism" delivers on the promise of its title.[19] For Latour, there are just two such bubbles, though he describes them in two separate ways:

(1) The Bubble of Trump's Opponents vs. The Bubble of his Supporters. The anti-Trump camp deserves to be called anti-realists for the obvious reason that they failed to take the threat posed by Trump seriously enough: "How could we have been so wrong? All the polls, all the newspapers, all the commentators, the entire intelligentsia."[20] We mocked and dismissed his supporters with a wave of the hand, then realized to our chagrin that there must have been real demographic forces in play: "'uneducated white men,' the ones that 'globalization left behind.'"[21] Latour writes in frustration that "despite having spent the past

six weeks at American universities, I have yet to hear a single account of those 'other people' that is realistic enough to truly unsettle us. They are, it seems, just as invisible, inaudible, and incomprehensible as the Barbarians outside the gates of Athens."[22] We, the anti-Trump intelligentsia, have somehow fallen out of touch with reality: the cardinal sin for any political realism. But this is not to say that Trump's supporters are any more in touch with reality, despite their unexpected victory: "The real tragedy … is that the others live in a bubble, too: a world of the past completely undisturbed by climate change."[23] Above all else, they are consciously deceived by their miserable leader: "Trump goes on lying and cheating without remorse, and what a pleasure it is to be misled … We can't expect [his followers] to play the roles of good, common-sense people, with their feet firmly planted on the ground. Their ideals are even more illusory than ours."[24]

(2) Instead of speaking of two groups of people, we can also speak of their two equally bankrupt idea of utopia: globalism for Hillary Clinton and nationalism for Donald Trump. Latour concedes briefly that the Clinton utopia might not have been much better, since "everyone now understands more or less clearly that there is no real material world in the offing corresponding to that vision of a promised land," meaning the promise of unlimited economic and human development under liberal democratic capitalism. "Just one year ago," he adds, "the United Nations Climate Change Conference served as a solemn declaration of this impossibility: the 'global' is simply too vast for the Earth." Yet of course the other side is surely even worse: "[For nationalists, it] hardly matters how tiny one's domain has become, as long as the borders are airtight. Each of the countries that contributed to the universal horizon of conquest and emancipation will now withdraw from institutions invented two centuries ago."[25]

Naturally, no one thinks that Trump is the *cause* of all this, or even that he is a unique symptom of it. Instead, he is part of an alarming general trend building over recent years: "The ongoing pattern of voluntary resignations is now terribly clear: first England [Brexit]; six months later the United States, which aspires to the lost grandeur of the 1950s. What next? If we heed the lessons of history, it is probably now France's turn, and then Germany's."[26] As of this writing—January 2019—France and Germany have managed to dam the flood of unreality somewhat, while Brexit is in trouble and Trump's popularity is in free fall amidst political failures and legal troubles. Nonetheless, even if we somehow return to the relatively stable situation of 2010 or so, it will not suffice to face up to reality. How might we rise to the occasion and do so? On this note, we turn to Latour's somewhat more detailed account in *Down to Earth*.

Latour on Trumpism

Down to Earth consists of twenty short sections, with Trump mentioned explicitly in numbers 1, 2, 6, 8, and 18, though he is central enough to the book's argument that his presence is almost ubiquitous. Let's begin by looking at these sections, so as to provide a sort of scaffolding for Latour's attempt at a positive post-Trumpian program.

Section 1 begins by telling us openly that Trump is the cause of the book's existence: "This essay uses the occasion of Donald Trump's election on November 6, 2016, to bring together three phenomena that commentators have already noted but without always seeing their connection."[27] The three phenomena in question—all originating in the post-1989 universe—are deregulation, growing inequality, and the systematic effort to deny the existence of climate change. Latour consolidates this trio into something that may strike his critics as a mere conspiracy theory: "This essay proposes to take these three phenomena as symptoms of a single historical situation; it is as though a significant segment of the ruling classes ... had concluded that the earth no longer had room enough for them and for everyone else."[28] But while we can certainly argue over the extent to which these "elites" were consciously aware of a plan to seize all resources for themselves, we can probably agree that the former horizon of modernism as a site for unlimited future development is coming to a close, and that the winners under the current system have become explicitly aware of this fact. Bearing this in mind, Latour diagnoses our situation as one in which a possible "common world" seems to be lacking.[29]

Section 2: Of course, when we speak of winners and losers, it is possible to speak of entire nations no less than wealthy individuals. The great geopolitical winner of the post-1989 era has of course been the United States, the hegemonic global power since the unexpected collapse of the Soviet Bloc. Thus, we should not be surprised by the unfolding tragedy of American national efforts to secede from the growing world crisis, paralleled by the behavior of individual billionaires fleeing to free-market Singapore or constructing bunkers in New Zealand. As has often been the case throughout history, America's boisterous exit from the Paris Climate Accord was foreshadowed by an earlier event in Britain: namely, the June 2016 vote to leave the European Union. As Latour aptly puts it: "Two of the greatest countries of the old 'free world' are saying to the others: 'Our history will no longer have anything to do with yours; you can go to hell!'"[30] In the wake of a growing migration crisis, we discover that we are all migrants, needing to find a new soil differing not only from globalizing modernism but also from nationalistic nostalgia: "Either we deny the existence of the problem, or else we *look for a place to land*. From now on, this is what divides us all, much more than our positions on the right or the left side of the political spectrum."[31] In short, Trumpism equals escapism, an attempt "to keep America floating in dreamland a few years longer, so as to postpone coming down to earth."[32]

Section 6: Here Latour notes "the epistemological delirium that has taken hold of the public stage since the election of Donald Trump."[33] The spreading flood of lies drives everyone insane, and hence Trump supporters are accused of gullibly accepting "alternative facts," without realizing the extent to which they too have been betrayed by the abandonment of the former common project of modernization for everyone.[34] Latour now ventures one of his biggest claims: "The issue of climate-change denial organizes all politics at the present time."[35] In passing, he makes a somewhat surprising appeal to "truth," complaining that "when journalists talk about 'post-truth' politics, they do so very lightly. They do not stress the reason why ordinary people have decided to keep on engaging in politics while voluntarily abandoning the link to the truth that (rightly!) terrified them."[36] For my part, I would note a different problem with speaking of "post-truth" in Trump's case: namely, the fact that no one is really in possession of a political truth, and that what we should be aiming for instead is a politics grounded in *reality*. What this means is that Trump is more of a "post-reality" than a "post-truth" figure.[37] Ironically, it is Latour himself who has done so much to show us that political realism is not exactly about *truth*. Is it possible, then, that he is simply speaking loosely when mentioning truth in a political context? No, he does so deliberately. On some level, Latour still thinks he knows where the root of political truth can be found: not in knowledge, but in *practice*. Consider his complaint about "the habitual vice of epistemology, which consists in attributing to intellectual deficits something that is quite simply a deficit in *shared practice*."[38] Latour is certainly not the first philosopher to rate praxis over theory as an alternative supply of truth: as if our practices somehow gave us more direct contact with reality than explicit propositional statements. No less a figure than Martin Heidegger grounded his major work *Being and Time* on a version of this very distinction.[39] More recently, Latour's close ally Isabelle Stengers glorifies a similar procedure in her two-volume *Cosmopolitics*, trying to root philosophy in what she calls an "ecology of practices."[40] Against this trend, I would argue, any full-blown realism must acknowledge that our practices come up short of reality no less than our most technical theories.

Section 8: This is probably the most important discussion of Trump in the book, and for this reason I postpone some of it for later. Latour begins by finding a silver lining in our recent series of Western political disasters: "If the Brexit campaign had failed in June 2016, if Hillary Clinton had been elected, or if after his election Trump had not withdrawn from the Paris Accord ... [w]e would still be weighing the benefits and drawbacks of globalization as if the modernization front remained intact."[41] However heinous a figure Trump may be, his platform is "a political innovation of a rare sort that needs to be taken seriously."[42] Although it is tempting to call Trump a fascist, Latour rejects this label on the grounds that fascism was still an avid modernization program. By contrast, "Trump's originality is to link, in a single gesture, first the *headlong rush* toward maximum profit while abandoning the rest of the world to its fate ... and second, the *headlong rush backward* of an entire people toward the return of national and ethnic categories."[43] If globalist capitalism and nationalist ethnocentrism were once opposed, Trump neatly combines both in a single stroke. It makes perfect sense that this monstrous fusion should have occurred in the United States, "The country *that had the most to lose* from a return to reality. Its material infrastructures are the most difficult to reorient quickly; its responsibilities in the current climactic situation are the most crushing."[44] Now backing away from the term "post-truth" after his fleeting embrace of it, Latour rightly notes that "Trumpian politics is not 'post-truth,' it is 'post-politics'– that is, literally, a politics *with no object*, since it rejects the world that it claims to inhabit."[45] Later in the book, this becomes a call for an "object-oriented politics." But it remains to be seen if Latour can prevent political objects from being conflated with his beloved category of political *practice*, since—among other things—the same political object might inspire numerous alternative practices.[46] But perhaps the most important remark about Trump in Section 8 concerns his place in Latour's scheme of four attractors, a topic left to the conclusion of this article.

Section 18: Trump is only mentioned once by name, but in the context of a fine *bon mot*: "His statement [following US withdrawal from the Paris Accord] was a declaration of war authorizing the occupation of all the other countries, if not with troops, at least with CO_2, which America retains the right to emit."[47]

To summarize, Latour reads Trump as an escapist rather than a fascist: as a sickening innovator who embraces both the globalizing modernism of successful plutocrats and the rancid ethnic resentment of "Build the Wall!" nationalism. At the same time, he tries to prevent us from noticing that these two models are really just mirror images of each other, insofar as neither makes contact with reality. As an alternative to this tangled ball of yarn, Latour insists that politics should be object-oriented in order to provide a common reality, though he is inclined nonetheless to proclaim that shared *practices* rather than shared political objects are what bring us together. Yet the real heart of *Down to Earth* is its theory of "attractors," a natural expansion of Latour's now-classic critique of modernism. It is to this topic that we now turn.

The Theory of Four Attractors

I am hardly alone in regarding Latour's *We Have Never Been Modern* as one of the most important works of philosophy since the Second World War. Indeed, I would go much further and claim that we cannot escape the congenital limits of modern thought without understanding how Latour's critique of modernism fundamentally changes the situation. The essence of his critique is that modernity makes a taxonomical split between two and only two kinds of entities: thought and world, which we might also call "culture" and "nature." Modernity makes the impossible attempt to purify these two zones from one another, asking of everything "Is it culture or nature?," even as it produces countless hybrid forms in which these two supposedly pure zones are hopelessly entangled. One can certainly ask whether Latour's nonmodern project is always carried out in convincing fashion. For example, the rejection of modernist purity need not entail that *all* entities are hybrids and therefore entangled with a human element, as often seems to be the case with Latour. This only undercuts his attempt at realism by entailing, for instance, that tuberculosis cannot exist until it is recognized by medical science.[48] But these are mere quibbles by contrast with the importance of the path he has shown beyond modernity.

In *Down to Earth*, Latour rhetorically simplifies his earlier account of modernism, speaking in terms of a passage to the Global that leaves whatever is outside its reach looking like a backwater to be called the Local. Once this opposition was identified and fixed, it was possible to "trace a pioneering front of modernization. This is the line drawn by the attempt to modernize, an injunction that prepared us for every sacrifice: for leaving our native province, abandoning our traditions, breaking with our habits, if we wanted to … participate in the general movement of development."[49] More succinctly, "we knew how to locate ourselves in the course of history."[50] Given the widely familiar sense of what modernizing ought to look like, any protestors could easily be dismissed "as reactionaries, or at least as anti-moderns, as dregs, rejects. They could certainly protest, but their whining only justified their critics."[51] Most importantly, "the arrow of time was going somewhere."[52] One could even afford to be politically smug about the process, since "this was [also] the vector along which the Left/Right distinction … had been projected."[53] Whatever the complexities of various concrete socio-political issues, it was possible to measure everyone's degree of progressive correctness in "the way one reads the temperature of a patient by following the gradations of a thermometer."[54] No matter the circumstances, there was "always *a single direction* that derived from the tension between the two poles of attraction, the Global and the Local."[55] And once the Global begins to falter, the Local seems to become more attractive once again. Yet the two sides are equally unworkable: "what is more unreal than Kaczyński's Poland, the National Front's France, the Northern League's Italy, Brexit's shrunken Great Britain, or Trump's deceitful great-again America?"[56]

Since both the unlimited development of modernism and the cornpone nostalgia of anti-modernism have come to seem impossible, we feel as if "something has come to twist the arrow of time."[57] The two familiar modern attractors of Global and Local now seem to be haunted by a third, one that is hard to put a finger on. Before attempting to name this third attractor directly, Latour identifies a more obvious fourth: "It is as though Trump had managed to identify a *fourth attractor*. This one is easy to name: it is the Out-of-This-World, the horizon of people who no longer belong to the realities of an earth that would react to their actions."[58] It is by contrast with this lamentable fourth attractor that we begin to sense the contours of the still under-described third one. One possible name for it is *Gaia*, and Latour refers us to his recent book on that topic.[59] For the moment, he settles on the "Terrestrial" as his name for the third attractor. The difference between the Terrestrial and our former notion of the world is that whereas the latter was a mostly unnoticed background for human action, the former is also a political agent in its own right, one that pushes back against us. What is so unnerving about the emergence of this new agent is that it "bars the modernizers from knowing *where they are, in what epoch*, and especially *what role* they will need to play from now on."[60] Or as Latour puts it, in a wonderful theatrical metaphor: "Today, the decor, the wings, the background, the whole building have come on stage and are competing with the actors for the principal role."[61] The situation is completely unprecedented, and not even the wisest past civilizations can help us with what we must now confront. "To modernize or to ecologize: this is now the crucial choice."[62]

Although Latour still sees the various Green parties as having been hampered by the inadequate modern concept of nature, he happily notes that these parties have "succeeded so well in transforming everything into vigorous controversies—from beef to the climate, by way of hedges, humid zones, corn, pesticides, diesel fuel, urban planning, and airports—that every material object has taken on its own 'ecological dimension.'"[63] Nonetheless, they have not managed "to get out of the trap set by the Moderns' temporal arrow."[64] Latour often speaks, in the spirit of Schmitt, of the political difference between friend and enemy. Who, then, are the enemies of his own new approach?[65] Plausibly enough, he says it will be those who continue to cling to the modern attractors of Global and Local, and above all those who adhere to Trump's Out-of-This-World Fourth Attractor. Yet somewhere there must also be *friends* of the Terrestrial, and they too must be found among the Global and Local factions. Perhaps the Terrestrial will have something to offer both groups.

The main reason that partisans of the Local become reactionary is that they are fleeing in fear before the deterritorializations of the modernist Global. Yet "if we stop fleeing, what does the desire for attachment look like?"[66] It is hard to imagine a more Latourian theme than attachment, given the extent to which modernism—his nemesis—was primarily about transcending, critiquing, ironically distancing, or cynically surveying something with which it *did not* feel itself entangled in the least. Stated more generally, we could say that nothing is more highly prized by the moderns than *freedom*, a noble value that—just like any other—degenerates into a vice when glorified piously at the expense of everything else.[67] Attachment is sometimes described negatively as a form of gullible naiveté. Yet in another respect, it is a neglected virtue that the Local might be able to teach us something about: provided we prevent it from lapsing into "ethnic homogeneity, a focus on patrimony, historicism, nostalgia, inauthentic authenticity," not to mention "Lebensraum [or] the back-to-the-land movement promoted in France by the Vichy government during the Second World War."[68] As for the partisans of the Global, they will perhaps be attracted by the Terrestrials' simultaneous insistence that "the Local is much too narrow, too shrunken, to accommodate the multiplicity of beings belonging to the terrestrial world."[69] Above all else, Terrestrials will need to avoid the modernist paralysis faced by the ecological movements when "they believed they faced a choice between focusing on social questions and focusing on ecological questions," as if it were a question of "*a priori* differences between humans and non-humans."[70] Insofar as we have wrongly accepted a purely human–social definition of politics, "on the whole, we have remained Marxist."[71] But a politics grounded in human society leaves too much of reality out of the picture: "To give a worldly definition of activity, one has to meet a world; to occupy a territory, one has to live on Earth; to take up *Realpolitik*, one has to be a realist."[72] Latour's case for a new way of looking at politics is helped by the fact that some alternative approaches are already available. For instance, in *Carbon Democracy* Timothy Mitchell has given a persuasive account of how politics is less about the class struggle between workers and owners than about the differing bonds of both groups with coal and oil, whose peculiar characteristics have unmistakable political effects.[73]

We close by returning to the theme of Latour's political realism, which ultimately has two—and only two—key features. The first is its tilt away from the assumption that politics is primarily about human beings, with Left and Right basically defined by their respectively optimistic and pessimistic conceptions of human nature. To quote again from Schmitt: "One could test all theories of state and political ideas according to their anthropology and thereby classify these as to whether they consciously or unconsciously presuppose man to be by nature evil or by nature good … [by their] answer to the question whether man is a dangerous being or not, a risky or a harmless creature."[74] Schmitt, of course, was among those who saw humans as dangerous. But this still leaves him on the same axis as someone like Rousseau, who took the opposite view; both thinkers tacitly agree that our conception of politics will follow from our conception of human nature.[75] Yet given the massive amount of work done by nonhuman entities in stabilizing our societies, it is no longer human nature that is the most important factor in politics, and thus the question of human (un)improvability is less important than modern conservatives and liberals have both imagined. In any case, the climate is becoming a more important political actor than any human, whether good or evil: "How could we deem 'realistic' a project of modernization that has 'forgotten' for two centuries to anticipate the reactions of the terraqueous globe to human actions?"[76] The second feature of Latour's new political realism, mentioned earlier in connection with Dewey, is that the polis is never fully knowable any more than the Constitution of matter is fully knowable. If politics must be object-oriented, it is because the object or issue in question will motivate certain political practices without being reducible to them.

At the start of this chapter, I mentioned Latour's notion of hybrids in connection with Barad's theory of entanglement, with which it has some definite resemblances. In closing, we are now in a position to say more about the key difference—as I see it—between these two influential theorists. In both authors we find a focused treatment of the entanglement between humans and nonhumans. Yet Latour calls for an "object-oriented politics," whereas Barad does not, and indeed it is hard to imagine her ever using such a phrase. The key difference is that Latour is more of a realist than a materialist, while Barad—despite her use of the phrase "agential realism"—is more of a materialist than a realist.[77] What, exactly, does this inversion mean? When Barad speaks of the entanglement of thought and world, she treats this as an "intra-action" between two mutually constituting poles rather than an "interaction" between two separate entities. This entails that thought and world, for Barad, are fully deployed in their mutual relation and do not exist as a surplus outside that relation. We have seen that Latour has strong tendencies in this direction himself, as when he says that an entity is nothing more than whatever it "modifies, transforms, perturbs, or creates."[78] Yet we also saw that his political theory contains a powerful realist counter-tendency: an "object-oriented" current aware that any political issue is always more than the specific practices through which it is confronted. When Latour accuses materialism of assuming it already knows in advance what matter is, he is taking another step in a realist direction.[79] Whether one prefers Barad's materialism or Latour's incipient realism, this is a debate well worth having.

Notes

1 Bruno Latour, *We Have Never Been Modern*, trans. Catherine Porter (Cambridge: Harvard University Press, 1993); Karen Barad, *Meeting the Universe Halfway: Quantum Physics and the Entanglement of Matter and Meaning* (Durham: Duke University Press, 2007).

2 James Lovelock, *Gaia: A New Look at Life on Earth* (Oxford: Oxford University Press, 2016).

3 Slavoj Žižek, "The Hillary Clinton Consensus Is Damaging Democracy," *Newsweek*, August 12, 2016.

4 Bruno Latour, "Two Bubbles of Unrealism: Learning from the Tragedy of Trump," trans. Clara Soudan and Jaeyoon Park, *The Los Angeles Review of Books*, November 17, 2016. https://lareviewofbooks.org/article/two-bubbles-unrealism-learning-tragedy-trump/ (accessed March 12, 2019).

5 Bruno Latour, *Down to Earth: Politics in the New Climactic Regime*, trans. Catherine Porter (Cambridge: Polity, 2018).

6   Ray Brassier, Iain Hamilton Grant, Graham Harman, and Quentin Meillassoux, "Speculative Realism," *Collapse* III (2007): 306–449; Graham Harman, *Speculative Realism: An Introduction* (Cambridge: Polity, 2018).
7   Bruno Latour, Graham Harman, and Peter Erdélyi, *The Prince and the Wolf: Latour and Harman at the LSE* (Winchester: Zero Books, 2011), 96.
8   Graham Harman, *Bruno Latour: Reassembling the Political* (London: Pluto, 2014), 32–55.
9   Bruno Latour, *We Have Never Been Modern*; Steven Shapin and Simon Schaffer, *Leviathan and the Air-Pump: Hobbes, Boyle, and the Experimental Life* (Princeton, NJ: Princeton University Press, 1985).
10 Bruno Latour, *Politics of Nature: How to Bring the Sciences into Democracy*, trans. Catherine Porter (Cambridge: Harvard University Press, 2004).
11 Bruno Latour, *An Inquiry into Modes of Existence: An Anthropology of the Moderns*, trans. Catherine Porter (Cambridge, MA: Harvard University Press, 2013).
12 Noortje Marres, "No Issue, No Public: Democratic Deficits after the Displacement of Politics," PhD dissertation, University of Amsterdam, The Netherlands, 2005; Noortje Marres, "Issues Spark a Public into Being: A Key but Often Forgotten Point of the Lippmann-Dewey Debate," in *Making Things Public: Atmospheres of Democracy*, ed. Peter Weibel and Bruno Latour, 208–17 (Cambridge: MIT Press, 2005); Noortje Marres, *Material Participation: Technology, the Environment, and Everyday Publics* (London: Palgrave Macmillan, 2015).
13 Walter Lippmann, *The Phantom Public* (New Brunswick: Transaction Publishers, 1993); John Dewey, *The Public and Its Problems: An Essay in Political Inquiry* (University Park: Penn State University Press, 2012).
14 Shirley Strum and Bruno Latour, "Redefining the Social Link: From Baboons to Humans." *Social Science Information* 26, no. 4 (1987): 783–802.
15 Harman, *Bruno Latour: Reassembling the Political*, 161–78.
16 Alfred North Whitehead, *Process and Reality: An Essay in Cosmology* (New York: Free Press, 1979).
17 Bruno Latour, *Pandora's Hope: Essays on the Reality of Science Studies* (Cambridge: Harvard University Press, 1999), 122.
18 Bruno Latour, "Can We Get Our Materialism Back, Please?" *Isis* 98 (2007): 138–42.
19 Latour, "Two Bubbles of Unrealism: Learning from the Tragedy of Trump."
20 Ibid.
21 Ibid.
22 Ibid.
23 Ibid.
24 Ibid.
25 Ibid.
26 Ibid.

27 Latour, *Down to Earth*, 1.
28 Ibid.
29 Ibid., 1–2.
30 Ibid., 4.
31 Ibid., 5.
32 Ibid.
33 Ibid., 22.
34 Ibid.
35 Ibid., 24.
36 Ibid.
37 Graham Harman, *Object-Oriented Ontology: A New Theory of Everything* (London: Pelican, 2018), 3–7.
38 Latour, *Down to Earth*, 25 Emphasis added.
39 Martin Heidegger, *Being and Time*, trans. John Macquarrie and Edward Robinson (New York: Harper, 2008); Graham Harman, *Tool-Being: Heidegger and the Metaphysics of Objects* (Chicago: Open Court, 2002).
40 Isabelle Stengers, *Cosmopolitics I*, trans. Robert Bononno (Minneapolis: University of Minnesota Press, 2011); Isabelle Stengers, *Cosmopolitics II*, trans. Robert Bononno (Minneapolis: University of Minnesota Press, 2011); Graham Harman, "Stengers on Emergence," *BioSocieties* 9, no. 1 (March 2014): 99–104.
41 Latour, *Down to Earth*, 33–4.
42 Ibid., 34.
43 Ibid., 35.
44 Ibid., 38.
45 Ibid.
46 Ibid., 52.
47 Ibid., 84.
48 Bruno Latour, "On the Partial Existence of Existing and Non-existing Objects," in *Biographies of Scientific Objects*, ed. Lorraine Daston, 247–69 (Chicago: University of Chicago Press, 2000).
49 Latour, *Down to Earth*, 27.
50 Ibid.
51 Ibid.
52 Ibid.
53 Ibid.
54 Ibid., 28.
55 Ibid., 28–9.
56 Ibid., 30.
57 Ibid., 32.
58 Ibid., 34–5.

59 Bruno Latour, *Facing Gaia: Eight Lectures on the New Climactic Regime*, trans. Catherine Porter (Cambridge: Polity, 2017).
60 Ibid., 41.
61 Ibid., 43.
62 Ibid., 46.
63 Ibid., 45.
64 Ibid., 46.
65 Carl Schmitt, *The Concept of the Political*, trans. George Schwab (Chicago: University of Chicago Press, 1996).
66 Latour, *Down to Earth*, 53.
67 Ibid., 82.
68 Ibid., 53.
69 Ibid., 54.
70 Ibid., 57.
71 Ibid., 59.
72 Ibid., 60.
73 Timothy Mitchell, *Carbon Democracy: Political Power in the Age of Oil* (London: Verso, 2011).
74 Schmitt, *The Concept of the Political*, 58.
75 Jean-Jacques Rousseau, *Discourse on the Origin of Inequality*, trans. Donald A. Cress (Indianapolis: Hackett, 1992).
76 Latour, *Down to Earth*, 66.
77 Graham Harman, "Agential and Speculative Realism: Remarks on Barad's Ontology." *Rhizomes: Cultural Studies in Emerging Knowledge* 30 (2016). http://www.rhizomes.net/issue30/harman.html (accessed 12 March 2019).
78 Latour, *Pandora's Hope*, 122.
79 Latour, "Can We Get Our Materialism Back, Please?"

Bibliography

Barad, Karen. *Meeting the Universe Halfway: Quantum Physics and the Entanglement of Matter and Meaning*. Durham: Duke University Press, 2007.

Brassier, Ray, Iain Hamilton Grant, Graham Harman, and Quentin Meillassoux. "Speculative Realism." *Collapse* III (2007): 306–449.

Dewey, John. *The Public and Its Problems: An Essay in Political Inquiry*. University Park: Penn State University Press, 2012.

Harman, Graham. "Agential and Speculative Realism: Remarks on Barad's Ontology." *Rhizomes: Cultural Studies in Emerging Knowledge* 30 (2016). http://www.rhizomes.net/issue30/harman.html (accessed March 12, 2019).

Harman, Graham. *Bruno Latour: Reassembling the Political*. London: Pluto, 2014.
Harman, Graham. *Object-oriented Ontology: A New Theory of Everything*. London: Pelican, 2018.
Harman, Graham. *Speculative Realism: An Introduction*. Cambridge: Polity, 2018.
Harman, Graham. "Stengers on Emergence." *BioSocieties* 9, no. 1 (March 2014): 99–104.
Harman, Graham. *Tool-Being: Heidegger and the Metaphysics of Objects*. Chicago: Open Court, 2002.
Heidegger, Martin. *Being and Time*. Translated by John Macquarrie and Edward Robinson. New York: Harper, 2008.
Latour, Bruno. *An Inquiry into Modes of Existence: An Anthropology of the Moderns*. Translated by Catherine Porter. Cambridge: Harvard University Press, 2013.
Latour, Bruno. "Two Bubbles of Unrealism: Learning from the Tragedy of Trump." Translated by Clara Soudan and Jaeyoon Park, *The Los Angeles Review of Books*, November 17, 2016. https://lareviewofbooks.org/article/two-bubbles-unrealism-learning-tragedy-trump/ (accessed March 12, 2019).
Latour, Bruno. "Can We Get Our Materialism Back, Please?" *Isis* 98 (2007): 138–42.
Latour, Bruno. *Down to Earth: Politics in the New Climactic Regime*. Translated by Catherine Porter. Cambridge: Polity, 2018.
Latour, Bruno. *Facing Gaia: Eight Lectures on the New Climactic Regime*. Translated by Catherine Porter. Cambridge: Polity, 2017.
Latour, Bruno. *Pandora's Hope: Essays on the Reality of Science Studies*. Cambridge: Harvard University Press, 1999.
Latour, Bruno. "On the Partial Existence of Existing and Non-existing Objects." In *Biographies of Scientific Objects*. Edited by Lorraine Daston, 247–69. Chicago: University of Chicago Press, 2000.
Latour, Bruno. *Politics of Nature: How to Bring the Sciences into Democracy*. Translated by Catherine Porter. Cambridge: Harvard University Press, 2004.
Latour, Bruno. *We Have Never Been Modern*. Translated by Catherine Porter. Cambridge: Harvard University Press, 2003.
Latour, Bruno, Graham Harman, and Peter Erdélyi. *The Prince and the Wolf: Latour and Harman at the LSE*. Winchester: Zero Books, 2011.
Lippmann, Walter. *The Phantom Public*. New Brunswick: Transaction Publishers, 1993.
Lovelock, James. *Gaia: A New Look at Life on Earth*. Oxford: Oxford University Press, 2016.
Marres, Noortje. "Issues Spark a Public into Being: A Key but Often Forgotten Point of the Lippmann-Dewey Debate." In *Making Things Public: Atmospheres of Democracy*. Edited by Peter Weibel and Bruno Latour. 208–17. Cambridge: MIT Press, 2005.
Marres, Noortje. *No Issue, No Public: Democratic Deficits after the Displacement of Politics*. PhD dissertation, University of Amsterdam, 2005. http://dare.uva.nl/record/165542 (accessed March 12, 2019).

Marres, Noortje. *Material Participation: Technology, the Environment, and Everyday Publics*. London: Palgrave Macmillan, 2015.
Mitchell, Timothy. *Carbon Democracy: Political Power in the Age of Oil*. London: Verso, 2011.
Rousseau, Jean-Jacques. *Discourse on the Origin of Inequality*. Translated by Donald A. Cress. Indianapolis: Hackett, 1992.
Schmitt, Carl. *The Concept of the Political*. Translated by George Schwab. Chicago: University of Chicago Press, 1996.
Shapin, Steven, and Simon Schaffer. *Leviathan and the Air-Pump: Hobbes, Boyle, and the Experimental Life*. Princeton: Princeton University Press, 1985.
Stengers, Isabelle. *Cosmopolitics I*. Translated by Robert Bononno. Minneapolis: University of Minnesota Press, 2011.
Stengers, Isabelle. *Cosmopolitics II*. Translated by Robert Bononno. Minneapolis: University of Minnesota Press, 2011.
Strum, Shirley, and Bruno Latour. "Redefining the Social Link: From Baboons to Humans." *Social Science Information* 26, no. 4 (1987): 783–802.
Whitehead, Alfred North. *Process and Reality: An Essay in Cosmology*. New York: Free Press, 1979.
Žižek, Slavoj. "The Hillary Clinton Consensus Is Damaging Democracy." *Newsweek*. August 12, 2016. https://www.newsweek.com/slavoj-zizek-hillary-clinton-donald-trump-us-presidential-election-bernie-489993 (accessed March 12, 2019).

10

Literary Worlds: Indigenous and Western Network Ethnography

Stephen Muecke

Within a Latourian framework, literary works are seen as compositions[1] embedded in a network of practices, rather than as communications that use language as the preeminent medium. How can literary works be neither communications from author to reader, or narrator to listener, nor texts abstracted from the layers of contexts that make them possible? The experiment to be performed in this chapter will examine the possibilities emerging from the conceptual architecture provided by Bruno Latour's *networks* and Isabelle Stengers's *cosmopolitics* and that enable an alternate compositional approach to literary works. In practical terms, seeing a reader as *networked* means locating that reader in a heterogeneous environment. To read well, one might need, for instance, a quiet room and a comfortable chair, but also a habit of reading, an anticipated pleasure (or, indeed, a duty: a reading group or tutorial for which one is reading), a familiarity with a national literary canon, a commitment to feminist theory, and so on. We can be fairly neutral and descriptive about a network, but as we attend to the compositions of worlds, we are faced with decisions about what can be added to or subtracted from them: such world-making decisions are *cosmopolitical*. Latour has a useful summary of his friend Isabelle's cosmopolitics:

> Stengers intends her use of *cosmopolitics* to alter what it means "to belong" or "to pertain." She has reinvented the word by representing it as a composite of the strongest meaning of cosmos and the strongest meaning of politics precisely because the usual meaning of the word *cosmopolite* supposed a certain theory of science that is now disputed. For her, the strength of one element checks any dulling in the strength of the other. The presence of *cosmos* in *cosmopolitics*

resists the tendency of *politics* to mean the give-and-take in an exclusive human club. The presence of *politics* in *cosmopolitics* resists the tendency of *cosmos* to mean a finite list of entities that must be taken into account. *Cosmos* protects against the premature closure of *politics*, and *politics* against the premature closure of *cosmos*.[2]

The experiment for this chapter takes place in an anthropological "laboratory" which has various pieces of theoretical apparatus at hand, plus a method: ethnographic writing. The premise is this: *literary networks cannot be perceived immediately in all their extensions by an observer. The observer, who is also a writer, has to move forward making the network real by following its extensions.* Here is my hypothetical question: is ethnography a good method for realizing networks in this way?

The aim of writing ethnographically about an indigenous world would thus be to *realize* this world, to make it real in the writing. I shall argue that that necessarily means seeing that world, and all worlds worthy of the name, as multiply real. But "seeing" and "writing" are only verbs with a limited purchase in an unknown ontologically diverse network stretching in all directions. It is for this reason that we cannot isolate "literary effects" just in language, as Latour cautions,[3] for what makes literature into literature always remains to be discovered, but where? It is not locked up in texts (the formalist focus), nor in reference to their binary opposite, context (which we will see not as a simple "real world out there" but as a plurality of contexts zigzagging along networks).[4] The text-context opposition, therefore, is not enough to constitute a world. Worlds are relabeled by Tobie Nathan as "multiple universe societies,"[5] while those that oppose subject and object, human mind and one external reality, have reduced complexity to the point where Isabelle Stengers draws a battle line: "The global West is not a 'world' and recognizes no world. Referring to Deleuze and Guattari I would rather characterize it as a 'machine,' destroying both politics and ontologies."[6]

Later, I will characterize earlier attempts at rendering Indigenous stories in print as machine-like, stripping away large swathes of their world, reducing a multiple universe society to one, reducing semiotic multimodality to a Standard English. That effectively removes Aboriginal poetics and style, assimilating what remains of the Aboriginal content.

As an ethnographer, I worked with Paddy Roe (*c.* 1912–2001), Nyigina elder in the Indigenous community of Broome, Western Australia, from the late 1970s. Someway into our working relationship, I realized I was turning him into an author. As we worked to establish literary texts based on his stories, a set of translations were performed to transform a corpus of artful oral narratives into artful written literature. That he became an "author" was not of great significance for the old man, but it was important for me because the habitual way of processing Indigenous peoples' words was to treat them as "informants" who would not have their name on the cover of the book, whose words were translated from traditional languages into standard written English for the page, who would not be in receipt of royalties nor any of the other legal and moral rights pertaining to authorship. One could say that the category "informant" was another of those roadblocks to decolonization, a subaltern category a long way from "teacher" or "colleague" that more enlightened anthropologists had started to use.[7] In the case of our first book, Paddy Roe was author and I was editor.[8]

It was not important for Roe to acquire a new identity as author, and books did not figure importantly in his world. Many of his descendants, who have learned to read and write in English, have little interest in books today. But they, like him, recognize their prestige and encourage my labors in producing them so that they will have some kind of positive impact in the *gardiya* world, the world of the white people. So, while I had a good practical knowledge of the world—or perhaps the "machine"—of "Western" literary production, I was a newcomer to the oral literatures of the Western Kimberley, and started to learn more as I sat with my patient teachers, Paddy Roe and Butcher Joe.

I learned that there were several genres of oral literary production. We spoke in Aboriginal English, a kind of creole, and I figured out that the genres that existed in Paddy's traditional languages—Nyigina, Yawuru, etc.—which I hadn't learned, carried over into Aboriginal English. Among the stories there were *bugarrigarra* stories, timeless stories from the Dreaming, and *trustori*, stories about events with real people from the recent past. "What about when you make stories up?" I asked, looking for something equivalent to "fiction." "Ah, we call-im liar story," Paddy replied with a laugh. "Might be I tell you snake behine that tree … You look? Ah, go on! Liar story!" Then I learned from Butcher Joe, the holder of songs, that he had a *nurlu*[9] and I saw it performed several times, and that there were other genres of songs, *jabi* and *lilyin* that the two men enjoyed translating for me.[10]

Without prompting, Butcher Joe would tell you where his *nurlu* came from. A spirit came to him in dreams. When I shared a camp with him early in our relationship, he would wake long before sunrise and I would hear him singing softly. Anthropologist Kim Akerman gives further details:

> Even as a young man, he had regularly experienced spirit visitations in the course of his dreams. In the mid-1920s, during one such visitation, the spirit of his dead "aunt" Kintimayi emerged from her grave at Wayikurrkurr on Dampier Downs. The spirit bestowed the Pelican Being, Mayata [*mayiarda*], upon Joe as a personal *jalnga* or spirit familiar and taught him the *marinji-rinji nulu*, a dance depicting the transformational processes by which spirits of the dead may reveal themselves and communicate benevolently with the living. Joe last performed the *Mayata nulu* [*mayiarda nurlu*], with its distinctive thread-cross headdress, in 1985.[11]

It was real all right. He would show you the headdress, and draw a picture with three figures: the pelican (*mayiarda*); the *balangan* (a skeleton, a spirit of the dead woman who gave him the songs), and a man dancing with body paint and his pelican headdress. His descendants perform a version of this *nurlu* today. To the extent that the spirit and the pelican as totem are part of their world, their universe is "multiple." And to the extent that the "Moderns," as Latour calls the colonizing Europeans, *subtracted* spirits from their cosmos and relegated them to the status of mere belief; then their world became impoverished, one dimensional and machine-like. They would borrow "objectivity" and "rationality" from scientific talk to give their limited realism more authority, as if that were the point: to empower the machine for destroying other worlds. All of Latour's institutional modes of existence would thus move in concert, the law, religion, science, economics, and aesthetics. But it is on this last one I should pause and continue so that I can eventually elaborate a description of a "multiple universe" literary world.

The Goolarabooloo Aesthetic

The Goolarabooloo aesthetic—"Goolarabooloo" is the term in the West Kimberley used to designate that set of "west coast cultures"—is territorial, or rather "earthbound," to use Latour's term.[12] Traditional peoples are tied to their sacred lands, refusing to budge, and no wonder: they have a pagan[13] god in every river and mountain, they have a vitalist and totemic extended kinship system that links humans to an array of animals and plants. Ancestors and spirits inhabit parallel universes to their own, and they use special techniques to interface with these other parts of their worlds. Among all the complex things that inhabit this world, you can't pick and choose: you can't suddenly decide you are not going to "believe" in *balangan* any longer, or stop protecting a special species of tree whose wood is used in a man-making ceremony. All of these things are tied together in a heterogeneous network with two fundamental concepts at its center: territory, called "country," and *bugarrigarra*, the law and culture of the Dreaming.

Underpinning the Moderns' aesthetic, on the other hand, is a singular concept of Nature, that they have sovereignty over. This is the *one* world, the "real" environment surrounding them, and it suits them to stand outside of this natural world, in their cultures, distant and somewhat omniscient (like their one god above them) and free to roam globally. It was a religion of the Book that went out proselytizing, for if God gave Moses the tablets of the covenant on Mt. Sinai, it is not the *mountain* that is significant, but the *text* and its communication. The cultures of the Book—religion, science, and law—spread around the world with an attitude of destruction that increased in intensity with modernization. Not only were colonized peoples' languages "mumbo-jumbo," but customs were superstition, and formulaic language along with spells and chants were disdained.

Table 10.1 sets out the opposition between these two kinds of aesthetic, borrowing on Tobie Nathan's type of tables.

Let's analyze how the first book I created with Paddy Roe was composed. The first division governing the selection was secret vs. public. Paddy was careful to announce at the outset that "[t]his is all public [...] for everybody: [c]hildren women, anybody."[14] This makes it implicit that there is a deeper,

Table 10.1 Two Kinds of Literary "Environments"

	One Universe Societies	**Multiple Universe Societies**
Era	Modern	Traditional
Media	The book	The word
Social actors	Individual	Collective
	Author	Muse
	Reader	Custodian
Pedagogy	Interpretation and techniques of the self	Repetition and mimesis
Technology	Mechanical reproduction	Corporeal and territorial
Human extension	Imaginative and non-real	Magical and powerful
Environment	Context	Linked universes

more restricted knowledge, that he knows, that only initiated men know. So, there are *bugarrigarra* and *trustori*, all of them tied to the territory by specific place names. As with Butcher Joe's *balangan*, his "muse" (a similar Western concept that modernity turned into something quaint), stories are immanent to country; they don't transcend it. When you travel that country, people will tell you stories about places as you pause there, or travel through, especially if you are on an old route, where each place might have a song, public or secret, and Paddy might start singing as he starts to remember further details.

Paddy is a skilled storyteller, on the way to being gathered up into another literary network that will receive him as an author, even though "illiterate" Aboriginal people had never been authors before. But what was storytelling for him? How did it connect him to country and to other people? "See … it's a thing like this," he might begin, picking up a stick to draw in the sand as he sits cross-legged under his old tamarind tree. A whitefella might have come asking about something. Often they wanted to build on a site or put in a road. Far from simply refusing, Paddy would offer to supplement the necessary information with the pleasure of listening to a story, and Paddy's authority would be folded into that of the *bugarrigarra* and the other law bosses who are beholden to it. It is the needs of the country that ultimately decide, and in mysterious ways, "something like that. We don't know, but it's a power." The authority is collective and intergenerational. Storytellers and songmen are *holders* of "the word," of heritage; their duty is to pass it on. "The word" and right to "hold" it carry responsibilities and practical information.

These compositional principles are internal to the text as well. A little textual analysis will show how this schema plays out all the way down to the structure of the text. The first story in the book begins like this:

> Yeah - - - - -
>   Well these people bin camping in Fisherman Bend him and his missus you know - -
>   Fisherman bend in Broome, *karnun* - -
>   We call-im *karnun* - - -[15]

In listening to Paddy Roe tell his story, I adapted a mode of transcription used by the famous pioneer in ethnopoetics, Dennis Tedlock.[16] He and I had both been trained in linguistics, so we were conscious of the need to transcribe accurately (I include dashes for end of line pauses). And because of a sense of meaningful linguistic variation, that is, poetics, we were aware that while people often didn't talk in sentences, verbal arts used different formulas to everyday speech.

Other peoples' oral literatures—folk tales, legends, myths—had often been transcribed by being standardized to proper sentences as they were removed from the context of performance. So, the above beginning of the story might have been rendered as:

> A man and his wife were living near Broome at a place called Fisherman's Bend. The local people call it *karnun*.

But Roe's technique is to alternate pause and speech. He breathes in the pause and each line of speech is a breath group. It is a corporeal technique, the same as is used in songs in the region.

Another technique is expansion through repetition: "these people" become "him and his missus" in the one line. Some redundancy of information, plus expansion. It makes it easy on the listener. A bit of redundancy makes it easier for you, doesn't it? And you can see that "Fisherman Bend" is repeated and then expanded to the regional location, Broome. That reference is destined for the listener outside of the region. The narrator includes a broader audience, as if he knows his story will become a book and be read in faraway places. But it is then translated into another world, the world of the Indigenous collective, the locals ("we") who know it by another name, *karnun*. This is a hint of the "multiple universes" to come. We will find out that the main character, Mirdinan, has magical powers that open a portal to a world inaccessible to non-Indigenous people.

My experiment at modernist rendering has taken away the collective "we" and hence Paddy Roe's authorship. This kind of radical textual violence was not unusual in the rewriting of Indigenous stories. But, even more violently, it removes the possibility of multiple universes, as the new third person narrator looks down on the *one real world*.

I wasn't aware of it at the time that I was coming from an environment where literary production was conceived of in relation to one (reduced) world to one where literary production saw its job as linking different parts of a multiple world. In the cities, writers were happy to invent other worlds imaginatively. They were called fiction; they were not real. But in Paddy Roe's country, there is no such thing as "fiction" (only *trustori*, "liar" stories (where you might trick people) and *bugarrigarra*, Dreaming stories). It is to this last category that magical portals to other parts of the cosmos are kept open through the arts of performance.

Now I could have listened to Paddy Roe over and over (as his family did) and become more attuned to the glimpses to these other universes that his performances afforded. But I was a young man in a hurry; I thought I had to get a book out quickly. So, I extended my capacity to listen with a clever piece of technology that was fairly new at the time, the cassette tape recorder, now vintage electronic nostalgia.

What was the literary environment like in which I got busy with my tape recorder? There were often other people present, interjecting, laughing, being consulted. These laughs and noises and interruptions all got transcribed, and I worked also with pen and notebook, sometimes doing interlinear translations of songs in the Nyigina, Ngumbal, or Jabirr-Jabirr languages. There was the occasional Malay word, since those men had come to Broome for the pearling industry in the early twentieth century. Paddy used to write with his finger in the sand, carefully smoothing a space, making his icons while telling his story; erasing it at the end with his hand, again carefully, and finishing by saying *mabu* (good). His story stayed where it was. Mine was captured by the alphabet, then by the notebook, to be taken away. And it was captured by the magnetized ferrous particles in the cassette tape. Then the technologies multiplied themselves. Imagine: back at my desk, I had my notebook, the cassette was now in a dictaphone machine, audio output to headphones, with a stop–start foot-pedal for transcription, my fingers flying over the keyboard of an electric typewriter, at the time. What a complex apparatus, and yet all the time I had imagined that Paddy was telling a story to me, one human to another, along a line of communication! How wrong I was; it was a network already, heterogeneously composed of humans, machines, concepts, habits, and feelings. All this just to make a book!

I had a feeling it could be a book, at any rate, and approached an editor—handed it over to Ray Coffey at Adelaide Writer's Week, editor of another enabling network, Fremantle Arts Centre Press, and a few months later the pages were flying through machines that had descended from Gutenberg, at Frank Daniels printery, Perth, typeset in 11/12 pt. IBM Press Roman, printed on 115 grams per square meter Satintone paper stock.

Such an actor network description of the literary environment has the usual effect of decentering the human. It turns to the literary ecology as an enabling composition, or even compost, debunking the old Weaver and Shannon "line of communication" model for literary ontology. That's long gone, but the humanist bias still exists in the form of the desire to enhance expressiveness and receptiveness, being "open" to the other, as in Barbara Smuts:

> Experience suggests that by opening more fully to the presence of "self" in others, including animals, we further develop that presence in ourselves and thus become more fully alive and awake participants in life.[17]

This generalized openness is far too imprecise, and focused on interiorities, to which I have an aversion (the article is called "Encounters with Animal Minds" and it is in the *Journal of Consciousness Studies*). I would rather specify all the mediations and heterogeneous network chains that go into literary composition. Maybe the Sony tape recorder was the most important actor in my literary environment with Paddy. Maybe, to paraphrase Debbie Bird Rose, "tape recorder makes us human," because the human is not given in advance (it is a work in progress).[18] The human has no capacity for *generalized* expansion. It can grow and extend its capacities, and this is of utmost importance, but it can only do so with *specific technologies*, with specific kinds of *craft*. To the extent that the tape recorder can make us listen really carefully, like we never could before, in a super-human way, then yes, "tape recorder makes us human" because it enables us to reproduce ourselves in a new and risky way, with a leap into a way of being human with a bit more capacity than we thought we had going for us.

So, to summarize and extend the argument, literary ecologies are all about the networked relations that are the compost with the right culture for something to germinate. Even a book burgeoning in a printing press required a lot of people to say "yes" to its potential, and they weren't just responding to "it," they were responding to a network of concepts, hunches about changing protocols and race relations, and institutional structures. To this I added the point that the literary experiments are about extensions of the human, without making much of a distinction between living and non-living things. An animal capacity, like a dog's sense of smell used in airport security, is networked to human capacities, and the tape recorder's capacity to listen is not essentially any different, except that the idea of purely technological extensions is a science fiction that has been particularly damaging to the living world: the hawk's eye is replaced by binoculars; the horse by a motorcycle; healing by medicine—these are all great steps for mankind, are they not?—and before long unique forms of life, each with its *umwelt*, become extinct. We never really needed Tasmanian tigers; they were just wild animals killing sheep.

This is not an argument for "our" preservation of pure natural forms that would be buying into the nature–culture opposition that obscures networks, a perspective that inhibits their descriptive realization. Without that opposition, we can create room for Nathan's "multiple universe" societies or for Latour's multiple "modes of existence."[19] Let me close with an example from each.

In the Paddy Roe story, the main character, Mirdinan, murders his wife and is pursued by the police. He evades them with his magical powers as a *maban* (sorcerer). They enable him to transform himself dramatically in a three-part repetition. First, he disappears from his chains and has to be recaptured. Then he transforms himself into a cat and walks out of prison, then finally into a totemic being, an eaglehawk. This demonstrates his power to articulate with a parallel dimension of the world that the police cannot even perceive. Mirdinan had techniques that open portals onto this other dimension. When you live in a multiple universe society like him, you live with ghosts, spirits of ancestors, and beings from the dreaming. But it is not like you and they are part of the *one society*, like you can go to the supermarket and see your great-great-grandmother buying yoghurt. Or that you are interested to find that the spirit of Captain Cook is a competitor for the job you are applying for. No, it is rather that there would be, in any animist, totemic, or multiple universe society, elaborate rituals and techniques for making contact with ancestor spirits: you have to enter another world to interact with their world. Precisely what the Moderns do if they go to church. You have to work at it, put a lot of elements in place for the magic to work. In the case of church—music, sacred words, incense, the flesh and blood of Christ, etc.—to break through into another dimension, the "actants" have to knot and bind in ritual that is precise and well-performed.

Now, turning to the modern literary ecology, the "mode of existence" that is privileged is FICtion, to use Latour's grapheme. To give it its full ontological weight, fiction has to be seen as not a mere construction of the real, a weak reflection best judged from a standpoint in the one and only "real world." As with multiple universe societies, you would have to be a bit crazy to spend all your life living with fictional characters. The usual procedure is to create special occasions on which fictions can be better understood, felt, and transformed into something else. These are necessarily somewhat ritualistic, because while you might come out of the experience of encountering Hamlet in school somewhat transformed, you still have to go back to "real life," before repeating the ritual again later on. These rituals or special occasions take place in classrooms, art galleries, or cinemas, with specific techniques that are open to description within the framework of an "ecology of practices."[20] These techniques constitute "know-how" rather than knowledge, minor skills often overlooked in the building up of disciplinary knowledge. Teaching *Hamlet*, then, would not be a matter of imparting the knowledge that the pupil should know, but a skillful description that ties the pupil's thoughts and desires into the "world" of Hamlet, a description that probably induces, in the pupil, admiration for both the teacher and Shakespeare *at the same time*.

So, you can see what I was trying to show that there is indeed a flowing together between so-called traditional societies seen as "multiple universe societies" and the Moderns with their multiple modes of existence, as restored by Latour, Stengers, and Nathan. The descriptive details are all different, and realization through the ethnographic description of practices will show networks that are not at all smooth and flat. Networks cross each other and knot and bind in ways I have described as ritualistic, rituals that have to be well-performed to keep these separate existences alive.

Notes

1   Bruno Latour, "An Attempt at a 'Compositionist Manifesto,'" *New Literary History* 41 (2010): 471–90.
2   Bruno Latour, "Whose Cosmos, Which Cosmopolitics? Comments on the Peace Terms of Ulrich Beck," *Common Knowledge* 10, no. 3 (2004): 454. For Stengers's notion of "cosmopolitics," see Isabelle Stengers, *Cosmopolitics I*, trans. Robert Bononno (Minneapolis: University of Minnesota Press, 2010).
3   "Language becomes an isolated domain only through the desperate effort to make the continuity of beings hold up despite the drift of beings-as-other: then, indeed, we find ourselves with a sign emptied of sense that seeks to catch what is fleeing from it and that, unable to do so, resigns itself to clinging to another sign to try to 'make world' in spite of everything; but it is a poor world, a world that has lost the world." Bruno Latour, *An Inquiry into Modes of Existence: An Anthropology of the Moderns*, trans. Catherine Porter (Cambridge: Harvard University Press, 2013), 257.
4   "Let us note first of all that with the notion and even the connotations of the word 'network' we have gained *room* and *space* where we can collect values without merely mouthing the words. If we get into the habit of speaking of trajectories and passes that are limited and specific to each occasion for the paths of persistence [REP], chains of reference [REF], law [LAW], or political autonomy [POL], the landscape spread out before the observer is already entirely different from the one that obliged him to believe himself surrounded on all sides by an 'external material world' that would have invaded the entire space and that would have forced all

the other values to retreat little by little. But to go where? Into the mind? Into the brain? Into language? Into symbolics? No one knew. It was a black hole. Stifling. Suffocating." (Latour, *An Inquiry into Modes of Existence*, 141. Original emphasis.)

5   Tobie Nathan has a number of "clinical tables" in a recent book that specify a number of factors that impinge on medical and healing contexts, contrasting "multiple" and "single" universe societies. The single universe is constituted by the "modern" subject/object division, such that the material universe is constituted by the objective world "out there." See Bruno Latour's numerous works critiquing this concept of a singular nature, and for the tables, see Tobie Nathan and Isabelle Stengers, *Doctors and Healers*, trans. Stephen Muecke (London: Polity Press, 2018).

6   Isabelle Stengers, "The Challenge to Ontological Politics," in *A World of Many Worlds*, ed. Marisol de la Cadena and Mario Blaser (Durham: Duke University Press, 2018), 88.

7   For instance, Deborah Bird Rose, *Dingo Makes Us Human: Life and Land in an Australian Aboriginal Culture* (Melbourne: Cambridge University Press, 1992).

8   Paddy Roe, *Gularabulu: Stories from the West Kimberley*, ed. Stephen Muecke (Crawley: University of Western Australia Press, 2016).

9   "Nurlu … refers to songs and dances which are performed by men and women in an 'open' context (no restrictions apply to who may participate in or watch performances) and which are believed to have originated comparatively recently, usually as a result of singers being given songs in dream from various spirit beings. The songs and dances belong to those same singers, which in all the cases I have documented are male. The songs are accompanied by pairs of boomerangs struck together and by body percussion. The dances may feature elaborate wanggararra, that is 'head gear' or 'totems' which are worn or carried by the performers." Ray Keogh, "Nurlu Songs of the West Kimberleys" (PhD dissertation, University of Sydney, 1990), 1. On p. 31 Keogh notes: "Butcher Joe's nurlu comprises over 50 songs and perhaps 20 dances."

10 Stephen Muecke, "The Great Tradition: Translating Durrudiya's Songs," in *Decolonizing the Landscape: Indigenous Cultures in Australia*, ed. Beate Neumeier and Kay Schaffer, 23–36 (Amsterdam: Rodopi, 2013).

11 Kim Akerman, "The Art of Butcher Joe Nangan," in *Likan'mirri—Connections: The AIATSIS Collection of Art*, ed. Wally Caruana (Canberra: Australian National University, 2004), 44; see also Stephen Muecke, *Butcher Joe*, Documenta 13: 100 Notizen—100 Gedanken No. 054 English/German (Hatje Cantz Verlag: Ostfildern, 2011).

12 Bruno Latour, *Facing Gaia. Eight Lectures on the New Climatic Regime*, trans. Catherine Porter (London: Polity Press, 2017), 248–53.

13 The etymology of *pagan* is Late Latin, *pagus*, "country."

14 Roe, *Gularabulu*, 1.
15 Ibid., 24.
16 *Finding the Center: Narrative Poetry of the Zuni Indians*, trans. Dennis Tedlock (Lincoln: University of Nebraska Press, 1978).
17 Barbara Smuts, "Encounters with Animal Minds," *Journal of Consciousness Studies* 8, no. 5–7 (2001): 308. I use this quotation chosen at random, as an example of language used. It is not meant to reflect on the considerable corpus of Smuts' ethological work.
18 Rose, *Dingo Makes Us Human*.
19 Latour, *An Inquiry into Modes of Existence*.
20 Isabelle Stengers, "Introductory Notes on an Ecology of Practices," *Cultural Studies Review* 11, no. 1 (2005): 183–96.

Bibliography

Akerman, Kim. "The Art of Butcher Joe Nangan." In *Likan'mirri—Connections: The AIATSIS Collection of Art*. Edited by Wally Caruana. Canberra: Australian National University, 2004.

Keogh, Ray. "Nurlu Songs of the West Kimberleys." PhD dissertation, University of Sydney, 1990.

Latour, Bruno. "An Attempt at a 'Compositionist Manifesto.'" *New Literary History* 41 (2010): 471–90.

Latour, Bruno. *Facing Gaia. Eight Lectures on the New Climatic Regime*. Translated by Catherine Porter. London: Polity Press, 2017.

Latour, Bruno. *An Inquiry into Modes of Existence: An Anthropology of the Moderns*. Cambridge: Harvard University Press, 2013.

Latour, Bruno. "Whose Cosmos, Which Cosmopolitics? Comments on the Peace Terms of Ulrich Beck." *Common Knowledge* 10, no. 3 (2004): 450–62.

Muecke, Stephen. *Butcher Joe*. Documenta 13: 100 Notizen—100 Gedanken No. 054 English/ German. Hatje Cantz Verlag: Ostfildern, 2011.

Muecke, Stephen. "The Great Tradition: Translating Durrudiya's Songs." In *Decolonizing the Landscape: Indigenous Cultures in Australia*. Edited by Beate Neumeier and Kay Schaffer. 23–36. Amsterdam: Rodopi, 2013.

Nathan, Tobie, and Isabelle Stengers. *Doctors and Healers*. Translated by Stephen Muecke. London: Polity Press, 2018.

Roe, Paddy. *Gularabulu: Stories from the West Kimberley*. Edited by Stephen Muecke. Crawley: University of Western Australia Press, 2016.

Rose, Deborah Bird. *Dingo Makes Us Human: Life and Land in an Australian Aboriginal Culture*. Melbourne: Cambridge University Press, 1992.

Stengers, Isabelle. "The Challenge of Ontological Politics." In *A World of Many Worlds*. Edited by Marisol de la Cadena and Mario Blaser, 83–111. Durham: Duke University Press, 2018.

Stengers, Isabelle. *Cosmopolitics I*. Translated by Robert Bononno. Minneapolis: University of Minnesota Press, 2010.

Stengers, Isabelle. "Introductory Notes on an Ecology of Practices." *Cultural Studies Review* 11, no. 1 (2005): 183–96.

Smuts, Barbara. "Encounters with Animal Minds." *Journal of Consciousness Studies* 8, no. 5–7 (2001): 293–309.

Tedlock, Dennis (trans.). *Finding the Center: Narrative Poetry of the Zuni Indians*. Lincoln: University of Nebraska Press, 1978.

Afterword
On the Ambiguities of the Modern

Rita Felski

What does Bruno Latour mean by the "nonmodern"? And how do the contributors to this volume employ or make use of the word? Are their concerns identical, adjacent, or diverging? And what is the modernity that is being questioned or reimagined? When and where is it situated, or seen to be situated? Is the modern a set of economic and material conditions, a philosophical picture, a relationship to time, an aesthetic sensibility? Does it possess an agreed-on set of features? Do understandings of the modern—and therefore of the nonmodern—converge, conflict, or shoot past each other? And what is the relation between Latour's account of the modern and recent discussions of "multiple modernities"?

Nonmodern, in its most common definition, means the premodern: being of, or characteristic of, an earlier time. It is commonly used to refer to those periods that precede modernity, such as the Middle Ages, as well as to currents of thought or cultural forms that are contemporaneous but that are seen as not being fully of their own time. (Religion, for example, has often been thought of as existing in modernity, but not being fully *of* modernity.)

This is not, of course, what Bruno Latour means by nonmodern. The nonmodern, he is at pains to stress, is neither the premodern nor the antimodern (and certainly not the postmodern!). Rather than a period, it denotes a certain *stance* toward the problematic of periodization. The point is to circumvent the conceptual scheme upon which appeals to the modern rely: modernity versus tradition; culture versus nature; subject versus object. (In a few places he avails himself of the term "amodern" to drive home the difference.) These oppositions, he argues, are the product of a "modern Constitution" that has molded Western thought over centuries, with often disastrous consequences: the treatment of the natural world as inert matter to be manipulated; the disdain for religion as an atavistic residue; the relegation of the non-Western world to the primitive and primordial.

This line of argument might seem to echo other influential accounts of modernity, such as Weber's analysis of instrumental rationality or Adorno and Horkheimer's diagnosis of the pathologies of enlightenment. Yet Latour has little patience for the doleful handwringing of cultural pessimists; we have never been disenchanted, he insists, and sweeping critiques of soulless bureaucracies or technology-as-domination impute a homogeneity to the modern world that does not exist. The key difference, then, lies in Latour's insistence that modern dichotomies cannot be sustained; that as well as separating and purifying, modernity also spawns countless hybrids and tangled networks. Even as Nature and Culture are opposed in principle, for example, the chemical composition of the atmosphere, scientific and industrial strategies, the concerns of politicians, and the fears of ecologists remain connected in practice. This line of argument leads Latour to offer his definition: "A nonmodern is anyone who takes simultaneously into account the moderns' Constitution and the populations of hybrids that the Constitution rejects and allows to proliferate."[1]

It is in this sense, then, that we have "never been modern"—the self-image of modernity is one that can never be realized. But how and where did this image arise, such that we came to think that modernity *did* exist? Here Latour engages in a lengthy discussion of *Leviathan and the Air Pump* by Shapin and Schaffer: an exercise in the sociology of scientific knowledge that zeroes in on a series of debates between Boyle and Hobbes in the 1670s. For Latour this disagreement heralds the birth of modern science and politics via a division of intellectual labor. From here on, the task of scientists will be to experiment with nature: to attend, as Latour puts it, to "the testimony of non-humans." Meanwhile politics will concern itself exclusively with the human world and with reason-based adjudications of demands for freedom and equality. "The modern Constitution invents a separation between the scientific power charged with representing things and the political power charged with representing subjects."[2] This scission of culture from nature and of persons from things will have far-reaching consequences.

How does this argument speak to literary critics and *their* conceptions of modernity? In her reflections on poetry, for example, Claire Lyu considers the reception of Mallarmé; meanwhile, William Paulson takes up related questions about literary autonomy in redescribing Flaubert as a nonmodern writer. Both chapters deal with the question of French literary modernity, which is usually traced back to the mid-nineteenth century and the poetry of Baudelaire. In much of the rest of Europe, meanwhile, the emergence of modernism is situated several decades later, in the writings of Kafka and Joyce, for example, that feature in Gabriel Hankins's chapter. In short, the onset of literary modernity is usually placed 200–250 years after the creation of Latour's "modern Constitution." What is the salience, if any, of this time lag? Is the modern a transhistorical formation, or does it look different in the late nineteenth century than it did two centuries earlier?

Further complicating matters is the fact that literary modernism is usually seen as being at odds with the sociological and philosophical meanings of the modern. If processes of modernization are synonymous with the consolidation of capitalism and an emphasis on means-end thinking, writers and critics will increasingly prize literature for its own sake, irrespective of its commercial value or practical use. If philosophical modernity ushers in a new age of reason, modern literature will delve into the chaos of consciousness and the unruliness of desire, testify to the fragility of language and the uncertainty of knowledge. Rather than affirming the tenets of the Enlightenment, it assails them. To what extent, then, is Latour's conception of the modern—with its focus on the early modern history of science and politics—relevant to the concerns of literary scholars? Indeed, an ANT perspective might cause us to query the assumption that modernity can be defined by a moment of origin—by a founding Constitution—in order to trace how it is *re*constituted and recomposed across different times and milieus.

Simon During, for example, contends that Latour's critique of modernity does not engage the humanities, which are neither modern nor nonmodern in Latour's terms. In contrast to the sciences, where earlier knowledge is soon rendered obsolete by new discoveries, there is no sense in which Aristotle and Plato, Shakespeare and Milton, Rembrandt and Bach, have been superseded. "The humanities," During writes, "have had, and still have, their own positive programs, many inherited from eras that predate the 'modern' by anyone's understanding of that term."[3] These programs of humanistic knowledge—involving forms of understanding, empathy, interpretation, and evaluation that stretch from Vico to Nussbaum—play virtually no part in *We Have Never Been Modern*. Meanwhile, During also expresses skepticism about Latour's claim that modernity is founded on schism and opposition—an all too familiar philosophical-historical narrative, he remarks, that drives countless critiques of modernity. Rather, he wants to describe how differing traditions, rhetorics, interests, and methods come together to make the history of the humanities.

And here the seventeenth-century English poet Abraham Cowley, who had personal connections to Hobbes and was familiar with Boyle, serves During as a counter-example to Latour's claims. In Cowley's writing, remarks During, we see a "broad understanding of the poet as simultaneously critic, intellectual, rhetorician, humanist involved in, but not overcome by, the new natural philosophy (i.e. science) and ethically responsible to the nation as a whole."[4] This is a discourse not of division, but of linkages between literary, scientific, ethical, and political domains. During points, for example, to Cowley's "creativism": his vision of the divine, human, and natural world as intimately connected rather than separated. Such a vision would seem to conflict with Latour's claim that modernity renders the mediation that creates hybrids "invisible, unthinkable, unrepresentable."[5] Meanwhile, the status of poetry as a form of communication that is held to be entertainable—rather than true in a scientific or a philosophical sense—allows for a tolerance of ambiguity and a flourishing of competing interpretations.

In short, Cowley exemplifies a tradition of literary creativity and thought that seems very different in kind to that outlined in the modern Constitution. Elsewhere, it should be said, Latour praises literature for very similar reasons—its attention to mediation and the distribution of agency—but During is right to note that such issues do not surface in *We Have Never Been Modern*. Perhaps Latour might respond by pointing out that even if nature and society are interwoven *within* literary works, this has little bearing on what is happening outside those works. Networks of actants have been forged, consolidated, and extended over centuries, shaped by the effects of the modern Constitution, such that—for example—the activities of a British MP have little in common with those of a theoretical physicist or a builder of hydroelectric dams.

The metaphor of the Constitution, however, tends to reinforce a sense of modernity as a single phenomenon: internally unstable, to be sure, yet a relatively coherent whole. In similar fashion, Latour repeatedly refers to "the moderns" as if they were a collective that speaks with one voice. Recent decades, however, have seen a sustained interest in "multiple modernities"—the claim that scrutinizing the modern through the prism of gender, or race, or sexuality alters our sense of what the modern means. I've argued, for example, that a focus on gender decenters sociological accounts of modernity based in economic production (Marx) or instrumental rationality (Weber), while also shaking up literary histories centered on the emblematic figures of Goethe's Faust and Baudelaire's flaneur (the heroes of Marshall Berman's *All That Is Sold Melts into*

Air). Instead, a rather different picture of modernity comes into view, composed of real and mythical female figures: the middle-class shopper entranced by the lavish displays of Parisian department stories; the lesbian who refuses the realm of "nature" and the norms of heterosexual reproduction; the fashion-conscious suffragette who seizes hold of public space; the author of female-centered fictions of the popular sublime; the male aesthete who identifies with an idea of transgressive femininity. Even as such figures came to represent modernity for both women and men in mid- to late-nineteenth-century Europe, they question many of the divisions on which Latour's modern Constitution depends.[6]

Similar arguments have been made around sexuality and race: see, for example, Henning Bech's account of how modern urban culture helped create a distinctively homosexual form of being; Paul Gilroy's recasting of modernity around the trope of the slave ship, or Arjun Appadurai's account of the non-synchrony of modern global flows.[7] Here we see a shift away from both sociological theories of modernization and literary theories of modernism toward what I've dubbed "cultural theories of modernity" that are more fully attuned to the experiences and practices of non-dominant groups, while avoiding identitarian thinking or segregational models—there can be no separate "women's modernity," for example, "the rich brew of ideas, images, and stories that defines the modern world is not simply imposed from above on a docile populace, but is constantly re-created through forms of negotiation and critical response."[8] Modernity is not just the creation of a few elite figures, whether Hobbes and Boyle or Kant and Marx; it is made from below as well as above. It is not just a matter of systems, ideas, or a symbolic Constitution, but of practices, negotiations, and everyday struggles.

This means, in turn, reckoning with the different resonances and functions of the language of the modern. What modernity means and the uses to which it is put are remarkably varied; the word "modern" is a powerful actor that hooks up with other co-actors to have differing and sometimes unpredictable effects across national cultures, intellectual fields, and political divides. *The Gender of Modernity*, for example, shows how women—defying gender divides that placed them on the side of nature and tradition—found inspiration in the language of the modern: whether fin-de-siecle suffragettes appropriating discourses of evolution and revolution or the artful embrace of "perverse" sexuality by the decadent writer Rachilde.

In this context, cultural studies scholar Lawrence Grossberg argues that Latour's line of thought tends to reduce modernity to a single epistemology grounded in a foundational set of divisions, "rather than offering an account of the multiplicity of vectors producing the complexity of actual modernities and struggles."[9] While appreciating many of Latour's insights, Grossberg finds his approach rather too abstract to account for the very diverse on-the-ground experiences of modernity. This complaint is more than a little ironic, given that so much of Latour's career has been devoted to an impassioned defense of the empirical; a call to "follow the actors" via the careful tracing of networks; vivid and eloquent accounts of humble objects from hotel room keys to revolving doors. Yet it's true that *We Have Never Been Modern* is pitched at a higher intellectual altitude than much of Latour's other work, including the—for me more foundational—arguments of *Reassembling the Social*.

All of this is to say that William Paulson is on the mark in observing that "literary modernity is not self-evidently the modernity questioned by Latour." I would push the point even further. Modernity possesses differing—often opposing—meanings in specific disciplines as well as national traditions, associated variously with increasing homogeneity or ever greater differentiation, with the sovereignty of reason (modernity as Enlightenment) or the dislocations and ironies, aesthetic intensities, and erotic possibilities of modern urban life (Simmel, Benjamin). In what is surely the most comprehensive essay on this topic, Susan Stanford Friedman traces out the dazzling array of paradoxes that define the modern. "What," she asks,

> is hidden within the proliferation of meanings for modern, modernity, and modernism? How might the dissonances and oppositions constitute fault lines inviting interpretation in and of themselves? What might such fault lines tell us about the contradictory and complex-ridden meanings and politics of the phenomena to which the terms refer as they change and vary in different historical moments and spatial locations?[10]

Her essay underscores the semantic slipperiness of the language of the modern: its capacities for metamorphosis, its potential to be recruited to varying intellectual, aesthetic, or political projects.

Yet there are also intriguing parallels between Latour's account of modernity and the concerns of literary and cultural studies, as shown by the illuminating essays in this volume. And here two especially salient issues come to the fore: *purification* and *periodization*, as they shape not only the creation of literature but also—perhaps more importantly—the discourses, frameworks, and assumptions through which literary studies sustains and reproduces itself as a field.

Paulson notes that "the invention of aesthetics as an autonomous discipline and the doctrine of art for art were among the most obvious moments of a purification process" that created polarities between art and life and between form and content. As his remark indicates, this process is stretched out over time; while Kant's treatise on aesthetics is published in the 1790s, it is only a century later that literary and artistic purification kicks into full gear. According to Clement Greenberg's well-known thesis, for example, modernist painting moves away from representation in order to focus on the distinctiveness of its own medium—its two dimensionality as a painted canvas—and thereby assert its autonomy. Meanwhile, we see in literary modernism a similar stress on medium and form via a heightened attention to the materiality and artifice of language. "Modern literature," Paulson continues, "came to require originality of form, self-purification from the suspicion of subservience either to content or to previous models and forms of writing."

Here, however, we are faced with a puzzle. How does this observation square with the point made earlier by During: that literature is characterized by its breadth and promiscuity, its ability to move into multiple worlds, draw from a plenitude of resources, including both scientific and humanistic thinking, and weave thick entanglements of humans and nonhumans? During is talking about seventeenth-century poetry, but the point would seem to hold even more strongly for nineteenth-century novels. The affordances of such novels, after all, include encyclopedic surveys of the mores and habits of differing social classes; a documenting of the everyday life of the present; a delving into psychic life and tracing of interpersonal interactions; and a staging of visual tableaus, such as Zola's famously vivid description of the cheeses on display at Les Halles. Are there not unambiguous traces of sociology, history, psychology, and painting at the very heart of literary representation? Countless—and hardly concealed—examples of mediation and cross-pollination? Meanwhile Balzac and Zola certainly cared about literary content, while across the channel novelists retained a deep commitment to ethics and politics and to forging ties to larger communities (George Eliot; Elizabeth Gaskell).

This apparent contradiction, however, might well confirm Latour's point; that purification is always accompanied by the creation of hybrids. On the one hand, literature and art develop a relative autonomy in modernity; on the other hand, they remain intimately concerned with and connected to other things. Moreover, as several essays in this volume remind us, at issue is not just the creation of literature but its reception—specifically, its academic reception, as shaped by dominant critical methods and regimes of interpretation.

Critics of poetry, Lyu suggests, have been especially invested in formalism and the idea of autonomy: "to read a poem is to treat it as an autonomous linguistic structure that has nothing to do with, and even negates, the world it refers to, the one who wrote it, and even the one who reads it." Lyu traces out this way of thinking as it influenced the French critical reception of Mallarmé; an analogous way of thinking—albeit less fixated on the negative—can be seen in New Criticism and its vision of the poem as a verbal icon or well-wrought urn. Yet novels can, of course, be treated in similar fashion, as Paulson shows in his account of the critical reception of *Madame Bovary*. Evacuated of content as well as its relations to the world around it, it was treated purely as an exercise in style and a novel "sur rien." One of the effects of the linguistic turn and the spread of deconstruction—the only branch of humanistic thought to be engaged in *We Have Never Been Modern*—was to universalize this way of reading, such that any literary work—indeed any piece of writing—could be taken to testify to the undecidability and indeterminacy of language. Here, Latour remarks, language becomes a law onto itself: bracketed off from any references to the natural world on the one hand and to persons on the other.[11]

And yet this way of thinking does not sum up or encapsulate the literary field. While poetry criticism remains strongly invested in formalist approaches, there are also counter-voices linking poetry to real world issues: postcolonial scholars of poetry such as Jahan Ramazani, for example, combine attention to form with political concerns and embrace hybridity as a guiding value.[12] At one point, this way of thinking might have been dubbed "postmodern" rather than modern—yet after several decades in the limelight, the idea of postmodernism has been stripped of its intellectual cachet.[13] Among the many criticisms it has received, perhaps most relevant is the objection that it simplifies and homogenizes the modernity against which it defines itself. The formalism of the mid-century New Critics, for example, existed alongside the ideas of critics such as Lionel Trilling or Edmund Wilson, who saw literature as deeply intertwined with social and ethical issues. In modern criticism as well as in modern art, purification coexists with—not just implicit but explicit—forms of combining and mixing.

Does the nonmodern avoid this problem of homogenizing the modern? In a significant sense, yes, insofar as Latour insists that in practice hybrids are inescapable and inevitable. Modernity is not something that needs to be overcome or moved beyond—as the language of "post" can imply—but to be reconceived in terms of its countless mediations. And yet it is also the case that modern ideas and thought patterns are sometimes portrayed in selective ways. *We Have Never Been Modern*, for example, zeroes in on E. O. Wilson, Bourdieu, and Derrida as exemplary thinkers who strive to explain the world via a single big idea: nature, society, and language, respectively. "Each of these forms of criticism is powerful in itself, yet impossible to combine with the other two," remarks Latour; "... we must not mix these three caustic acids."[14] The point is well-taken; yet, the cards have already been stacked (as Latour admits, "a bit unfairly") to support the thesis that the modern denies mediation and mixing. Citing other scholars with cross-disciplinary commitments—Charles Taylor, Dipesh Chakrabarty, Clifford Geertz, or Martha Nussbaum—would result in quite a different picture.

Yet this difference can hardly be clarified by dubbing Bourdieu "modern" and Nussbaum "nonmodern." We are talking, at least in part, about divergences in intellectual temperament: the thinker as single-issue hedgehog or as promiscuous fox. Modernity may encourage the breeding of hedgehogs, but foxes are far from extinct. Similarly, while modernity and purification are connected, they are far from synonymous. After all, if anthropologists (Mary Douglas, Levi-Strauss) are to be believed, all cultures are preoccupied with purity and organize the world in terms of dichotomies. We cannot lay all human shortcomings at the door of modernity. While a pushback against the excesses of purification is certainly merited—and can gain crucial ammunition from Latour and actor network theory—the analytical benefits of casting this disagreement as a battle between moderns and nonmoderns are not entirely self-evident.

What about the question of periodization, whether in literary studies and elsewhere? Whatever else it may signify, modern is a temporal term that treats the new as a value in itself, while causing words such as "old-fashioned" or "behind the times" to acquire pejorative connotations. "What is the source of the very modern impression that we are living a new time that breaks with the past?" asks Latour. As he notes, it is the binding together of elements into coherent bundles—which we call periods—that allow us to conceive of time as a sequence of stages. This model can take on various forms; whereas evolutionary history combines continuity and change, revolutionary time posits irrevocable breaks and ruptures. Yet in both cases temporal schemes are saturated with ethical values; "modernity designates a combat in which there are victors and vanquished."[15]

While such schemes fuel the modern political imagination, they also drive literature and the arts. In the nineteenth century an idea arises of writers and artists as not just separate from society, but *ahead* of society—a vanguard that repudiates the past and that points the way forward to a better future. The consequences of such thought are not always or automatically negative. The desire to revolt, to innovate, to break with the past, has often served as a source of artistic inspiration and a motor of creativity, whether one thinks of the French Realists voicing their scorn at pallid imitations of past styles or avant-gardes manifestos calling for the destruction of museums, libraries, and academies. The history of modern literature and art has been fueled by passionate time-oriented exhortations: "Il faut être de son temps" and "make it new."

Yet a tension exists—yet again—between theory and practice: modern art works have a more ambiguous and multi-faceted relation to time than such slogans convey. "The past remains, therefore, and even returns," writes Latour, but "this resurgence is incomprehensible to the moderns."[16] This is another instance of a statement that does not square with the humanities. After all, the presence of the past is vividly actualized in works of modern literature and art. Even as they experiment with new forms and styles, they are bound, by countless intertextual ties, to what came before. Andromache pops up in Baudelaire's poetry; the very title of James Joyce's masterpiece calls to mind the ancient Greeks; Picasso's paintings are replete with mythological references; H. D. calls up the spirit of Sappho. As more sophisticated theories of modernism have long acknowledged, modern literature or art never constituted any kind of clean break.

The reception of literature, moreover, is an inherently transtemporal affair. In reading novels or plays or poems, we listen to, and sometimes converse with, the dead. The question of time thus plays out very differently in the humanities than in the natural sciences (or even the social sciences). That a piece of writing originated hundreds or even thousands of years ago has no bearing on its value—Aristotle is still hailed by some as the greatest philosopher of all time. In the institutional transmission of literature, several different value regimes hold sway: the modern masterpiece (prized for its formal innovation), the window onto the world (valued for its political or historical perspectives), and the classic, often seen as foundational and associated with Greek and Roman literature, or perhaps with Shakespeare.[17] There is no sense in which newness automatically trumps or wins out over pastness.

At a phenomenological level, moreover, engaging with literature brings it into the reader's own time, as Gadamer and others have argued. Historical distance does not preclude the possibility of a felt immediacy, as the words of the past are reactivated and reanimated in the present. "I sit with Shakespeare, and he winces not. Across the color line I move arm in arm with Balzac and Dumas, where smiling men and welcoming women glide in gilded halls ... I summon Aristotle and Aurelius and what soul I will, and they come all graciously with no scorn nor condescension."[18] Du Bois's often-cited words rail against the exclusion of African Americans from education and high culture; yet, they also depict literature and philosophy as resonating across time rather than being quarantined within a single time. While the sway of historicism over recent decades rendered such issues taboo, we are now seeing a renewed interest in theorizing transtemporal affinities and connections.[19]

In another turn of the screw, however, there is a sense in which temporal frameworks *do* remain pertinent to reception and to regimes of aesthetic value. Moliere and Milton are prized as exemplary figures of their own time; meanwhile, they can also be freely cited by contemporary writers, whether in a spirit of homage or irony. Yet anyone nowadays who tried to faithfully imitate Moliere or Milton—to write in the exact same manner—would be met with incomprehension or derision. What could such an effort signify (Pierre Menard nonwithstanding!) beyond a pointless exercise in antiquarianism? While the reception of works can cut across centuries, we expect the creation of works to be timely—that is, to speak to the conditions of their own time.

This expectation is not necessarily misguided, but problems arise when it is too quickly conflated with innovation in form—so that, say, a realist novelist of the 1930s is thereby summarily dismissed as failing to be authentically modern. Here I'm very much in sympathy with Maxime Goergen's remark that nonmodernity can "help us make sense of specific works and authors that have become unreadable or out of fashion under the restrictive paradigm of modernity." (Along similar lines, *The Gender of Modernity* argued that Marie Corelli—writer of sentimental and supernatural bestsellers, often with Orientalist overtones—was no less authentically modern, no less attuned to her time, than the avant-garde Rachilde.)

That the scholarship on multiple modernities is not engaged in *We Have Never Been Modern* is hardly surprising; when Latour's book was published, in 1993, this work had barely begun. That it still remains unacknowledged in the mainstream of French intellectual culture, meanwhile, has much to do with an academic milieu that, as Goergen shows, remains caught up in a battle with the heritage of Marxism but pays little attention to current work on gender, race, or sexuality. Beyond the question of social movements, however, there are also disciplinary issues at stake. If literary modernity has always an ambivalent relationship to sociopolitical modernity, what are the stakes of defining this ambivalence as nonmodern rather than differently modern? A potential risk of such a shift in vocabulary is that mainstream sociologists or philosophers will acquire exclusive rights to define what the modern means—in textbooks, encyclopedias, survey courses, and other places where the word "modern" remains central.

Goergen shows persuasively that a Latourian lens renders writers such as Michelet newly interesting by freeing them from fixed historical frames and endowing them with a new dynamism and transtemporal mobility. We can "read the French nineteenth century anew, as both unfamiliar and yet surprisingly relevant for early twenty-first century readers." Meanwhile, Gabriel Hankins's chapter brings my reflections on the ambiguities of the modern full circle. Kafka's work has been a goldmine for critical theorists intent on denouncing the Law (see Lacan); instrumental rationality (the Frankfurt School, and disciplinary regimes (Foucault)). Leaning on Latour, Hankins gives us an unexpected but compelling account of Kafka's world: one that includes useless papers and empty ink bottles, the vital importance of desks, chairs, and junk rooms, and occasional moments of satisfaction or even obscure joy that complicate a single-minded story of modern disenchantment. Kafka, from an ANT perspective, turns out not be not so utterly Kafkaesque after all!

Unspooling a single thread—rather than attempting to do justice to all of the rich and stimulating essays in this volume—I've sought to convey my longstanding debt to Latour's work, while making connections to other influential reassessments of the modern. And here the variations in terminology—the nonmodern versus multiple modernities—are ultimately less salient than the many affinities of outlook among those of us who are committed to rethinking the theory and history of modernity. Such affinities are best conveyed in one of Latour's telling aphorisms: "Modernity is much more than an illusion and much less than an essence."[20]

Notes

1 Bruno Latour, *We Have Never Been Modern*, trans. Catherine Porter (Cambridge: Harvard University Press, 1993), 47.
2 Ibid., 29.
3 Simon During, "Are the Humanities Modern?" in *Latour and the Humanities*, ed. Rita Felski and Stephen Muecke (Baltimore: Johns Hopkins University Press, 2020).
4 Ibid.
5 Latour, *We Have Never Been Modern*, 32.

6   Rita Felski, *The Gender of Modernity* (Cambridge: Harvard University Press, 1995).
7   Paul Gilroy, *The Black Atlantic: Modernity and Double Consciousness* (Cambridge: Harvard University Press, 1993); Henning Bech, *When Men Meet: Homosexuality and Modernity* (Chicago: University of Chicago Press, 1997); Arjun Appadurai, *Modernity at Large: Cultural Dimensions of Globalization* (Minneapolis: University of Minnesota Press, 1996).
8   Rita Felski, "New Cultural Theories of Modernity," in *Doing Time, Feminist Theory and Postmodern Culture* (New York: New York University Press, 2000), 59.
9   Lawrence Grossberg, *Cultural Studies in the Future Tense* (Durham: Duke University Press, 2010), 89.
10 Susan Stanford Friedman, "Definitional Excursions: The Meanings of Modern/Modernity/Modernism," *Modernism/Modernity* 8, no. 3 (2001): 499.
11 Latour, *We Have Never Been Modern*, 63.
12 Jahan Ramazani, *A Transnational Poetics* (Chicago: University of Chicago Press, 2009).
13 For the most trenchant critique of the concept of postmodernism, see John Frow, "What Was Postmodernism?" in *Time and Commodity Culture* (Oxford: Clarendon Press, 1997), 13–63.
14 Latour, *We Have Never Been Modern*, 6.
15 Ibid., 10.
16 Ibid., 69.
17 David Damrosch, *What Is World Literature?* (Princeton, NJ: Princeton University Press, 2003), 15.
18 W. E. B. Du Bois, *The Souls of Black Folk* (New York: Oxford University Press, 2014), 52.
19 See, for example, Rita Felski, "Context Stinks!" *New Literary History* 42, no. 4 (2011): 573–91, and Wai Chee Dimock, "A Theory of Resonance," *PMLA* 112, no. 5 (1997): 1060–71.
20 Latour, *We Have Never Been Modern*, 40.

Bibliography

Appadurai, Arjun. *Modernity at Large: Cultural Dimensions of Globalization*. Minneapolis: University of Minnesota Press, 1996.

Bech, Henning. *When Men Meet: Homosexuality and Modernity*. Chicago: University of Chicago Press, 1997.

Damrosch, David. *What Is World Literature?* Princeton: Princeton University Press, 2003.

Dimock, Wai Chee. "A Theory of Resonance." *PMLA* 112, no. 5 (1997): 1060–71.
Du Bois, W. E. B. *The Souls of Black Folk*. New York: Oxford University Press, 2014.
During, Simon. "Are the Humanities Modern?" In *Latour and the Humanities*. Edited by Rita Felski and Stephen Muecke. Baltimore: Johns Hopkins University Press, 2020.
Felski, Rita. "Context Stinks!" *New Literary History* 42, no. 4 (2011): 573–91.
Felski, Rita. *The Gender of Modernity*. Cambridge: Harvard University Press, 1995.
Felski, Rita. "New Cultural Theories of Modernity." Chapter 2 in *Doing Time, Feminist Theory and Postmodern Culture*. New York: New York University Press, 2000.
Friedman, Susan Stanford. "Definitional Excursions: The Meanings of Modern/Modernity/Modernism." *Modernism/Modernity* 8, no. 3 (2001): 493–513.
Frow, John. "What Was Postmodernism?" Chapter 1 in *Time and Commodity Culture: Essays in Cultural Theory and Postmodernity*. Oxford: Clarendon Press, 1997.
Gilroy, Paul. *The Black Atlantic: Modernity and Double Consciousness*. Cambridge: Harvard University Press, 1993.
Grossberg, Lawrence. *Cultural Studies in the Future Tense*. Durham: Duke University Press, 2010.
Latour, Bruno Latour. *We Have Never Been Modern*. Translated by Catherine Porter. Cambridge: Harvard University Press, 1993.
Ramazani, Jahan. *A Transnational Poetics*. Chicago: University of Chicago Press, 2009.

Contributors

Elisabeth Arnould-Bloomfield is Associate Professor of French at the University of Colorado, Boulder. She has published essays on contemporary literature and theory and is the author of an essay on Georges Bataille, entitled *Georges Bataille, la terreur et les lettres* (2009). She is currently working on a study of modern and postmodern animal discourses in philosophy, literature, and science, entitled *Animal Encounters of a closer kind*. In addition to her research on animals, she is interested in literary theory and the link between knowledge and practice, most notably in the works of Bruno Latour, Isabelle Stengers, Donna Haraway, and Vinciane Despret.

Vinciane Despret is Professor of Philosophy at the University of Liège. Her body of work, inspired by Isabelle Stengers and Bruno Latour, is at the intersection of ethology, human psychology, and politics. A fundamental thinker in the field of animal studies, she has won multiple awards, including the Prix des Humanités Scientifiques and the Prix du Fond international Wernaers. She is the author of many books and articles, including *Women Who Make a Fuss* (2015 [2011 for original edition in French]) and more recently of *What Would Animals Say If We Asked the Right Questions?* (2016 [2012 for original edition in French]).

Rita Felski is William R. Kenan Jr Professor of English at the University of Virginia and Niels Bohr Professor at the University of Southern Denmark. Her most recent books are *Uses of Literature* (2008), *The Limits of Critique* (2015), and *Hooked: Art and Attachment* (2020). She is currently writing a book on the contemporary Frankfurt School.

Maxime Goergen is Lecturer in French studies at the University of Sheffield. His work focuses on literature and ideology in the longer nineteenth-century and on nineteenth- and twentieth-century French intellectual history. Publications include articles on Balzac, Hugo, Saint-Simonianism, and the post-1968 intellectual field. Among his current projects are a monograph on the question of generations in Balzac and a research on the recuperation of the figure of Victor Hugo in the 1980s.

Gabriel Hankins is Assistant Professor of English at Clemson University. He has published articles in which Latour's works are brought to bear on literature ("The Objects of Ethics: Rilke and Woolf with Latour" [2015] and "The Weak Powers of Digital Modernist Studies" [2018]). His first book is *Interwar Modernism and the Liberal World Order* (2019), and he plans to take up the politics of the digital humanities in his next book and as series co-editor of the Cambridge *Elements in Digital Literary Studies*. He is a co-founder of the *Twentieth-Century Literary Letters Project*.

Graham Harman is Distinguished Professor of Philosophy at SCI-Arc in Los Angeles and a faculty member of the European Graduate School (EGS). His work on the metaphysics of objects led to the development of object-oriented ontology. He is a central figure in the field of speculative realism in contemporary philosophy. He has published eighteen books and has worked extensively on Latour (*Prince of Networks: Bruno Latour and Metaphysics* [2009] and *Bruno Latour: Reassembling the Political* [2014]). He also co-authored *The Prince and the Wolf: Latour and Harman at the LSE* (2011) with Latour and Peter Erdélyi.

Claire Chi-ah Lyu is Associate Professor of French at the University of Virginia and works in the field of modern French poetry and literary theory with a particular emphasis on Mallarmé and modern theorizations of poetry. She is author of *A Sun within a Sun: The Power and Elegance of Poetry* (2006) and is currently working on the notion and practice of blank space, entitled *From Empty to Open: Blank Space in Modern French Literature and Theory*. Guided by the works of Stengers, Latour, Haraway, Despret, and Hearne, she has begun recently to explore how language connects us to the nonhuman world.

Jan Miernowski is Douglas Kelly Professor of French at the University of Wisconsin-Madison, United States and Visiting Professor at the University of Warsaw, Poland. His works focus on the aesthetic response of literature to the diverse discourses of early modern and contemporary philosophy, theology, science, and politics. His latest books include *Beauté de la haine* (2014), an edited volume on the intersection between the grotesque and the sublime (*Le Sublime et le grotesque*, 2014) and another one on the dialog between early modern humanism and postmodern anti-humanism (*Early Modern Humanism and Postmodern Antihumanism in Dialogue*, 2016). His current project tests the conditions of possibility of a humanism for our posthuman times.

Stephen Muecke is Professor of Creative Writing at Flinders University, South Australia and a Fellow of the Australian Academy of the Humanities. He is a writer specializing in innovative cross-generic work; a recent publication is *The Mother's Day Protest and Other Fictocritical Essays* (Rowman and Littlefield International, 2016). He also works on literary theory, with a special edition of *New Literary History* ("Recomposing the Humanities—with Bruno Latour"), 2016. He has carried out research with Indigenous people (a new edition of Paddy Roe's *Gularabulu: Stories from the West Kimberley*, 2016), and current research involves ethnographic documentation of Goolarabooloo county north of Broome, Western Australia, using a "multirealist" approach. He has also translated two books by Isabelle Stengers: *Another Science Is Possible*, (2018) and (with Tobie Nathan) *Doctors and Healers* (2018).

William Paulson is the Edward Lorraine Walter Collegiate Professor of Romance Languages and Literatures at the University of Michigan. He has published extensively on literary and cultural theory, concentrating on the forms and institutions of modern literature and their relations to science, technology, history, and society. He is among the early group of scholars to introduce the works of Bruno Latour and Isabelle Stengers to US literary scholars. Among his books are *The Noise of Culture* (1988), *Literary Culture in a World Transformed* (2001), and a critical study of Flaubert's *Sentimental Education*. In 2011 and 2013, he directed Mellon Foundation Dissertation Seminars on science studies and cultural theory. He is currently completing a book manuscript entitled *Thinking in Real Time*.

Oumelbanine Zhiri is Professor of Literature at the University of California, San Diego, where she teaches French, Arabic, and Comparative literature. She has published books and articles on early modern cultures and authors, such as Leo Africanus (*L'Afrique au miroir de l'Europe, Fortunes de Jean Léon l'Africain à la Renaissance,* Geneva, 1991) and François Rabelais (*L'Extase et ses paradoxes,* Paris, 1999). Her current research is devoted to the literature of travel between Europe and the Orient and to mapping the development of early modern Oriental studies in a transcultural context as a circulation of objects, manuscripts, knowledge, technologies, and people between East and West.

Index

Acquisto, Joseph 91, 93
   Poetry's Knowing Ignorance 104 n.14
actants 38, 145, 189, 226, 234
Actor Network Theory (ANT) 1, 6, 52, 57, 153, 200, 239, 242
Adorno, Theodor 115, 123, 232
   Prisms 127 n.8
aesthetics 9, 16-17, 71, 77-8, 80, 122, 124, 134, 138-9, 185, 231, 236-7, 241
   Goolarabooloo aesthetic 220-7
Agamben, Giorgio 178, 181
agency 1, 11-13, 57, 90, 93, 97, 99-100, 116, 135, 140, 142-4, 146, 185, 234
agential realism 210
Akerman, Kim 219-20
   "The Art of Butcher Joe Nangan" 228 n.11
al-Hajari, Ahmad (Ahmad ibn al-Qâsim al-Hajarî Afuqay) 15, 58, 60
   and Golius 57-8, 62
   The Supporter of Religion against the Infidels 56
Allee, Warder Clyde 165, 168
   Principles of Animal Ecology 172 n.49
Alsworth, David 1
   "Latour and Literature" 19 n.3
Althusser, Louis 113, 118
Altum, Bernard 160-1
amodern 231
animal science/birds 175-81
   animal awareness 177-9
   animal realism 175
   baboons, study of (society and) 153-6, 162-3
   behavior 184
      bat's 186
      conventional 157
      geopolitical 17, 157-9
   birds, study of 159-68
   borders and space of (territory) 17, 157-69

   conflicts, territorial 167-8
   "dear enemy effect" 168
   dwelling place 159
   "nasty neighbor effect" 168
   political society/relations 156-8
   population of 165-6
   postmodern 176
Anthropocene 27-9
anthropocentrism 32, 34, 90, 176-7, 179
anthropology 8, 10-12, 14, 20 n.17, 31-2, 169, 209
anthropomorphism 179
antimodern/antimodernism 2-4, 16, 70, 81-2, 131, 136, 138, 140, 207
Antiquity 29, 33, 82
anti-realism/anti-realists 201
Appadurai, Arjun 235
   Modernity at Large: Cultural Dimensions of Globalization 243 n.7
Aristotle 233, 240
   l'Historia Animalium 171 n.31
Armstrong, Nancy 120
   How Novels Think: The Limits of Individualism from 1719–1900 127 n.20
Arnould-Bloomfield, Elisabeth 17-18
Attridge, Derek, *Acts of Literature* 107 n.71
Aubin, Thierry, "When to Be a Dear Enemy: Flexible Acoustic Relationships of Neighbouring Skylarks, *Alauda arvensis*" 172 n.55
Aurelius 240
Australian literature 18
auto-noetic nature 183-4
auto-poietic nature 183-5
avant-garde 123, 240

bacteriology 35-6
Bailly, Jean-Christophe 18, 188
   animal science 176-80
   The Animal Side 17, 175, 181-2, 186

Index

empiricism 186–7
ethology 181–5, 187, 189
"Le Moindre souffle" ("The Slightest Breath") 185
balangan (skeleton) 220–2
Balzac, Honoré de 77, 140, 237, 240
Barad, Karen 5, 18, 92–3, 102
  agential realism 210
  entanglement 18, 93, 197, 209–10
  intra-action 6, 20 n.20, 93, 210
  Meeting the Universe Halfway: Quantum Physics and the Entanglement of Matter and Meaning 105 n.24, 210 n.1
  posthumanist performativity 93, 99
  "Posthumanist Performativity: Toward an Understanding of How Matter comes to Matter" 104 nn.20–1
Baratay, Eric 190
Barinaga, Ester, "A Performative View of Language—Methodological Considerations and Consequences for the Study of Culture" 104 n.21
Barthes, Roland 74, 85 n.52, 143, 146
  bourgeois writing 70
  Michelet 148 n.31
  "Michelet's Modernity" 148 n.41
  Writing Degree Zero 84 n.3, 105 n.34
Baudelaire, Charles 17, 240
  modernity 138, 140–1, 233
  The Painter of Modern Life and Other Essays 147 n.15
Baudrillard, Jean 10
  La Gauche divine (*The Divine Left*) 136
Bayle, Pierre, *Dictionnaire historique et critique* 53–4
Bech, Henning 235
  When Men Meet: Homosexuality and Modernity 243 n.7
Bénichou, Paul 135, 142
  Le Temps des prophètes: Doctrines de l'âge romantique 147 n.25
Benjamin, Walter 105 n.31, 236
Bennett, Jane
  transfer 177
  Vibrant Matter: A Political Ecology of Things 105 n.23

Bevilacqua, Alexander, *The Republic of Arabic Letters. Islam and the European Enlightenment* 63 n.7
Bildung 28, 119
bildungsroman 17, 120
birds. *See* animal science/birds
Blanchard, Barbara 162
Blanchot, Maurice 16, 94–7, 99–100, 106 n.36
  "Literature and the Right to Death" 105 n.27, 105 n.34
  "The Myth of Mallarmé" 106 n.39
Bleich, David, *The Materiality of Language: Gender, Politics, and the University* 106 n.49
Bloch, R. Howard, *One Toss of the Dice: The Incredible Story of How a Poem Made Us Modern* 108 n.75
Blok, Anders, *Bruno Latour: Hybrid Thoughts in a Hybrid World* 63 n.10
Boileau 71, 83
Bonaparte, Louis-Napoléon 142
Bourdieu, Pierre 10, 16, 113, 118, 125, 238–9
  Distinction: A Social Critique of the Judgement of Taste 126
  The Rules of Art: Genesis and Structure of the Literary Field 139
Bovelles, Charles de 32
  In hoc volumine continentur ... De Nihilo ... 47 n.49
Boyle, Robert 3, 5, 199, 232, 234–5
Briefer, Elodie, "When to Be a Dear Enemy: Flexible Acoustic Relationships of Neighbouring Skylarks, *Alauda arvensis*" 172 n.55
bugarrigarra (dreaming) 18, 219, 221–3
bureau 117
bureaucracy 116–18, 125, 232
Butler, Judith 10, 192 n.43

capitalism 135, 202, 205, 233
Çelebi, Kâtib 50
Charbonnier, Pierre 136
  "Les Aventures écologiques du libéralisme" 147 n.7
  "Prendre les animaux au sérieux: de l'animal politique à la politique des animaux" 170 n.18

Citton, Yves, *Lire, interpréter, actualiser: Pourquoi les études littéraires?* 108 n.82
Clarke, Bruce 104 n.8
climate change 16, 30, 89–90, 94, 98–9, 101, 197, 202–4
Clinton, Hillary 202, 205
Cole, Sarah 119
   At the Violet Hour 127 n.16
Colet, Louise 77, 80, 82–3
Collot, Michel 91, 93
   La Poésie moderne et la structure d'horizon 104 n.12
Compagnon, Antoine 138, 140
   Les Antimodernes. De Joseph de Maistre à Roland Barthes 147 n.18
constitutional analysis 11, 14, 20 n.10
constructivism/constructivist 9–10, 33–4
Corelli, Marie 241
Corngold, Stanley 117
cosmopolitics 217–18
Cowley, Abraham 234
Czar Nicolas II 121

d'Alembert, Jean le Rond 70
Damrosch, David, *What Is World Literature?* 243 n.17
Dante, Alighieri 49, 94
Daston, Lorraine, "Introduction: The Age of the New" 65 n.29
"dear enemy effect" 168
Debaise, Didier, *Philosophie des possessions* 172 n.50
DeLanda, Manuel, *Intensive Science and Virtual Philosophy* 20 n.23
Deleuze, Gilles 5, 116–17, 181–2, 218
   A Thousand Plateaus: Capitalism and Schizophrenia 192 n.23
de-modernizing approach 8
Demorcy, Didier 170 n.10
Derrida, Jacques 100–1, 176–7, 238
   Acts of Literature 107 n.71
   The Animal That Therefore I Am 175
   "La Double séance" 108 n.77
   Limited Inc. 104 n.20
Descartes, René 28, 72, 132
Despret, Vinciane 17–18, 170 n.10, 190
   "From Secret Agents to Interagency" 191 n.22
   Naissance d'une théorie éthologique: La danse du cratérope écaillé 171 n.30
   territories 17
   What Would Animals Say If we Asked the Right Questions? 171 n.30
Dewar, J. M. 161
   "The Relation of the Oyster-Catcher to its Natural Environment" 171 n.36
Dewey, John 18, 200–1
   The Public and its Problems: An Essay in Political Inquiry 211 n.13
d'Herbelot, Barthélemy, *Bibliothèque Orientale* 50
dialogic poetics 91
Diego Bejarano. *See* al-Hajari, Ahmad (Ahmad ibn al-Qâsim al-Hajarî Afuqay)
Dimock, Wai Chee, "A Theory of Resonance" 243 n.19
discipline 13, 16–17, 35, 40
   disciplinary power 16–17, 113, 115, 118–19, 121, 124
displacement 28, 37–40, 73, 184
diversity 2, 162–3
Dosse, François, "1989 moment" 133
dualism 3, 5–8, 10–11, 14, 16, 32, 39–40, 83, 187
Du Bois, W. E. B. 240
   The Souls of Black Folk 243 n.18
During, Simon 233–4, 237
   "Are the Humanities Modern?" 242 n.3
Dutch Republic 52, 54–6

early modern Orientalism 50–1, 59–62
echolocation 186, 190
ecology 154–5, 165, 197, 204, 207–8
   literary 224–6
   modern 190, 226
   political 193 n.49
effectuation process 188
empiricism 18, 186–7, 189
Enlightenment 4, 35, 57, 82, 232–3
   first Enlightenment 3
   post-Enlightenment 28, 32
   second Enlightenment 28, 132
entanglement 5, 12, 49, 51–2, 60, 89, 93, 138, 197, 209–10, 237

epistemology 2, 6–7, 15, 17–18, 28, 31, 33–5, 49–50, 60, 62, 132, 177–9, 182, 187–8, 190, 204, 235
Erasmus 29, 32–3, 43
   Querela Pacis 36
Erdélyi, Peter, *The Prince and the Wolf: Latour and Harman at the LSE* 211 n.7
Erpenius, Thomas 15, 53–4, 57
   Grammatica Arabica 56
escapism/escapist 18, 201, 204–5
ethnocentrism 205
ethnography 18, 218, 227
ethology 17, 175, 177–8, 181–5, 187, 189
Eurocentrism 32
Europe 30, 52–3, 55–6, 58, 60, 133, 233
   modern 50
   post-medieval 16
   Western 28, 31, 49
exegesis 35, 37, 39–40

fascism 18, 205
Felski, Rita 1, 13–14, 18, 21 n.46, 113
   "Context Stinks!" 243 n.19
   The Gender of Modernity 235, 241
   The Limits of Critique 65 n.26, 108 n.82, 127 n.1
   "New Cultural Theories of Modernity" 243 n.8
   Uses of Literature 108 n.82
feminist materialism 198
fiction 18, 77, 79–80, 145–6, 188, 219, 223, 225–6, 235
Flaubert, Gustave 70, 79, 81, 85 n.38, 85 n.52, 125, 139, 232
   and Colet 77, 80, 82–3
   Correspondance 85 n.30
   favorite writers of 82–3
   La Tentation de Saint-Antoine 78, 80
   on Leconte's work 82
   L'Education sentimentale (*Sentimental Education*) 77–8
   livre sur rien 76–8, 80
   Madame Bovary 16, 69, 73–6, 78–82, 238
   nonmodern views of 82
formalism 16, 74, 77, 79, 237–8
   with phenomenology and psychoanalysis 91
Foucault, Michel 10, 16, 50, 60, 86 n.52, 113

épistemè 70
governmentality 126
The Order of Things: An Archaeology of the Human Sciences 83 n.2
Security, Territory, Population: Lectures at the Collège de France 128 n.36
France 17, 30–1, 36, 56, 82, 135–6, 138, 142, 144, 202, 208
   French Revolution 17, 132–3, 137–8, 141–2
   post-Revolutionary France 135
Fressoz, Jean-Baptiste 137
   "The Lessons of Disaster: A Historical Perspective of Postmodern Optimism" 147 n.14
Friedman, Susan Stanford 236
   "Definitional Excursions: The Meanings of Modern/Modernity/Modernism" 243 n.10
Frow, John, "What Was Postmodernism?" 243 n.13
Furet, François 134, 137–8
   Interpreting the Revolution 133

Gaia 43, 90, 98–102, 103 n.8, 104 n.10, 197, 207
Gemayel, Nasser, *Les Échanges culturels entre les Maronites et l'Europe* 64 n.20
Germany 202
Gilroy, Paul 235
   The Black Atlantic: Modernity and Double Consciousness 243 n.7
global warming 90, 98, 100
God 27, 32, 42–4, 96, 105 n.31, 135, 142, 220–1
Goergen, Maxime 17, 241–2
Golius, Jacobus 15, 53–5, 59–61
   and al-Hajari 57–8, 62
Goolarabooloo aesthetic 220–7
Gossman, Lionel 143, 145
   "Michelet's Gospel of Revolution" 148 n.29
governmentality 126
Gramsci, Antonio 50
"Great Bifurcation" 28, 31, 33, 39–40, 42–3
Great Divide 83, 89, 91, 93, 97
Greenberg, Clement 237

Grossberg, Lawrence 235–6
  Cultural Studies in the Future Tense 243 n.9
Guattari, Félix 116–17, 218
  A Thousand Plateaus: Capitalism and Schizophrenia 192 n.23

Hamayon, Roberta 157
Hankins, Gabriel 16–17, 233, 242
Haraway, Donna 5, 10, 12, 15, 92, 102, 190
  contact zone 100
  material-semiotic technology 92–3
  situated knowledges 99
  "Situated Knowledges: The Science Question in Feminism and the Privilege of Partial Perspective" 105 n.22, 107 n.62
  When Species Meet 21 n.49, 22 n.66, 107 n.69, 188
Harman, Graham 1, 18
  "Agential and Speculative Realism: Remarks on Barad's Ontology" 213 n.77
  Bruno Latour: Reassembling the Political 147 n.21, 211 n.8
  Object-Oriented Ontology: A New Theory of Everything 212 n.37
  The Prince and the Wolf: Latour and Harman at the LSE 211 n.7
  Speculative Realism: An Introduction 211 n.6
  "Stengers on Emergence" 212 n.40
Harpham, Goeffrey Galt, *Language Alone: The Critical Fetish of Modernity* 104 n.19
Hearne, Vicky 190
Hegel, Georg Wilhelm Friedrich 96, 99, 106 n.36
Heidegger, Martin 178–9, 182, 184
  Being and Time 204
Hinde, Robert 163
  "The Biological Significance of the Territory of Birds" 171 n.41
Hobbes, Thomas 28, 232, 234–5
  politics 3, 18, 198–201
Hours, Bernard 136
  "Compte-rendu de *Nous n'avons jamais été modernes*" 147 n.11

Howard, Eliot 167
  The British Warbler 161
  Territory of Bird Life 161
Hubert, Étienne 56
Hugo, Victor 49, 134–6
human exceptionalism 28, 92, 100, 176
human/human being 6, 9, 15, 27, 32–7, 61, 69–70, 72, 79–80, 83, 89–90, 92, 95, 102, 116, 132, 136, 144, 157, 179, 200. *See also* nonhuman
  Latour's relational approach 17–18
  nature and 4, 31–2, 184
  politics 156, 209
  and technologies 225
humanism 3, 15, 27–8, 32, 34
  humanist 18, 27–9, 32, 34–6, 177, 234
  exegesis 35–8
  metaphysics 31–5
  practice 27, 29–30, 39, 44
  rhetoric 39–42
  theology 42–4
  nonmodern 15, 28, 35
  Renaissance 28–9, 32–3, 36, 40–2, 45 n.15
humanitarianism 116, 122, 135
humanities/humanity 1, 8, 43, 59–60, 115, 197, 233, 240
hybrids 3–4, 6, 11–13, 16, 28, 31–2, 43–4, 72, 80, 91, 131, 137, 190, 209, 234, 237–8
  classes of 5
  literary 140
  natural-cultural 8, 95, 176, 197, 206, 232
  premodern 96
  sociotechnical 70
hygienists 37, 40

illuminism 134
imagology 51, 57
immanentism 189
Indigenous community, literature 18, 218–20
  Goolarabooloo aesthetic 220–7
  karnun 222–3

Jakobson, Roman
  "Closing Statement: Linguistics and Poetics" 103 n.7
  poetic function 90–1
James, Henry 74, 189

James, William 12, 20 n.25
Jauss, H.-R. 138
  "Modernity and Literary Tradition" 147 n.16
Jensen, Torben Elgaard, *Bruno Latour: Hybrid Thoughts in a Hybrid World* 63 n.10
Joe, Butcher 219–20, 222
Joyce, James 233, 240
  "Hangman God" 115, 119
  non serviam 119, 123
  A Portrait of the Artist as a Young Man 16, 118–26
  Ulysses 127 n.7

Kafka, Franz 233, 242
  The Trial 16, 114–19
Kant, Immanuel 9, 27, 132, 235
  on aesthetics 237
  neo-Kantian 28, 32, 176
Kaufmann, Vincent, *La Faute à Mallarmé: L'aventure de la théorie littéraire* 107 n.72
Keogh, Ray, "Nurlu Songs of the West Kimberleys" 228 n.9
Kojève, A. 96, 99
  Introduction to the Reading of Hegel 106 n.36
Kummer, Hans, *Vies de singes. Mœurs et structures sociales des babouins hamadryas* 170 n.10

Lack, David 161–2
  "Territoriality Reviewed" 171 n.37
language 40, 53, 70–3, 79, 85 n.52, 91, 119–21, 224, 227 n.3, 235–8. *See also* poetry
  literary 106 n.48, 218
  materiality of 96–7
  mathematical 96
  modern poetry 93–4, 96
  performative model of 92–3
  poetic 12, 14, 92, 94, 96–8, 103
  of premodern 96
  self-referentiality 16, 90, 92, 95–7
  traditional 219
Lapoujade, David 164
  Les Existences moindres 172 n.47

Latour, Bruno 2, 44 n.7, 49, 57, 60, 70, 89, 93–4, 97–8, 100, 102, 105 n.29, 124, 126, 131–2, 136–7, 140–1, 144–5, 155, 158–9, 169, 186, 190, 217
  "An Attempt at a Compositionist Manifesto" 193 n.44, 227 n.1
  ANT (*see* Actor Network Theory (ANT))
  "A Texbook Case Revisited: Knowledge as a Mode of Existence" 192 n.38
  attachment 208
  "Can We Get Our Materialism Back, Please?" 201
  circulating reference 7, 20 n.28, 83
  Cogitamus. Six lettres sur les humanités scientifiques 44 n.6, 147 n.19
  crossed-out God 135, 142
  Down to Earth: Politics in the New Climate Regime 18, 30, 159, 198, 200, 202–3, 206
  experimental metaphysics 32–4, 36, 39
  Facing Gaia: Eight Lectures on the New Climatic Regime 86 n.52, 105 n.30, 170 n.21
  "Furry sociologists" 153–6, 169 n.2
  Gaia Global Circus 94, 100–2
  governmentality 126
  Green parties 208
  "How to Talk about the Body? The Normative Dimension of Science Studies" 187
  as humanist 27–30
  "Human Social Origins: Please Tell Us another Story" 172 n.43
  immanentism 189
  Inquiry into Modes of Existence 18
  "in the middle" (au milieu) 192 n.43
  Irreductions 33, 41
  "La Société comme possession: La 'preuve par l'orchestre,'" in *Philosophie des possessions* 172 n.50
  literary criticism 1–2, 7–8, 11, 13–14, 19
  The Los Angeles Review of Books 198
  The Making of Law: An Ethnography of the Conseil D'état 116
  metaphysical realism 200–1
  On the Modern Cult of the Factish Gods 148 n.40

on modernism/modernity 3–4, 19, 59, 69, 72, 79, 91, 136, 139, 197, 206, 232–4, 236, 240, 242
modern West 61, 69
modes of existence 13, 199, 220, 226–7
morality 199–200
morphism 170 n.21
nonmodern/nonmodernity of 2, 5–8, 10–11, 15, 17, 90, 133–4, 139, 143, 176, 206, 231–2
"On the Partial Existence of Existing and Non-existing Objects" 212 n.48
Pandora's Hope: Essays on the Reality of Science Studies 200–1
parody of Christian mysticism 43
and Pasteur (Pasteurians) 35–7, 39–41
The Pasteurization of France 29–30, 33, 131
political realism 198–201, 209
political sociology 113
Politics of Nature: How to Bring the Sciences into Democracy 31, 190
The Prince and the Wolf: Latour and Harman at the LSE 211 n.7
"Qui a la parole ? Anti- ou multi-espèce?" 173 n.59
Reassembling the Social. An Introduction to Actor-Network-Theory 153, 236
"Redécouvrir la terre" 169 n.1
"Redefining the Social Link: from Baboons to Humans" 153–4
relational approach 1, 5–6, 10, 15, 17, 39, 51–2, 177
science 199–200
on Trump (Trumpism) 197–8, 201–6
"Two Bubbles of Unrealism" 18, 198, 201
We Have Never Been Modern 2, 8, 18–19, 61, 95, 131–3, 137–8, 199, 206, 234, 236, 238, 241
"A Well-articulated Primatology. Reflections of a Fellow Traveler" 170 n.11
"Whose Cosmos, Which Cosmopolitics? Comments on the Peace Terms of Ulrich Beck" 227 n.2
"Why Has Critique Run Out of Steam? From Matters of Fact to Matters of Concern" 106 n.53

Leconte de Lisle 85 n.47
Poèmes antiques 82
Le Gendre, Thomas 52–5, 58–61
European Orientalism 55
Lewis, Wyndham 115, 126
The Art of Being Ruled 128 n.35
liberalism 122
line of communication model 224
Lippman, Walter 200
The Phantom Public 211 n.13
"Literary Actor Network Theory" 2
literature 1, 14, 19, 70, 72, 75, 113, 131, 141, 218, 234, 240–1
Australian 18
compositions 217, 222
and criticism 7–8, 14
French 82–3, 132, 232
Indigenous community 218–20
literary
anthropology 11
criticism 1–2, 14, 19, 71, 140
environments 221, 224–5
history 2, 10, 17, 139–41
works 217–18, 234
Madame Bovary 16, 69, 73–6
modern 8–11, 14, 16, 51, 71, 86 n.52, 89, 137–9, 233, 236–7, 239, 241
nonmodern 14, 141, 146
slopes of 97
Loop, Jan, *Johann Heinrich Hottinger. Arabic and Islamic Studies in the Seventeenth Century* 64 n.13
Lorenz, Konrad 161, 165
territorial conflicts 167
Love, Heather, "Close but not Deep: Literary Ethics and the Descriptive Turn" 108 n.82
Lovelock, James 103 n.8
Gaia: A New Look at Life on Earth 210 n.2
Gaia theory 197
Lyu, Claire Chi-ah 16, 232, 237–8

Macé, Marielle, *Façons de lire, manières d'être* 108 n.82
Macherey, Pierre 113
Machiavelli, Niccolò 29, 198–9
Malherbe, François de 71, 83

Mallarmé, Stéphane 16, 125, 232, 238
  "A Throw of Dice Will Never Abolish Chance" 94, 100–2
  "Crise de vers" 107 n.74
Mandrou, Robert, "Pourquoi relire Le Peuple" 148 n.32
Manganiello, Dominic 123
  Joyce's Politics 128 n.26
Marres, Noortje 18, 200–1
  "Issues Spark a Public into Being: A Key but Often Forgotten Point of the Lippmann-Dewey Debate" 211 n.12
  Material Participation: Technology, the Environment, and Everyday Publics 211 n.12
  "No Issue, No Public: Democratic Deficits after the Displacement of Politics" 211 n.12
Marxism/Marxist 133, 135, 209, 241
Marx, Karl 49, 234–5
materialism 198, 201, 210
material-semiotic technology 92–3
"median point" 10–11
mediation 2, 4–7, 10–13, 15–16, 36, 39, 78, 81, 89, 91, 94, 96–7, 99, 103, 136–7, 139–41, 143, 146
Meizoz, Jérôme 140
Merleau-Ponty, Maurice 177, 182–4
  Nature: Course Notes from the College de France 192 n.23
metaphor 12, 39, 120–4, 234
  gas 7
  material 80
  optical 6–7
  theatrical 207
  "war" 35–6, 40
metaphysics 15, 31–6, 38–42, 200
  metaphysical realism 200–1
Michelet, Jules 17, 78, 132, 134, 139, 141, 143–4, 242
  Grace 142
  History of the French Revolution 148 n.27
  The Insect 141
  Introduction to World History 141
  The Mountain 144

nonmodernity of 145–6
  The People 141, 144
  Preface to the History of France 145
  The Sea 141
  The Sorceress 131
middle-knowledge 17, 176, 192 n.43
Miernowski, Jan 15
Miller, D. A. 113
Mill, John Stuart 117
Milton, John 233, 241
mimesis 93–4, 102, 139
Mirandola, Pico della 32
Mitchell, Timothy, Carbon Democracy 209
Mitterrand, François 135
Mitzman, Arthur 142
  "Michelet and Social Romanticism: Religion, Revolution, Nature" 147 n.26
modern Constitution 2–4, 69, 79, 94–5, 137, 142, 231–5
modern imperialism 15, 50, 58
modern/modernism/modernist/modernity 2–3, 13, 16, 18, 33, 61–2, 70, 73–4, 78, 82, 115, 131–4, 136–8, 140–1, 189, 197, 203–4, 231, 233, 235–6, 238–9, 242
  Anglophone 118
  autonomy in 237
  capitalist 120
  collapse of 136
  ecology 190, 226
  Latour's view on 3–4, 16, 19, 59, 69, 72, 79, 91, 136, 139, 197, 206, 232–4, 236, 240, 242
  literary 16, 70, 72–4, 80, 137–9, 233, 236–7, 241
  modernismo 70
  "multiple modernities" 19, 231, 234, 241–2
  Orientalism 50–1, 55, 60–1
  philosophical 233
  poetry 16, 89, 91, 93–4, 96, 98, 100, 103
  religion 231–2
  sociopolitical 241
  twentieth-century 3
  women's 235
Moffat, Charles 160–1
  "The Spring Rivalry of Birds" 171 n.33

Molière 241
mononaturalism 32
Montaigne, Michel de 15, 29, 34, 36–7, 40–1, 45 n.10, 82
  Essays 29–30, 33–4, 44
Moreri, Louis, *Grand dictionnaire* 53–4
Moretti, Franco 120
  The Way of the World: The Bildungsroman in European Culture 127 n.20
Morisco 56–8
Morizot, Baptiste 156–9, 168, 172 n.44
  Les Diplomates: Cohabiter avec les loups sur une autre carte du vivant 170 n.19
  Old Viking law 171 n.32
Morizot, Philippe 190
Morocco 52–3, 55–6, 59–60
Morris, Karl Philip 180
  Anton Reiser 191 n.14
Muecke, Stephen 18
  "The Great Tradition: Translating Durrudiya's Songs" 228 n.10
Mufti, Aamir 51
  Forget English! Orientalisms and World Literatures 63 n.9
multiculturalism 32–3
multiple universe society 218, 220–1, 223, 226–7
Muray, Philippe 135–6
  Le 19e siècle à travers les âges (*The 19th Century through the Ages*) 134
Musil, Robert, *Young Törless* 118

Napoléon Bonaparte 36, 50
"nasty neighbor effect" 168
Nathan, Tobie 218, 221, 226–7, 228 n.5
naturalism 73–4, 132, 134, 189
nature 3–4, 8–9, 32, 35, 40, 42, 71, 143, 163, 183–5, 221
  and culture 3–6, 8–9, 28, 30–1, 33, 61, 69, 89, 91–3, 132, 176, 190, 206, 225, 232
  knowledge 186
  and society 8–9, 69–70, 101, 134, 140, 142, 234
network analysis 11–14
New Criticism 238

new materialism 198
Nice, Margaret Morse 164
  "The role of territory in bird Life" 171 n.31
nineteenth century 3, 9, 17, 28, 35, 37, 43, 50, 55–6, 59, 70–2, 76, 131–2, 134, 136–7, 139–41, 146, 160, 233, 237, 239, 242
nonhuman 5–6, 16, 27, 31–2, 35–6, 44, 61, 69–70, 79–80, 89–92, 94, 96–7, 102, 132, 136, 143–4, 200, 232. *See also* human/human being
nonmodern/nonmodernity 1, 14, 16, 28–9, 33, 61–2, 71–2, 76, 82–3, 86 n.52, 89, 102, 131–3, 136–7, 141, 238
  humanism/humanist 15, 28, 37
  in humanities 197
  Latour's 2, 5–8, 10–11, 15, 17, 90, 133–4, 139, 143, 176, 206, 231–2
  Michelet's 145–6
  performative language 93–4, 100, 102–3
  poetry 91, 93, 95, 103
Nora, Pierre, *Lieux de mémoire* (*Rethinking France*) 133
nouveau roman 74, 77
Nurlu 219–20, 228 n.9
Nussbaum, Martha 233, 239

object-oriented politics 205–6, 210
Olina, Giovanni Pietro, *L'Uccelliera* 171 n.31
one/single universe society 221, 226
Ong, Walter J., rhetorical culture 71
ontology 1, 3, 33–6, 40, 182, 199
  flat 6, 92
  literary 224
  Michelet's 144
  providentialist 136
  relational 1, 6
  religious 184
open 15, 22 n.66, 177–81
optical model of knowledge 20 n.24
Orientalism 15, 55, 58–62
  early modern (*see* early modern Orientalism)
  European 55, 58
  humanities and technology 59–60

imperialist tradition 50
and Orient 49–55, 61
Orientalists 15, 51, 53–5, 57, 61–2
Oriental Other 54
Orientals 51–2, 55–6, 58–9, 61–2
premodern 61
Said's definition of 49–52

Paré, Ambroise 32
Des monstres et prodiges 45 n.15
parnassianism 73
Pasteur, Louis 36–40
bacteriology 35–6
Pasteurians 37–8, 40–1
"war on microbes" 15
Paulhan, Jean 72–3
Flowers of Tarbes, or, Terror in Literature 106 n.48
language and thought 72
Les Fleurs de Tarbes ou la terreur dans les lettres 71
"Literature and the Right to Death" 106 n.48
terror 71–2
Paulson, William 1, 14–16, 89, 140, 232, 236, 238
cosmopolitical philology 91
"For a Cosmopolitical Philology: Lessons from Science Studies" 103 n.1
Literary Culture in a World Transformed: A Future for the Humanities 19 n.2, 103 n.1, 108 n.82
"Nous n'avons jamais été dix-neuviémistes, ou l'avenir d'un avant-dernier siècle" 147 n.20
Péguy, Charles, *Clio. Dialogue de l'histoire et de l'âme païenne* 146 n.1
pelican (*mayiarda*) 220
performative 8, 16, 18, 154
performative model of language 92–3
performative model of naming 98
periodization 19, 231, 236, 239
Petitier, Paule, "Un Discours sur la mort: Michelet et le modèle de *L'Insecte*" 148 n.30
philosophical realism 201
Plato 33, 36, 233
hermeneia 185

Plotinus 183–4
Enneads 185
poetry 14, 16, 42, 90–1. *See also* language
criticism 238
dialogic poetics 91
modern 16, 89, 91, 93–4, 96, 98, 100, 103
naming in 94–6, 98–100
nonmodern 91, 93, 95, 103
performative model of 93–4
poetic studies 89–93
representational 93–4
transnational poetics 91
poiesis 93–4, 102
politics 3, 5, 8, 18, 29, 31, 36, 89, 123, 132
bureaucracy 117
human 156, 209
object-oriented 205–6, 210
political animal 156–7
political philosophy 134, 157, 199, 201
political realism 198–200, 202, 209
political sociology 113, 115
political theology 115
'post-truth' 204–5
Ponge, Francis 22 n.57
"Oyster" 11–14
posthumanism 35
posthumanist performative approach 92–3, 99, 176
postmodern/postmodernism 1–4, 10, 13, 28, 136, 176, 190, 238, 243 n.13
poststructuralism 90, 93
"posture auctoriale" (auctorial posture/author's image) 140
Pratt, Mary Louise 57
Imperial Eyes: Travel Writing and Transculturation 64 n.18
premodern/premodernity 3–4, 28–9, 32–3, 35, 37, 43, 61–2, 69–71, 82–3, 231
Prigent, Christian 89
L'Incontenable: Essais 103 n.3
poetic language 92
Protagoras 33–4
purification 5, 7, 11, 15–16, 19, 89–91, 97, 99, 135, 137, 139–40, 236–7, 239

quasi-objects 4, 10, 99, 131, 141

Rabelais, François 29, 42, 82
Rachilde 235, 241
Ramazani, Jahan 93, 238
  notions of poetics 91
  Poetry and Its Others: News, Prayer, Song, and the Dialogue of Genres 104 n.13
  A Transnational Poetics 104 n.13, 243 n.12
Ray, John, *Ornithology of Francis Willughby* 171 n.31
realism 16, 32, 72, 74, 77, 141, 210
  agential 210
  metaphysical 200–1
  philosophical 201
  political 198–200
Realpolitik 209
receptive 181
Reiser, Anton 180–1
Renaissance humanism/humanists 28–9, 32–3, 36, 40–2, 45 n.15
Republic of Letters, European 54, 56–7
rhetorical culture 71
Rilke, Rainer Maria 178–9, 181
Roe, Paddy, storytelling 18, 218–19, 221–6
  Gularabulu: Stories from the West Kimberley 228 n.8
  techniques 223
Romanticism 71–2, 141
Ronsard, Pierre de 82–3
Rooney, Sally, *Normal People* 125
Rose, Debbie Bird 225
  Dingo Makes Us Human: Life and Land in an Australian Aboriginal Culture 228 n.7
Rousseau, Jacques 41, 199, 209
  Discourse on the Origin of Inequality 213 n.75
Rousset, Jean 76
  "*Madame Bovary*: Flaubert's Anti-Novel" 84 n.27
Rowell, Thelma 15, 170 n.10, 190
Ruyl, Albert 54, 59
Rybak, Fanny, "When to Be a Dear Enemy: Flexible Acoustic Relationships of Neighbouring Skylarks, *Alauda arvensis*" 172 n.55

Said, Edward 15
  on Orientalism 49–52
  Orientalism: Western Conceptions of the Orient 60
Saint-Amour, Paul, "Weak Theory, Weak Modernism" 127 n.2
Sainte-Beuve, Charles Augustin 73
Sarraute, Nathalie 74–5, 77–8, 85 n.38
  argument on Flaubert's work 74–6
  "Flaubert le précurseur" 74
  Œuvres uvres complètes 84 n.17
Sartre, Jean-Paul 27, 41–2
Schaeffer, Jean-Marie 103 n.4
Schaffer, Simon 199–200
  Leviathan and the Air Pump 232
Schmidt, Jan, *The Joys of Philology. Studies in Ottoman Literature, History and Orientalism* 64 n.22
Schmitt, Carl 198–9, 208–9
  The Concept of the Political 213 n.65
science 1, 3, 5–6, 9, 13, 40, 43, 69–70, 132
  Latour's 199–200
  modern 71, 190
  and technology 31, 60, 62
Scientific Revolution 62
Second World War 27, 206, 208
self-referentiality 91–3, 99
  self-referential language 16, 92, 95–6
  self-referential negativity 89–90, 94, 100
  solipsistic 92
Selous, Edmund 163
  Evolution of Habits in Birds 162
Serres, Michel 131–2, 164
  Hermès I: la communication 146 n.2
  Le Mal propre: Polluer pour s'approprier? 172 n.45
Shakespeare, William 82, 233, 240
  Hamlet 226–7
Shapin, Steven 199–200
  Leviathan and the Air Pump 232
Shelley, Percy 123
  A Defense of Poetry 128 n.27
skepticism 15, 33–4, 176, 180, 189, 233
Smuts, Barbara 224
  "Encounters with Animal Minds" 225
"social" (society) 154
  study of baboons 153–6

theory of dominance 155
socialism 132, 134, 136
sociology 8, 13, 16–17, 153–4
   association with social 154
   critical 113, 125–6
   traditional 154
Socrates 33, 36–7
Speculative Realist movement 198
States General (*Staten-Generaal*) 63 n.11
Stead, W. T., *The United States of Europe* 121
Stengers, Isabelle 10, 89–90, 94, 98–100, 102, 104 n.9, 227
   In Catastrophic Times: Resisting the Coming Barbarism 105 n.30
   "The Challenge to Ontological Politics" 228 n.6
   cosmopolitics 217–18
   Cosmopolitics (I and II) 204
   "Gaia: The Urgency to Think (and Feel)" 105 n.28
   "Introductory Notes on an Ecology of Practices" 229 n.20
   Thinking with Whitehead: A Free and Wild Creation of Concepts 191 n.12
structuralism 74, 93
Strum, Shirley 17, 155, 158–9
   "Human Social Origins: Please Tell Us another Story" 172 n.43
   "Redefining the Social Link: from Baboons to Humans" 153–4
symbolism 73

tape recorder 225
technology 31, 59–60, 62, 75–6, 92, 117, 135, 224, 232
Tedlock, Dennis 222
theology 15, 30, 42–3, 115–16
theory of dominance, social 155
Tinbergen, Nikolaas 162
Tocqueville, Alexis de 134–6
   Democracy in America 135
Tolstoï, Leo 36, 39
Toulmin, Stephen, *Cosmopolis: The Hidden Agenda of Modernity* 86 n.52
transcendence 9, 11, 42, 90, 95, 102, 123, 145, 189

transformative approach 7, 12
translation 4–5, 7, 12, 18, 28, 35, 37–42, 52, 60, 81, 95, 101, 144, 146, 159, 176, 185, 189–90, 219, 224
transnational poetics 91
Trilling, Lionel 238
Trump, Donald J. 18, 197, 201–2, 207
   Latour on 197–8, 201–6
trustori (stories) 219, 222–3
"truth" 3, 7, 33–4, 73, 77, 95, 131, 198–200, 204–5

Uexküll, Jakob von 164, 178, 181–2
   animal umwelt 182
   "A Stroll through the Worlds of Animals and Men: A Picture Book of Invisible Worlds" 191 n.20
   ethology 184
umwelt theory 182, 184, 225
The United Nations Climate Change Conference 202
The United States 135, 202
   exit from Paris Climate Accord 203, 205
   president of (*see* Trump, Donald J.)
unity 80, 136, 143, 145

Valéry, Paul 102
   "*Le coup de dés*. Lettre au Directeur des *Marges*" 108 n.81
van Dijksterhuis, Fooko, *The Making of the Humanities. Volume II—From Early Modern to Modern Disciplines* 65 n.24
Vanuxem, Sarah 165
Vargas Llosa, Mario 74, 78–9
   The Perpetual Orgy: Flaubert and Madame Bovary 85 n.32
Vattimo, Gianni 114
Viala, Alain 140
Vigo, Jean, *Zéro de conduite* 118
Vismann, Cornelia 117
   Files: Law and Media Technology 127 n.12
vital materialism 198
Voegelin, Eric 198
Voltaire 83

war 30–1, 35–6, 39–40
"war machine" 37
weak program in literary studies 113–14
Weber, Max 117, 234
    instrumental rationality 232
west coast cultures 220
Whitehead, Alfred North 28, 186, 189, 200
    Process and Reality: An Essay in Cosmology 192 n.36, 211 n.16
    "Theories of the Bifurcation of Nature" 192 n.26
Wiegers, G. A., "Moriscos and Arabic Studies in Europe" 64 n.20
Wilson, Edmund 238

Witkam, J. J., "The Leiden Manuscript of the '*Kitâb al-Musta'înî*' 64 n.17

"year of miracles" 132, 136, 143, 146

Zahavi, Amotz 159
Zaydân, Mûlay 52–3, 56, 59–60
Zhiri, Oumelbanine 15
    "The Task of the Morisco Translator in the Early Modern Maghrib" 64 n.21
Žižek, Slavoj 198
    "The Hillary Clinton Consensus is Damaging Democracy" 210 n.3
Zola, Émile 16, 73–4, 237

www.ingramcontent.com/pod-product-compliance
Lightning Source LLC
Chambersburg PA
CBHW072134290426
44111CB00012B/1873